"*The Next Board* is a practical tool for effective board service grounded in industry leaders' insights to help aspiring and existing board members."

Rod Adkins, *board member at United Parcel Service (UPS), PayPal, Grainger, and Avnet*

"*The Next Board* is an incredible book. Given the chaos and uncertainty in the world today, it is also more timely than ever. The insights support the board's forward thinking. As such it helps businesses to look through the 'drama' of the day to the future to enhance ability to build ongoing, sustainable success."

Kathleen Bailey-Lord, *chair at ed-tech company Janison and member of the board at Datacom, AMP, and St. Vincents*

"Many interesting best practice examples from modern boards providing practical hands-on guidance for Board Chairs, Board Members and CEOs. Based on my own experience, a very worthwhile read."

Pius Baschera, *experienced board member and former board chair of Hilti*

"The authors have covered the wide range of challenges facing boards across differing geographies, industries, scales, and ownership structures in a way that provides insights and questions to consider for any director or senior member of management. And they have brought the text alive with the direct thoughts of a diverse group of experienced directors."

Jeff Campbell, *former vice-chairman and CFO of American Express, former CFO of McKesson and American Airlines, and current director at AON plc, Marathon Petroleum Corp., and Hexcel Corp*

"*The Next Board* provides practical insights into how to build boards that can handle the increased workloads most boards face while not losing sight of the future. A valuable support for modern boards and a must read."

Ian Carter, *board chair of Watches of Switzerland plc*

"*The Next Board* is a very useful read for anyone involved in modern corporate governance. Thomas Keil and Marianna Zangrillo provide a comprehensive framework to navigate the complexities of today's board responsibilities, offering practical insights and strategies to build effective, future-ready boards. As someone who has witnessed the evolving challenges in boardrooms firsthand, I found this book to be a very valuable resource for board members and executives alike."

Jean-Pierre Clamadieu, *chair of French energy company Engie and director of Airbus and TE Connectivity*

"Boards today are operating in an environment marked by economic fluctuations and policy shifts. The pace of change is overwhelming, and the expansion of scope is irreversible. *The Next Board* is an essential resource for navigating the expanded responsibilities of today's boards. Based on interviews with over 100 experienced board members and enriched with real-world examples and insights, this book offers actionable frameworks to address challenges such as enhanced oversight duties, strategic involvement, risk management, and stakeholder engagement. It uniquely emphasizes the differences across various corporate holding structures, providing tailored guidance for diverse boardroom contexts. The book can serve as a foundational resource, complementing other tools to navigate the rapidly evolving business landscape."

Xiaoqun Clever-Steg, *director at multiple international corporations*

"This book helps understanding the boards of today. It provides practical advice how to navigate its increasingly complex challenges. A must-read for newly elected board members and interested outsiders to understand modern board practices."

Dr Christoph Franz, *vice-chair of the board of Zurich Insurance, member of the board of Stadler Rail, Artemis Holding, Chugai Pharmaceutical, and former Chairman of the board of Roche*

"Finally, a clear framework that helps boards tackle today's demands and anticipate tomorrow's challenges."

Erik Huggers, *board member at Hexagon and several other privately owned companies and former board member of ProSieben*

"Boards have evolved from being exclusive clubs to professionally managed teams that play a central role in the company's success. *The Next Board* provides invaluable advice on how to play that role."

Johannes Huth, *former partner at private equity firm KKR, lead independent director at Coty Inc, and director at Axel Springer*

"*The Next Board* is a must read for any engaged Chair or Director. It offers state of the art research with hands-on insights from leaders and world class companies."

Jan Jenisch, *former board chair of Holcim, chairman and CEO of Amrize*

"A delightful guide of the ideal board that will inspire both experienced and aspiring non-executive directors, at a time when governance is confronted to strong headwinds: repeated disruptions, geopolitical confrontations and questioning around the mission of corporate businesses in the XXI century economy."

Anne Lange, *director at Pernod-Ricard, Orange, and Inditex*

"Grounded in rigorous, multi-year research, this book offers deep insights into board governance in today's increasingly complex business environment. Rich in examples from major international companies and featuring candid insights from experienced board directors, it equips readers with practical frameworks and actionable advice. A timely read for board members and senior executives navigating today's board challenges."

Kalidas Madhavpeddi, *chair of Glencore*

"*The Next Board* is a must read for board chairs, board members and those aspiring to join boards. As a reader one finds a wealth of practical advice from board practitioners of top organizations, that the authors have translated into a practical guide to increase board effectiveness."

Luka Mucic, *director at Heidelberg Materials*

"Future-proof boards are strategic partners, not just supervisors, ensuring long-term value creation and responsible corporate governance. The book offers an excellent guide and many practical examples of how to get there."

Dr. Stefan Nöken, *supervisory board member at Vaillant, Vorwerk and Peri Group, former member of the executive board of Hilti Corporation*

"Effective boards are diverse in skills, experience and short and long-term thinking of their members. This book offers valuable insights for successful management of the demanding ecosystem at the top of a company."

Joerg Reinhardt, *chair of Novartis and member of the board of SwissRe*

"Master the boardroom. Get practical insights and guiding principles to navigate any board challenge. Essential for all fiduciaries."

Kaj-Erik Relander, *board member of Louis Dreyfuss Corporation, SES Satellites and a number of other privately held corporations*

"Boards are more important than ever. *The Next Board* provides a conceptual frame and lots of practical tools to help boards to excel at their tasks. A useful and enjoyable read for both experienced and aspiring board members."

Andreas Umbach, *former chair of SIG Group AG*

"*The Next Board* is thoroughly researched and full of practical insights – an indispensable guide for board members navigating today's most pressing challenges."

Peter Voser, *board chair at ABB, PSA International, and member of the board at IBM*

The Next Board

Hardly a month goes by without news of a high-profile corporate failure that raises the question of the role of the board. Why do boards of directors find it so difficult to steer the company and its management team? Topics such as digitalization, cybersecurity, AI, and sustainability have taken center stage, while multiple crises and the new geopolitical environment are forcing firms to operate in highly turbulent environments.

Illustrated with real-life examples from interviews with board chairs, board members, CEOs, executives, and investors, *The Next Board* provides unique insights on how boards can master the dual challenge of implementing the best practices of today while future-proofing an organization for the emerging challenges of tomorrow. Through the lens of the "board diamond" – purpose, people, structures and processes, leadership, and performance evaluation – this book introduces the building blocks that are central to implementing best practice. Furthermore, it provides a practical framework to configure them differently depending on the context of the company. These practices are brought to life with case studies and interviews with directors from some of the most successful firms from across the globe, including ABB, ASML, Avnet, Bertelsmann, Engie, Ericsson, IBM, Inditex, Kellogg, McKesson, Nestlé, Nokia, Novartis, Paypal, Santander, Target, and UPS.

This book provides directors, board chairs, CEOs, senior executives, and C-suite managers, who are preparing for future board assignments, with tangible advice on how to develop their boards and how to succeed as directors.

Thomas Keil is a professor at the University of Zurich, Switzerland, where he teaches strategy and international management, and partner at The Next Advisors.

Marianna Zangrillo is a corporate leader, business angel, investor, author, and partner at The Next Advisors.

The Next Board

Delivering Value Today
while Making the Board
Fit for Tomorrow

Thomas Keil and Marianna Zangrillo

Routledge
Taylor & Francis Group

LONDON AND NEW YORK

Designed cover image: Getty Images - gerenme

First published 2026
by Routledge
4 Park Square, Milton Park, Abingdon, Oxon OX14 4RN

and by Routledge
605 Third Avenue, New York, NY 10158

Routledge is an imprint of the Taylor & Francis Group, an informa business

British Library Cataloguing-in-Publication Data
A catalogue record for this book is available from the British Library

ISBN: 978-1-032-87350-3 (hbk)
ISBN: 978-1-032-86520-1 (pbk)
ISBN: 978-1-003-53220-0 (ebk)

DOI: 10.4324/9781003532200

Typeset in Adobe Garamond Pro
by codeMantra

Contents

Acknowledgments

This volume marks the third installment in our exploration of the strategic apex in corporate life, and with every book, our appreciation for those who shared their time, insights, and expertise deepens. We are profoundly grateful to everyone who played a role in making this publication a reality. Without your time and support, it could not have been completed.

First and foremost, we owe a great debt to every CEO, board member, and chairperson who participated in our interviews, offered their reflections, challenged our thinking, and helped shape this manuscript with genuine, real-world perspectives. Over the course of our trilogy, we have been fortunate to stay in touch with many of you, as your leadership journeys often evolved from CEO or executive positions to guiding boards. Your commitment to thoughtful deliberation on what truly drives success in complex organizations sparked countless illuminating conversations. While some of you are mentioned by name within these pages, others chose to remain unnamed. However, each contribution was equally significant, occasionally allowing us to voice issues that would not be possible to openly share with a name attached. We are humbled by your dedication, your clarity of thought, and your passion for furthering knowledge – qualities that pushed us to keep refining our ideas.

In addition to those interviewed, we would like to acknowledge some individuals whose exceptional involvement and dedication have significantly advanced our thinking and guided the creation of this volume.

Stuart Crainer and Des Dearlove at Thinkers50 once again provided indispensable guidance and incisive critique, refining our initial ideas into a coherent narrative. Their influence on this book cannot be overstated, and we remain deeply appreciative of their persistent encouragement.

We extend our heartfelt thanks to Professor Martin Hilb of the University of St. Gallen, who invited us to contribute to some board programs and whose early suggestion that we broaden our study on CEO succession inspired us to produce a series intended for board members, senior executives, and organizational leaders alike.

We are also profoundly grateful to our editor at Routledge, Rebecca Marsh, whose proactive approach and collaborative spirit made the entire publishing process far more rewarding, and Lisa Humphries for her meticulous copyediting, which helped us hone our writing and clarify the key messages.

Although our writing is focused on board chairs and members, CEOs, and senior executives as our primary audience, this book is firmly grounded in extensive academic research. We are particularly indebted to David Seidl, Professor of Organization and Management at the University of Zurich, for granting us permission to use anonymized material from a joint research project. Many of the anonymous quotations in this book originate from that study. We also express our appreciation to Alexander Thiel, senior partner at McKinsey & Company, who kindly allowed us to draw upon interview material gathered with Thomas during an earlier collaboration. Our sincere thanks go to Stevo Pavićević, Associate Professor of Strategy at Frankfurt School of Finance and Management, whose thoughtful suggestions and critical insights over multiple projects have once again elevated our work in many ways.

We also want to acknowledge the tireless support of Gian-Luca Asquini, whose research assistance proved invaluable while he was simultaneously working toward his doctoral degree. In our friendly contest to see who would cross the finish line first, we must admit that Gian-Luca emerged victorious by completing his dissertation before we wrapped up this manuscript.

The process of crafting this third volume required yet another marathon of evenings and weekends, inevitably taking time away from our children, family, and friends. Thank you for your patience.

Finally, we keep thanking our parents, who instilled in us a love of learning, a sense of curiosity, and the discipline to persevere even when the journey felt daunting. Their unwavering support and guidance form the foundation of our accomplishments, and for that, we are eternally grateful.

Introduction

The role of the board of directors in corporations has never been more important than it is today. Yet the increasing complexity of board responsibilities has made it more challenging for them to fulfill their mandate, and the meaning of a high-performance board is no longer straightforward.

In contemporary governance, companies are run day-to-day by the CEO and their leadership team, and boards operate mostly in the background. Despite this seemingly invisible role, boards can have a profound impact that can make or break an organization. In the words of a European board chair: "In today's governance, the board plays a pivotal role in making strategic decisions, supporting and monitoring management, and steering the company towards the topics of tomorrow."

Boards are responsible for appointing CEOs and dismissing them when they underperform. They also play a critical role in selecting and replacing other top executives. A strong board serves as a strategic advisor and sounding board to leadership while respecting management's operational autonomy. Boards hold ultimate authority on major strategic decisions and provide oversight over management's activities.

Not only do boards matter more than ever, but the demands placed on them have also expanded dramatically. Relatively new topics such as digitalization, cybersecurity, AI, sustainability, and ESG have taken center stage, while multiple crises in recent years have further complicated board agendas. Suzanne Thoma, executive chair of Sulzer, the Swiss-based industrial engineering and manufacturing firm specializing in fluid engineering, underlined this trend: "Driven by the unprecedented change in the world and facilitated by the pressure from governance rules and proxy advisors, the role of the board has become bigger and more important. More and more is required from the modern board."

An abundant body of academic[1] and practice-oriented[2] research has emerged that backs up the central role of the board and shows that boards significantly influence whether a company succeeds or fails. Studies suggest that various aspects of board composition, structure, and behavior – ranging from directors' characteristics

DOI: 10.4324/9781003532200-1

1

to board size, compensation, and processes – are closely linked to board effectiveness and organizational performance.[3]

While boards play an important role in modern governance, due to the nature of their work, they frequently do so behind the scenes. Discussions take place and decisions are made behind closed doors, and it's the CEO and executive team that typically receive the credit when initiatives are enacted. As Phoebe Wood, who serves on the boards of Invesco, Ltd., PPL Corporation, and Leggett and Platt Corporation, put it: "As a board member, we add value out of the public eye – by offering critical insights on strategy or resolving issues before they escalate into something much bigger."

Likewise, a chair in a US stock exchange-listed firm explained:

> We saw the problems with the CEO coming for a while. Initially, we tried to work with him, but as time progressed, it became increasingly clear that he wasn't the right person to lead the company through the changes the business required. In the end, we decided that a change at the top was the only way to initiate the strategic renewal that we wanted. We then spent months working intensely as a board to identify a new CEO. During that period, I stepped in as interim CEO and, together with the board, we kick-started the strategy process. Once we had our new CEO in place, I stepped back to the role of chair.

The work of boards typically attracts public attention only when problems escalate and prompt questions about the board's oversight. Consider Boeing's recent decline. Although Boeing had been a market leader for decades, it lost that position after a series of accidents raised serious concerns about the safety and quality of its products. In 2019, following two crashes and 346 fatalities, its 737 MAX airliners were grounded, and all further deliveries were suspended. The severity of the incidents prompted strong action from the board. It fired CEO and chair Dennis Muilenberg, replacing him with two outside directors: David Calhoun as CEO and Lawrence Kellner as chair. However, quality issues persisted across different product lines, and Boeing's reputation continued to deteriorate. Problems continued for four years, culminating in a near-catastrophic incident when a faulty plane door blew off mid-flight, endangering passengers and crew. It was only after this dramatic accident that the board took further action and removed CEO David Calhoun – a decision that many viewed as too little, too late.

Another example is the collapse of Credit Suisse (CS),[4] once a leading international bank based in Switzerland. After the 2007–2008 financial crisis, the bank's performance steadily declined. In 2015, the board of directors took decisive action by appointing an industry outsider as CEO, Tidjane Thiam, to lead a major restructuring effort. While this initially brought some financial stability, deeper issues persisted and, following a corporate espionage scandal, the board replaced Thiam with Thomas Gottstein, a long-serving and successful executive from within the company. Beyond this, however, the board remained largely passive, and the second shift at the top did little to steer the bank back toward success. Instead, a series of failed deals further undermined confidence in its risk management capabilities.

In addition, the board created instability of its own when the recently appointed new chair, António Horta-Osório, was forced to resign after only nine months following irregularities in the use of corporate jets and repeated violations of COVID-19 quarantine rules. Axel Lehmann took over, and the bank followed its usual pattern of leadership changes, appointing Ulrich Körner as CEO in August 2022 to spearhead yet another restructuring effort.

Despite a flurry of activity, shareholders and customers increasingly lost faith in the company and withdrew funds. The outflow of capital eventually became so dramatic that in March 2023, the Swiss government stepped in and brokered a forced acquisition by CS's Swiss competitor, UBS. While many lessons can be drawn from the demise of CS, in the context of this book, this case illustrates the vital need for a strong board – one that takes decisive action in times of turmoil to address underperformance, while also providing steady leadership. At CS, the board did neither, instead becoming yet another source of instability.

Why do some boards successfully steer their companies through the turbulent changes of today's business environment while others seem to lose control and spiral into decline? What can board chairs and board members do to improve the impact of their work? How can they enhance the effectiveness of their boards to future-proof their organizations? Starting with these questions, we engaged in a multi-year research program that took us on a global journey through the boardrooms of some of the world's leading companies across Australia, the US and Canada, the UK, the Nordics, and continental Europe. While our ambition with this book is to provide an international perspective, we will not address the specific challenges of governance in much of Asia, Africa, and South America, given that the institutional environment in these markets often follows different principles from those that tend to apply to Western countries. Nonetheless, we believe many of the insights from this book should be of interest in these markets too.

During our journey through the boardrooms, we interviewed well over 100 board chairs, board members, investors, CEOs, and executives, some of them several times. During these conversations, we exchanged ideas and insights on what makes the board a functioning body and what various organizations have tried, successfully or less successfully, to make their boards more impactful. Many participants generously allowed us to share their experiences and advice, while others chose to stay anonymous to speak more candidly about the obstacles they faced in their board environments. We have quoted both sets of participants throughout this book but have carefully removed identifying details upon request.

Our research also built on our previous two books, *The Next CEO: Board and CEO Perspectives for Successful CEO Succession*[5] and *The Next Leadership Team: How to Select, Build, and Optimize Your Top Team*,[6] in which we analyzed some of the key tasks of the board[7] and developed some leadership principles[8] that apply to any governing body – including boards. We further enriched our primary research with in-depth case studies of selected boards and a survey of the academic literature on corporate governance.

In our conversations with board chairs, board members, CEOs, and investors, three dominant themes emerged that have inspired and shaped the ideas and contents of this book.

1. The dual challenge

First, today's boards face what we call a dual challenge of governance. On the one hand, the past 15 years have seen a qualitative change in the requirements of a board, with scandals and the financial crisis of 2007–2008 prompting a push for more professional, accountable boards. On the other hand, the last five years have seen a second challenge emerge, arising from a vastly altered business landscape. Digitalization; AI; multiple global crises; de-globalization and the emergence of new protectionism; political tension between the US, Europe, and China; and the drive to integrate sustainability into core business practices have fundamentally altered the business environment for many corporations and boards need to reinvent strategy and business models to respond to these changes – and future-proof the board and the company. This dual challenge forces boards to sharpen their existing standards and practices while also reinventing themselves to address new demands. Although the most effective boards have made significant progress with this transformation, others are still in the early stages of the process.

2. Lack of frameworks

Secondly, our discussions confirmed that many board members, committee chairs, and board chairs need simple frameworks to help them navigate their responsibilities. Although there has been extensive academic and practical research on boards, easy-to-use frameworks remain scarce, and there is a lack of guidance on how to create boards that are effective today and prepared for tomorrow.

3. Context matters

Finally, we were fortunate to speak with board members, board chairs, owners, and investors representing a diverse range of ownership structures – public companies with dispersed ownership, private-equity-controlled businesses, and family- or founder-owned firms – across various national governance models and stages of the corporate life cycle, from turnarounds to stable operations and high-growth environments. These conversations underscored the critical role of context and company-specific circumstances in shaping board design, operations, and leadership. While universal frameworks are valuable, the effectiveness of board strategies ultimately hinges on each organization's unique ownership structure and distinct challenges.

This book builds on these three insights and introduces ideas, frameworks, and tools designed to support seasoned board members, those new to board service, and executives aspiring to join a board, as they engage in the important work that boards do.

Let's take a little deeper dive into our three insights.

The changing requirements of modern boards

Modern boards face a dual challenge that is summarized in Figure 0.1. Following the scandals of the early 2000s and the 2007–2008 financial crisis, regulators, proxy advisors, and investors worldwide increased their demands for stronger corporate governance. New laws and regulations have multiplied and changed the expectations placed on the board, as Don Knauss, director of US-based Kellogg's, McKesson, and Target, highlighted: "The requirements for oversight have changed dramatically, and that means that we need to support management teams to an extent never seen before." Consequently, boards have had to professionalize, and adopting best practices in corporate governance has become more important.

However, our journey through the boardrooms around the globe also highlighted that there is still much room for improvement. Some boards we studied stood out for using state-of-the-art governance and leadership approaches, whereas others retained a "clubby" atmosphere more characteristic of the past. Many boards still have a long journey ahead to reach the levels of excellence we observed in a handful of truly world-class boards. In other words, the journey of professionalizing through deploying current best practices is a work-in-progress for many, if not most, boards.

Figure 0.1   The Dual Challenge of Modern Boards: Balancing Present-Orientation and Future-Orientation

Moreover, merely responding to the challenges of today is not enough; boards are facing a number of changes that have created a level of uncertainty and complexity not seen before. Technological developments (digitalization and AI, for example) are testing the capabilities and business models of most organizations, with project after project failing or not generating the desired results, ultimately forcing companies to reinvent their strategy.

Further complicating matters, the shift from globalization to de-globalization, international polarization, geopolitical tensions, and new trade conflicts have not only made operational planning and risk management far more complex for large international organizations but also increasingly led many firms to rethink their geographic strategy fundamentally.

Despite the recent political backlash, many analysts and investors now also view sustainability as a critical measure of corporate performance, compelling boards and executives to adopt a broader, stakeholder-focused view of strategy and value creation. Sustainability is just one of many governance issues requiring boards to expand their understanding of the business, as well as their responsibilities.

On top of these changes, multiple consecutive global crises – from the COVID-19 pandemic to the war in Ukraine and the conflict in the Middle East – have tested companies' resilience and agility in unprecedented ways.

The uncertainty and complexity created by these changes place a premium on strategic thinking and foresight, agility in response, and resilience to shocks. Boards may not be well positioned to respond, as Thomas Thune Andersen, chair at Lloyd's Register Group and VKR Holding, and member of the board at BW Group and IMI plc, provocatively stated:

> I am not convinced that boards as we know them today are still relevant or up to the task. Increasing compliance combined with a new need to think differently about the business and challenge the strategy with different eyes cannot be accomplished with the current board structures.

How, then, can boards address the dual challenge of maintaining and fine-tuning current best practices while future-proofing for the transformations waiting on the horizon? This book aims to offer some guidance for board chairs, individual board members, and boards as a whole on how to try and square this circle by identifying and mapping out some possible changes in standards, expectations, and requirements while at the same time implementing the practices demanded by the current environment.

Addressing changing requirements through the board diamond

During our conversations with existing board members, calls arose for simple frameworks and tools that help them master their tasks. We propose a simple framework of five dimensions of board design that together help boards to achieve both goals of the dual challenge:

1. Board roles and purpose
2. People
3. Board structures and processes
4. Board leadership
5. Performance evaluation and development

While these dimensions are well established in organization design and the design of leadership teams,[9] we use this framework, which we refer to as the "*diamond model of board effectiveness*," or short "*Board Diamond*," as a lens to focus our discussion on the key dimensions of board design, management, and leadership.

To be at the leading edge of current practice, boards must be thoughtful about defining the board's purpose and the board roles that arise from this purpose; select the right people for the board; identify structures and processes that drive efficiency and effectiveness; identify leadership practices suitable for the context of the board; and engage in meaningful evaluation practices and performance management. While these measures can help a board function at the top level today, they are insufficient to ensure future relevance. Along each of these five dimensions, we identify new challenges boards must tackle to remain effective and forward-looking.

Adapting boards to different environments

Together, the board, the CEO, and the top leadership team make up what we call "the strategic apex of the firm." Like the pieces of a puzzle, they need to align and complement one another. Consequently, boards must be carefully crafted to integrate seamlessly with the broader leadership structure. In addition, as we discussed in our previous books[10] in relation to the role of the CEO and the top leadership team, the requirements, profile, and personalities of the key players – in particular, the role of the chair and the structures and processes – need to be aligned with the specific context and situation of the company.

Our research shows that a company's ownership structure is particularly influential in determining how the board should be set up. For example, Pauline Van der Meer Mohr, chair of the Dutch semiconductor equipment manufacturer ASM and director of Ahold Delhaize, NN Group, told us: "There are important differences between boards of widely held companies, private-equity-owned companies, and family-owned companies. How decisions are made, who has a say, and what the time horizons are. It is all different." For instance, boards in widely held public corporations face different constraints in terms of structure and composition than boards in private firms. Family- or founder-controlled firms may have long-term time horizons that stretch decades or generations ahead. In contrast, private-equity or widely held public firms might take a shorter-term perspective measured in years or even quarters. Board design, management, and leadership must consider these differences to create effective boards tailored to the specific ownership structure.

A company's strategic situation also has profound implications for board design. Although some boards may strive to remain independent of strategic pressures, our findings suggest that boards may need to evolve their behaviors, structures, or even their composition in response to strategic shifts. Our study suggests that boards need to reconfigure different dimensions of the "board diamond" to fit the requirements of key strategic situations such as growth, maturity, and crisis to remain effective.

Finally, differences in national regulatory frameworks also shape boards in meaningful ways. Even in today's interconnected markets and with proxy advisors that may not differentiate much across geographies, US-based corporate governance rules create different requirements for the board than governance rules in Germany, France, or the UK.

Johannes Huth, former partner at private equity firm KKR, senior independent director of Coty Inc., and director at Axel Springer, emphasized this:

> What legal system and governance structure you work in matters a lot. Are you operating in a two-tier board, as we usually have in Germany or France, or in a one-tier set-up, as in the UK or America? It's different whether the CEO is part of the board, sometimes even as the chair, or whether they are supervised by a chair and an independent board. And then there is this difference in the power of the chair. The chair of a Swiss board has much more influence than a German Supervisory Board Chair. The legal regime and governance structure also influence how the board acts.

While a complete discussion of the differences in corporate governance rules across the countries studied is beyond the scope of this book, we will discuss similarities and, most importantly, differences arising from these institutional differences. These differences across countries have become even more important because the recent change in the US government has created new challenges for boards in international corporations to reconcile the divergent demands of different countries.

Structure of the book

The Next Board provides practical, hands-on guidance for board chairs, board members, CEOs, and executives who interact with the board and anyone aspiring to become a board member. The book is organized into four parts and 11 chapters based on the core ideas just introduced. Each chapter explores key challenges and presents concepts to tackle them, offering practical tools and actionable advice supported by insights from our interviews, examples, and case studies.

Part I lays out the dual challenges that modern boards face and introduces the board diamond framework to address them. Chapter 1 focuses on the changed operating environment of modern companies and the implications for the boards that govern them, using the dual challenge concept of simultaneously adopting current best practices while future-proofing the board. Chapter 2 introduces the board diamond as a systematic framework to identify the key areas for current best practices and areas for planning future readiness.

In Part II, we dive deeper into the different dimensions of the board diamond. For each dimension, we identify current best practices that well-functioning boards should implement and highlight areas that should be addressed to make the board future-fit.

Chapter 3 focuses on the importance of defining the board's purpose and roles and how to design a board fit for purpose. Chapter 4 asks the question of who should be on the board, using the purpose of the board as the starting point to define the roles required, board size and composition, and the profile of board members in terms of competencies, experience, and personality. Chapter 5 explores the structures and processes of modern boards, highlighting their role in transforming boards from loosely facilitated peer groups into professional organizations. Chapter 6 introduces the central role of the board chair, or lead independent director, and leading the board more generally. Chapter 7 focuses on board evaluation and development, discussing how boards can create effective evaluation and performance management systems.

In Part III, we highlight how the board's roles and purpose, composition, structures, processes, and practices discussed in Part II are configured depending on the situation and context of the company. In Chapter 8, we address the special characteristics of boards for widely held, family-controlled, or private-equity-owned companies. In Chapter 9, we discuss how boards can reconfigure different dimensions of the "board diamond" to fit the requirements of key strategic situations such as growth, maturity, and crisis and offer some implications for the board as a whole, its chair, and individual board members. In Chapter 10, we discuss the impact of different institutional environments, particularly specific national frameworks that shape corporate governance and set boundary conditions for board work.

In Part IV, we turn our discussion to the future of governance. In the final Chapter 11, we discuss development areas where boards should experiment with new practices on how to become efficient, more agile, and resilient to both discontinuous changes and an ever-changing business environment.

By the end of *The Next Board*, we hope readers will not only have a grasp of the core elements of effective boards but also feel prepared to help shape the next generation of board governance – one that meets today's expectations *and* tomorrow's challenges.

Notes

1. The academic research on boards and corporate governance is too large to do justice within this book, given that it not only spans decades of work but also crosses multiple disciplines, including management, finance, and law. Our focus here is a management perspective, and, for the interested reader, we recommend the following books

and reviews that provide an overview of at least some of the key questions that have been asked: Steven Boivie, Michael K. Bednar, Ruth V. Aguilera, and Joel L. Andrus, "Are Boards Designed to Fail? The Implausibility of Effective Board Monitoring," *Academy of Management Annals* 10, no. 1 (2016); Ruth V. Aguilera, J. A. Aragón-Correa, V. Marano, and P. A. Tashman, "The Corporate Governance of Environmental Sustainability: A Review and Proposal for More Integrated Research," *Journal of Management* 47, no. 6 (July 2021); Ruth V. Aguilera, K. Desender, M. K. Bednar, and J. H. Lee, "Connecting the Dots: Bringing External Corporate Governance into the Corporate Governance Puzzle," *Academy of Management Annals* 9, no. 1 (2015); Ruth V. Aguilera and G. Jackson, "Comparative and International Corporate Governance," *Academy of Management Annals* 4 (2010); Ruth V. Aguilera and A. Cuervo-Cazurra, "Codes of Good Governance," *Corporate Governance: An International Review* 17, no. 3 (May 2009); R. Federo, Y. Ponomareva, Ruth V. Aguilera, A. Saz-Carranza, and C. Losada, "Bringing Owners Back on Board: A Review of the Role of Ownership Type in Board Governance," *Corporate Governance: An International Review* 28, no. 6 (November 2020); D. R. Dalton and C. M. Dalton, "Integration of Micro and Macro Studies in Governance Research: CEO Duality, Board Composition, and Financial Performance," *Journal of Management* 37, no. 2 (March 2011); B. K. Boyd and A. M. Solarino, "Ownership of Corporations: A Review, Synthesis, and Research Agenda," *Journal of Management* 42, no. 5 (July 2016); P. J. Bezemer, A. Pugliese, G. Nicholson, and A. Zattoni, "Toward a Synthesis of the Board-Strategy Relationship: A Literature Review and Future Research Agenda," *Corporate Governance: An International Review* 31, no. 1 (January 2023); A. Pugliese, P. J. Bezemer, A. Zattoni, M. Huse, F. A. J. Van den Bosch, and H. W. Volberda, "Boards of Directors' Contribution to Strategy: A Literature Review and Research Agenda," *Corporate Governance: An International Review* 17, no. 3 (May 2009); H. Van Ees, J. Gabrielsson, and M. Huse, "Towards a Behavioral Theory of Boards and Corporate Governance," *Corporate Governance: An International Review* 17, no. 3 (2009); Federo et al., "Bringing Owners Back on Board: A Review of the Role of Ownership Type in Board Governance."; A. Banerjee, M. Nordqvist, and K. Hellerstedt, "The Role of the Board Chair—A Literature Review and Suggestions for Future Research," *Corporate Governance: An International Review* 28, no. 6 (November 2020); A. Eirola, P. J. Bezemer, and S. Reinhold, "Boardroom Dissent: An Integrative Review and Future Research Agenda," *Corporate Governance: An International Review* (2024 July 2024); P. Deb, V. Sreekumar, P. Sen, A. Duru, and D. L. Brannon, "New Venture Governance: An Integrative, Multidisciplinary Review," *Academy of Management Annals* 18, no. 2 (July 2024); S. G. Johnson, K. Schnatterly, and A. D. Hill, "Board Composition Beyond Independence: Social Capital, Human Capital, and Demographics," *Journal of Management* 39, no. 1 (January 2013); R. Krause, M. Semadeni, and A. A. Cannella, "CEO Duality: A Review and Research Agenda," *Journal of Management* 40, no. 1 (January 2014); R. Krause, M. C. Withers, and M. J. Waller, "Leading the Board in a Crisis: Strategy and Performance Implications of Board Chair Directive Leadership," *Journal of Management* 50, no. 2 (February 2024); C. Chet Miller, Sana Chiu, Curtis L. Wesley II, Dusya Vera, and Derek R. Avery, "Cognitive Diversity at the Strategic Apex: Assessing Evidence on the Value of Different Perspectives and Ideas among Senior Leaders," *Academy of Management Annals* 16, no. 2 (2022); S. Paruchuri, E. A. Hoempler, A. P. Cowen, A. A. Cannella, and P. I. Nahm, "Governance Failure and Governance under Failure: Reviewing the Role of Directors in Organizational Misconduct," *Journal of Management* (February 2024); Boivie et al., "Are Boards Designed to Fail? The Implausibility of Effective Board Monitoring."; Steven Boivie, Michael C. Withers, Scott D. Graffin, and Kevin G. Corley, "Corporate Directors' Implicit Theories of the Roles and Duties of Boards," *Strategic Management Journal* 42, no. 9 (2021); J. D. Westphal and E. J. Zajac, "A Behavioral Theory of Corporate Governance: Explicating the Mechanisms of Socially Situated and Socially Constituted Agency," *Academy of Management Annals* 7, no. 1 (June 2013); Withers Michael C. and Fitza Markus A., "Do Board Chairs Matter? The Influence of Board Chairs on Firm Performance," *Strategic Management Journal* 38, no. 6 (2017); S. Finkelstein, D. C. Hambrick, and A. A. Cannella, *Strategic Leadership: Theory and Research on Executives, Top Management Teams, and Boards* (New York: Oxford University Press, 2009); Morten Huse, *Boards, Governance and Value Creation: The Human Side of Corporate Governance* (Cambridge: Cambridge University Press, 2007).

2. For some of the most notable practitioner oriented books on boards, see, for instance, Ram Charan, Dennis Carey, and Michael Useem, *Boards That Lead: When to Take Charge, When to Partner, and When to Stay Out of the Way* (Boston, MA: Harvard Business Review Press, 2014); Dambisa Moyo, *How Boards Work: And How They Can Work Better in a Chaotic World* (London: Bridge Street Press, 2021); Martin K. Welge and Marc Eulerich, *Corporate-Governance-Management*, 2nd ed. (Wiesbaden: Springer Gabler, 2014); Gerry Brown and Randall S. Peterson, *Disaster in the Boardroom: Six Dysfunctions Everyone Should Understand* (Cham: Springer/Palgrave McMillan, 2022); Didier Cossin, *High Performance Boards: Improving and Energizing Your Governance* (Chichester: John Wiley & Sons, 2024); Philip Stiles, *Board Dynamics* (Cambridge: Cambridge University Press, 2021); Martin Hilb, *Integrierte Corporate Governance*, 6th ed. (Berlin: Springer, 2016); Jay William Lorsch, *The Future of Boards: Meeting the Governance Challenges of the Twenty-First Century* (Boston, MA: Harvard Business Review Press, 2012); Leslie Brissett, Mannie Sher, and Tazi Lorraine Smith, *Dynamics at Boardroom Level: A Tavistock Primer for Leaders, Coaches and Consultants* (London: Routledge, 2020); Richard Leblanc, *The Handbook of Board Governance: A Comprehensive Guide for Public, Private, and Not-for-Profit Board Members* (Hoboken, NJ: John Wiley & Sons, 2020); David Larcker and Brian Tayan, *Corporate Governance Matters: A Closer Look at Organizational Choices and Their Consequences*, 3rd ed. (London: Pearson/FT Press, 2020).

3. For a review of the research on boards, see, for instance, Larcker and Tayan, *Corporate Governance Matters: A Closer Look at Organizational Choices and Their Consequences.* for a review of the research on boards.

4. George (Yiorgos) Allayannis, Boban Markovic, and Gerry Yemen, *The End of Credit Suisse*, Case Study: UVA-F-2064 (Charlottesville, VA: Darden Business Publishing, December 20, 2023).

5. Thomas Keil and Marianna Zangrillo, *The Next CEO: Board and CEO Perspectives for Successful CEO Succession* (London: Routledge, 2021).

6. Thomas Keil and Marianna Zangrillo, *The Next Leadership Team: How to Select, Build, and Optimize Your Top Team* (London: Routledge, 2023).

7. Keil and Zangrillo, *The Next CEO: Board and CEO Perspectives for Successful CEO Succession.*

8. Keil and Zangrillo, *The Next CEO: Board and CEO Perspectives for Successful CEO Succession.*

9. See, for instance, Keil and Zangrillo, *The Next Leadership Team: How to Select, Build, and Optimize Your Top Team.*

10. Keil and Zangrillo, *The Next CEO: Board and CEO Perspectives for Successful CEO Succession*; Keil and Zangrillo, *The Next Leadership Team: How to Select, Build, and Optimize Your Top Team.*

Part I

Boards' struggle between the challenges of today and tomorrow

Chapter 1

The dual challenge
of the modern board

Carla Smits-Nusteling was preparing for an upcoming board meeting at Nokia, the Finnish telecommunications infrastructure provider. She joined Nokia's board in 2016, shortly before the merger with Alcatel-Lucent, which solidified Nokia's market position. She has also served on the board of Dutch ASML and Swedish TELE2 AB.

Recent years have been a wild ride for Nokia. After exiting the mobile phone business in 2013, the company switched its focus to supplying the technology that powers mobile and fixed telecommunications networks for telecommunications operators around the world. Through a series of mergers and acquisitions, it became one of the top three industry players. Yet competition remained fierce, intensified by continuous technological change.

In each of its board meetings, Nokia's board members had to deal with an increasing number of critical issues. Competition was tougher than ever, largely because the telecommunications operators that formed Nokia's client base were under tremendous cost pressures themselves, pushing their vendors to cut costs. Given that each country typically had at most three or four telecom operators – each required to invest billions in building and maintaining networks – the large, infrequent deals these investments created had the power to shape a vendor's profitability for years to come. Following the COVID-19 pandemic, global semiconductor shortages and supply chain disruptions demanded significant attention from both management and boards. Adding to this complexity, the escalating US-China trade conflict further politicized the telecommunications equipment market. Under US pressure, several governments opted to exclude Huawei, Nokia's strongest competitor from China, from their national telecommunications infrastructure. At the same time, China's growing political influence raised the risk of retaliation in nations more closely aligned with its interests. Compounding these challenges, sustainability and corporate responsibility emerged as critical priorities, commanding a substantial share of the board's focus.

As Smits-Nusteling prepared for the meeting, she reflected on how the role of a board member has evolved:

> Ten years ago, being on the board was a well-paid side job with a lot of status. You came to the office five or six times a year, had a nice dinner and some strategic conversations. Today, it is a professional job. The expectations from shareholders and the general public on what the board can and cannot influence, or is supposed to influence, have skyrocketed, especially when things go wrong.

Smits-Nusteling is not alone in her assessment of the changing demands on modern boards. Almost every board member interviewed for this book mentioned the sheer increase in issues that boards now handle. As Johannes Huth, former partner at private equity firm KKR, senior independent director of Coty Inc, and director at Axel Springer, explained: "The issues are not necessarily new, but the environment has become more complex and faster paced. There are more changes and uncertainties that challenge companies, and the boards have to adapt to that."

However, many board members stressed that it is not just a quantitative shift. There has also been a qualitative change in expectations by many investors. Luka Mucic, director at Heidelberg Materials, explained:

> We have a huge sustainability challenge. Sustainability is having a massive impact on our core business. It can either be the driver of great value creation or, conversely, can really call the core principles of operations into question. We need to reinvent ourselves to address it.

However, some directors were more cautious in their assessment following the change of government in the US in early 2025. For instance, one director of a large US company who preferred to remain anonymous explained:

> The one overwhelming change in the business environment in past years has been that investors have forced boards to hold management accountable on sustainability. And that has created quite important new requirements that never existed before. But in the current political environment, we do not know if it is here to stay. For now, investors continue to keep it on the board's agenda but that could change, especially here in the US.

In this first chapter, we examine these shifts and what they mean for boards, laying the groundwork for the chapters that follow.

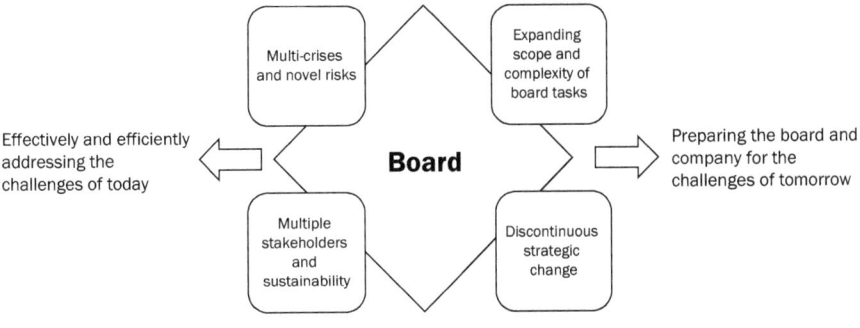

Figure 1.1   The New Forcefield of Board Work and the Dual Challenge of Modern Boards

As shown in Figure 1.1, today, boards are operating in a forcefield shaped by at least four broad forces that together create a dual challenge. Following the COVID-19 pandemic, boards have had to learn to steer companies through successive large-scale crises on a global scale and to deal with novel types of risk. At the same time, governments, regulators, investors, and proxy advisors have introduced many new items to the board's agenda. These new priorities have forced boards to become more effective and efficient in handling an increasingly complex workload.

Addressing today's challenges alone does not guarantee a corporation's success in the current environment. Companies have become subject to more intense pressures from multiple stakeholders and must find ways to build sustainability into their core strategy. Meeting these demands involves more than simply being effective and efficient; it calls for fundamentally rethinking how both the corporation and the board conduct business. Technological changes, new business models, and a shift in the global political environment toward de-globalization have also created discontinuous strategic change in many corporations' operating environments and elevated the need for strategic thinking to a new level. To fulfill these strategic responsibilities while managing an ever-expanding array of governance tasks requires unprecedented agility.

Multi-crisis and novel risks

One factor behind the intensifying demands on boards is that today's business environment is best described as a multi-crisis or poly-crisis context.[1] Over the past five years, businesses have had to deal with a pandemic, the Russian invasion of Ukraine, the escalating conflict between Israel and its neighbors, global inflation and economic volatility at a level not seen for a long time, a surge in climate change-related natural disasters, and supply chain disruptions following these disasters. In light of these crises, companies, their boards, and their leadership teams must cultivate a new level of resilience and agility to keep pace and respond effectively to ever-new shocks.[2] Johannes Huth, former partner at KKR, senior independent director of Coty Inc., and director at Axel Springer, highlighted this:

> With some of my boards, we have monthly calls, update calls, deep dives with business heads. You are simply in a much faster and more intensive interaction with the company now than in the past to deal with all the events happening around you.

More specifically, in light of consecutive crises spanning economic, environmental, and political spheres, boards face heightened expectations for robust risk management.[3] A much-enlarged spectrum of risks, including but not limited to technological, financial, environmental, and geopolitical risks, now falls under the board's purview. Many of these risks are novel, calling for the implementation of structured frameworks for risk management to mitigate potential operational failures and reputational damage.

Moreover, governments, regulators, proxy advisors, and shareholders demand more transparency, accountability, and stronger performance on risk issues. For instance, Jean-Pierre Clamadieu, chair of French energy company Engie and director of Airbus and TE Connectivity, put it this way: "Shareholders are putting a lot of expectations onto the board and there is a new level of pressure for accountability."

Consequently, boards find themselves under growing scrutiny. They must justify decisions to a diverse range of stakeholders and face potentially serious pushback if outcomes do not meet expectations. This increased pressure forces boards to spend more time and energy on robust risk oversight and adds complexity to their work. Put simply, boards must be both highly responsive and proactive in discharging their governance duties.

Expanding the scope and complexity of board responsibilities

Another driver of the increasing demands on board work is the expanding scope of their responsibilities. A number of issues have been escalated to the board level in recent years, including digital transformation,[4] artificial intelligence,[5] cybersecurity,[6] and supply chain, to name only a few. While some of these challenges are fundamentally new and would normally come under the board's remit, given the potential implications for the firm's overall strategy – AI and digitalization, for example – others simply have temporarily risen in importance. The question is whether they all belong on the board agenda in the long term. When an issue is escalated to board level, it is usually a signal of its importance and a call for a new director with a specific skillset, along with regular discussion.[7]

The increasing workload and complexity that result from this upswing in board responsibilities pose challenges to maintaining depth in any of the areas and could potentially impact overall governance quality.[8] Joerg Reinhardt, chair of Novartis and member of the board of SwissRe, conveyed this concern: "Individual board members spend more and more time on board work than ever before. There are more meetings of the full board, more committees, and more work outside of meetings and committees. It is becoming a challenge."

Board members are beginning to question if the board has the capacity and the skillset needed to fulfill this expanding scope without overextending members or diluting focus on strategic issues.

In fact, during our research, multiple board members raised the possibility that an expansion of the scope of the board's oversight and advisory role could, in fact, come at the expense of a meaningful role in strategy work. For instance, Jeff Campbell, former vice chairman and CFO of American Express, former CFO of McKesson and American Airlines, and current director at AON plc, Marathon Petroleum Corp., and Hexcel Corp, shared: "The expectations of regulators and other stakeholders to get deep into a lot of new topics make it very challenging to raise the board back up to thinking about strategy."

Riet Cadonau, experienced board chair and director and current director at the Zehnder Group AG, expressed a more provocative view:

> In my opinion, reporting and compliance are getting out of control in publicly listed companies. These [compliance] reports, if you add them all up, annual report, governance report, sustainability report, remuneration report, etc., add up to several hundred pages, even for a medium-sized company. And the board must be on top of all of that. My concern is that the board is too busy with all these compliance issues and has too little time for the core strategic issues, for markets, for technology and innovation, or for HR topics.

To keep focus on strategy, today's boards must carefully prioritize what topics to take on board and be selective and strategic in determining where to focus their attention to avoid overextension.[9] Jean-Pierre Clamadieu, chair of French energy company Engie and director of Airbus and TE Connectivity, highlighted the importance of careful prioritization:

> When we do our yearly board assessment, there is always a long list of additional subjects that board members would like to add to the topics to be discussed. But what we really should ask is, "What should we stop doing in return for adding a topic?" That's a bigger challenge.

If the board is constantly reacting to new demands, it risks allocating insufficient time to forward-looking activities, potentially missing growth opportunities.[10] Similarly, adding new members or creating new committees is not the right solution to address these demands, but rather careful consideration should be taken on what tasks to take on and to ensure alignment with strategic priorities to maintain effective governance.

Discontinuous strategic change

Taken on their own, the multi-crisis environment and the expanding scope of board work create demands that could be addressed by strict implementation of good governance practices, as specified in many governance codices and recent books on high-performing boards.[11] However, running parallel to these two developments are several trends that radically increase the uncertainty and complexity of the business environment and, therefore, compel boards to renew their focus on strategy.[12] Peter Voser, board chair at ABB, PSA International, and member of the board at IBM, emphasized: "One thing which has clearly changed in the business environment is the importance of setting, discussing, monitoring and challenging the strategy."

Specifically, corporations face several strategic discontinuities that require a rethinking of strategy and a stark shift in focus from today to the future. In fact, at the time of writing, topics such as the strategic implications of AI and the new global geopolitical environment and its impact on worldwide trade and international relations have joined, if not replaced, sustainability as the most discussed subject at Davos, an indicator of what is on the agenda for many boards.[13]

The rise of digitalization and especially AI is a technological discontinuity that is diffusing across most industries. For many companies, it creates the opportunity or even necessity to reinvent their business model or strategic direction. Few companies can afford to ignore the strategic implications of these game-changing technologies.[14]

Also, in the geopolitical arena, a fundamental shift has taken place from decades of increasing globalization to de-globalization, the rise of new protectionism, trade conflicts, and bloc-building. Following the appointment of a new government in the US, traditional political alliances have been put into question, and at the final stages of writing this book, wide-ranging tariffs imposed by the US have put the global trade paradigm of decades at risk, with implications for corporations that are difficult to predict. These changes have forced companies and their boards to reevaluate their international exposure and approach to avoid becoming collateral damage of changing political priorities in many countries. In this new geopolitical environment, operational planning and risk management have taken on a new level of complexity. More importantly, in a fragmenting world characterized by rising nationalism, protectionism, trade conflicts, and increasingly unpredictable political changes, firms must fundamentally reevaluate their geographic footprint and international strategy.[15]

To play an active role in these changes, boards must shift focus from compliance and overseeing the past toward creating future opportunities and innovation, and providing strategic foresight. They must reconcile their focus on immediate financial pressures with a focus on long-term strategy, growth, and sustainability objectives. Pauline Van der Meer, Mohr chair of the Dutch semiconductor equipment manufacturer ASM and director of Ahold Delhaize, NN Group, described this balancing act:

> There is always a dilemma between long term and short term. Many companies are starting to think about and define their goals in the

context of longer-term sustainability. But it is often disconnected from the shorter-term perspective and decision-making. There is too little integrated thinking, and boards often do not connect the dots.

The rapidly changing business environment, characterized by technological advancements and evolving market conditions, requires boards to engage in continuous strategic discussions. The best boards intentionally dedicate substantial portions of every meeting to strategic conversations focused on future planning and strategic issues. For instance, one director from a large French corporation illustrated this practice: "Strategy is in every board meeting and often takes half of each session. We have a continuous view of the strategic topics and focus on the long-term issues."

Especially during times of unprecedented levels of uncertainty, a premium for constant monitoring and re-evaluation of the environment by the board exists to gain a thorough understanding of challenges and opportunities that emerge.

Ongoing strategic conversations enable boards to stay ahead of market trends and make proactive decisions. By focusing on the future, they can provide greater value through strategic insights, counsel, and guidance to management. In times of uncertainty, a future-oriented approach is essential for fostering necessary innovation, ensuring long-term sustainable value creation, and sustaining competitive advantage. It entails cultivating a culture where change and new opportunities are embraced rather than treated as disruptions.

Multi-stakeholders and sustainability

The heightened uncertainty and complexity arising from geopolitical changes and discontinuous technological changes are not the only drivers that force boards to renew their focus on strategy. Luka Mucic, director at Heidelberg Materials, underscored the transformative effect of sustainability and multiple stakeholders on companies and the board's work:

> We have a huge sustainability challenge. It is a topic that we are all still learning, but it is having a massive impact on our core business. It can either be the driver of great value creation or, conversely, can really call the core principles of operations into question.

In line with the magnitude of the challenge, scholars and practitioners have called
f   rds to shift from focusing solely on financial metrics toward a holistic view
           ces financial, social, and environmental outcomes.[16] Simply put, boards
              ʳ weigh profit against sustainability as separate or competing goals.
                 ˢt develop strategies that integrate both objectives.
                    ʲnal boardroom thinking, especially in the Anglo-Saxon con-
                       ` on shareholder returns, there has been a marked shift over

the past decade toward addressing a wider range of stakeholders – employees, communities, governments, and society at large.[17] Kalidas Madhavpeddi, chair of Glencore, described the changed expectations:

> Over the last decade, the focus of the Board and management team has continued to evolve. We now have to think 360 degrees, for example, from climate to your communities, your social presence, and your internet presence, as opposed to being focused on profit and the ten degrees that you are operating in. And that requires a different mindset from boards and from management, as they need to be much more in tune with what is happening 360 degrees around.

By adopting this broader perspective, boards can more effectively tackle social, environmental, and governance challenges, building organizational resilience and delivering a positive societal impact.[18] Boards need to balance the interests of shareholders with those of other stakeholders, requiring changed governance frameworks and a focus on a clear definition of corporate purpose.[19]

In some regions of the world, particularly in the US, efforts toward sustainability have faced renewed opposition due to political polarization,[20] often conflating concepts such as ESG (Environmental, Social, and Governance) with leftist politics and political wokeness. However, addressing fundamental issues like climate change and social equity remains critical, and integrating them into corporate strategy simply makes good business sense as they align with stakeholder expectations, especially among younger customers and employees,[21] and are essential for long-term value creation. In this book, we focus on the notion of sustainability (rather than using loaded terms such as ESG) to capture the idea that stakeholders in most countries demand corporate performance on sustainability metrics alongside financial performance, which makes sustainability a strategic, not just a reporting, issue.

Becoming serious about sustainability, however, requires fundamental strategic rethinking by many boards and corporations. Many organizations continue to treat sustainability as a mere exercise in compliance, which diverts attention away from strategic opportunities, and, therefore, they prefer to relegate it to a committee rather than using it to stimulate strategic innovation. And despite public commitments to stakeholder interests, many companies have not significantly altered governance structures. For instance, in 2019, the Business Roundtable pledged to shift from shareholder primacy to a stakeholder-oriented approach. While the pledge was seen as a significant moment for corporate governance, potentially initiating a shift to a broader incorporation of sustainability as the main goal of the firm, the actual change has been limited. Most companies that signed the pledge have kept their governance structures the same; shareholder interests still dominate the decision-making process, and sustainability is not a priority.[22]

Risto Siilasmaa, former board chair (until 2020) of Nokia, offered a stark example of the gap between words and actions:

> Many companies talk in one way and act in another way. Taxes are a good litmus test for this. Every year, at Nokia, we had a target for the taxes we pay, and that had ranged around 24–28 percent. Other companies choose to minimize their taxes, maybe to as little as 10 percent or less. As long as that is practice, I believe that we have a major issue with being a good corporate citizen.

Following the recent shift toward a conservative government in the US, many companies have pulled back their pledges. Some have been forced to do so by aggressive shareholder lawsuits.

In our view, boards should continue to explore how sustainability can become core to both their own purpose and the broader purpose of the company and inform strategy in a way that is value-creating; however, they need to do so in a manner that is shareholder value-creating and compliant with public policy. Boards should strive to create both societal impact and financial returns, as this aligns with the expectations of many investors, customers, employees, and other key stakeholders, even in the current environment. This will require a fundamental strategic rethinking from the side of the board. Delivering on this vision requires reimagining the board's role and modes of operation. Many boards are not yet prepared for this shift and will need to adapt how they function in response.

From new forces toward the dual challenge of boards

Taken together, the forces outlined in this chapter create a dual challenge for modern boards and the organizations they govern. On the one hand, boards must be razor-focused on driving efficiency and effectiveness by refining and streamlining governance processes so they can effectively handle the risks emanating from multiple crises and incorporate the growing number of new requirements into the board agenda. For the many boards that are still catching up to the current standards of good governance and best practices, this alone demands a significant upgrade in their processes and skill sets. However, spending too much time on regulatory and compliance matters may prioritize the focus on the present, arguably diverting discussions away from strategy. Dedicating excessive time to regulatory and compliance issues carries the risk of overshadowing strategic discussions crucial for the company's future, and a compliance-heavy approach may hinder the board's ability to identify and capitalize on emerging trends and innovations or address new challenges in a timely manner.

This is where the second part of the dual challenge becomes paramount. The discontinuities and fundamental strategic shifts that arise from sustainability, technological change, new business models, and geopolitical shifts require a new level of focus on strategy and a level of board agility that demand new approaches to governance and novel practices. Boards may have to collaborate with management in new ways, fostering a culture of innovation and speed that meets the realities of an evolving market. The need to develop new practices for the future, while continuing to refine today's governance standards, is a core challenge, even for boards that consider themselves best-in-class. Luka Mucic, member of the board of Heidelberg Materials, summed up this tension:

> The question of how a board can have the capability to not only monitor a management team in this more challenging global environment, but also provide meaningful strategic support and advice for the future, has become the central challenge of many boards.

This dual challenge is the focus of the core of this book. In the next chapter, we introduce a framework designed to help board chairs and directors navigate the dimensions of these complex demands.

Notes

1. https://www.weforum.org/stories/2023/03/polycrisis-adam-tooze-historian-explains/.
2. Thomas Keil and Marianna Zangrillo, "Building Organizational Resilience: When the Entire Organization Should Be Engaged and Power Unleashed," in *Building Resilient Organizations*, ed. Stuart Crainer (Newtown Square, PA: Thinkers50/Brightline, 2022).
3. Gaizka Ormazabal, "Risk Oversight: What Every Director Should Know," *IESE Insight* 28, no. 28 (2016).
4. Linda M. Sama, Abraham Stefanidis, and R. Mitch Casselman, "Rethinking Corporate Governance in the Digital Economy: The Role of Stewardship," *Business Horizons* 65, no. 5 (2022).
5. Vivek Sharma and David C. Edelman, "It's Time for Boards to Take AI Seriously," *HBR.org, Harvard Business Review*, November 02, 2023, https://hbr.org/2023/11/its-time-for-boards-to-take-ai-seriously.
6. Ray A. Rothrock, James Kaplan, and Friso Van Der Oord, "The Board's Role in Managing Cybersecurity Risks," *MIT Sloan Management Review* 59, no. 2 (2018); Chon Abraham, Sasha Cohen O'Connell, Iria Giuffrida, and Ronald R. Sims, "Adding Cybersecurity Expertise to Your Board," *MIT Sloan Management Review* 65, no. 2 (2024).
7. Peter Weill, Thomas Apel, Stephanie L. Woerner, and Jennifer S. Banner. "It Pays to Have a Digitally Savvy Board," *MIT Sloan Management Review* 60, no. 3 (Spring 2019); Mason A. Carpenter, Wm Gerard Sanders, and Hal B. Gregersen, "Bundling Human Capital with Organizational Context: The Impact of International Assignment Experience on Multinational Firm Performance and CEO Pay," *Academy of Management Journal* 44, no. 3 (June 2001); M. L. McDonald, J. D. Westphal, and M. E. Graebner, "What Do They Know? The Effects of Outside Director Acquisition

Experience on Firm Acquisition Performance," *Strategic Management Journal* 29, no. 11 (November 2008).

8. Stevo Pavićević, Thomas Keil, and Zahra Shaker, *A Board Capital Perspective on Corporate Entrepreneurship in Technology-Intensive Firms*, Working Paper (Frankfurt: Frankfurt School of Finance and Management, 2025).

9. Christopher S. Tuggle, Karen Schnatterly, and Richard A. Johnson, "Attention Patterns in the Boardroom: How Board Composition and Processes Affect Discussion of Entrepreneurial Issues," *Academy of Management Journal* 53, no. 3 (June 2010); Christopher S. Tuggle, David G. Sirmon, Christopher R. Reutzel, and Leonard Bierman. "Commanding Board of Director Attention: Investigating How Organizational Performance and CEO Duality Affect Board Members' Attention to Monitoring," *Strategic Management Journal* 31, no. 9 (2010); Pavićević, Keil, and Shaker, *A Board Capital Perspective on Corporate Entrepreneurship in Technology-Intensive Firms*.

10. Larry Bennigson and Frank S. Leonard, "Bringing Opportunity Oversight onto the Boards Agenda," *MIT Sloan Management Review* 54, no. 3 (2013).

11. Richard Leblanc, *The Handbook of Board Governance: A Comprehensive Guide for Public, Private, and Not-for-Profit Board Members* (Hoboken, NJ: John Wiley & Sons, 2020); Gerry Brown and Randall S. Peterson, *Disaster in the Boardroom: Six Dysfunctions Everyone Should Understand* (Cham: Springer/Palgrave McMillan, 2022); Didier Cossin, *High Performance Boards: Improving and Energizing Your Governance* (Chichester: John Wiley & Sons, 2024).

12. Dunigan O'Keeffe, Karen Harris, and Austin Kimson, "How to Succeed in an Era of Volatility (Cover Story)," Article, *Harvard Business Review* 102, no. 2 (2024).

13. Gayle Markovitz, Kate Whiting, and Spencer Feingold, "5 Takeaways from Davos 2025," *World Economic Forum*, Jan 24, 2025, https://www.weforum.org/stories/2025/01/5-key-takeaways-davos-2025/.

14. Scott Cook, Andrei Hagiu, and Julian Wright, "Turn Generative AI from an Existential Threat into a Competitive Advantage," Article, *Harvard Business Review* 102, no. 1 (2024); Toby E. Stuart, "Could Gen AI End Incumbent Firms' Competitive Advantage?," *HBR.org*, *Harvard Business Review*, November 21, 2024, https://hbr.org/2024/11/could-gen-ai-end-incumbent-firms-competitive-advantage; Ajay Agrawal, Joshua Gans, and Avi Goldfarb, "How AI Will Change Strategy: A Thought Experiment," *HBR.org*. *Harvard Business Review,* October 3, 2017, https://hbr.org/2017/10/how-ai-will-change-strategy-a-thought-experiment; David Edelman and Vivek Sharma, "It's Time for Boards to Take AI Seriously," *HBR.org*, *Harvard Business Review*, November 2, 2023, https://hbr.org/2023/11/its-time-for-boards-to-take-ai-seriously; Milan Miric, "Strategy, Not Technology, Is the Key to Winning with Genai," *HBR.org*, *Harvard Business Review*, December 6, 2023, https://hbr.org/2023/12/strategy-not-technology-is-the-key-to-winning-with-genai; Tomas Chamorro-Premuzic and Darko Lovric, "How to Decide If AI Should Be Part of Your Growth Strategy," *HBR.org*, *Harvard Business Review*, March 20, 2024, https://hbr.org/2024/03/how-to-decide-if-ai-should-be-part-of-your-growth-strategy; David Kiron, Michael Schrage, François Candelon, Shervin Khodabandeh, and Michael Chu, "Governance for Smarter KPIs: Effective Governance Enables Kpis to Evolve, Remain Aligned with Strategic Goals, and Gain Workers' and Managers' Trust," *sloanreview.mit.edu*. *MIT Sloan Management Review*, November 06, 2023, https://sloanreview.mit.edu/article/governance-for-smarter-kpis/; Kartik Hosanagar and Ramayya Krishnan, "Who Profits the Most from Generative Ai?," *MIT Sloan Management Review* 65, no. 3 (Spring 2024); David Kiron and Michael Schrage, "Strategy for and with AI," *MIT Sloan Management Review* 60, no. 4 (Summer 2019).

15. Tobias Feakin, "Navigating the New Geopolitics of Tech," *HBR.org*, *Harvard Business Review*, November 11, 2024, https://hbr.org/2024/11/navigating-the-new-geopolitics-of-tech; Dambisa Moyo, "Are Businesses Ready for Deglobalization?," *HBR.org*, *Harvard Business Review*, December 6, 2019, https://hbr.org/2019/12/are-businesses-ready-for-deglobalization; David Garfield, "Supply Chains Belong at the Top of a CEO's Agenda: Five Ways Leaders Can Navigate the Growing Risks of Instability and Disruption without Getting Bogged Down in Tactical Issues," *HBR.org*, *Harvard Business Review*, September 30, 2024, https://hbr.org/2024/09/supply-chains-belong-at-the-top-of-a-ceos-agenda; Vijay Govindarajan, Anup Srivastava, Hussein Warsame, and Luminita Enache, "Tech Giants, Taxes, and a Looming Global Trade War," *HBR.org*, *Harvard Business Review*, August 24, 2020, https://hbr.org/2020/08/tech-giants-taxes-and-a-looming-global-trade-war; Pankaj Ghemawat, "Globalization in the Age of Trump: Protectionism Will Change How Companies Do Business – But Not in the Ways You Think," *Harvard Business Review* 95, no. 4 (2017); Omri Nahmias, "Deglobalization," *MIT Sloan Management Review* 65, no. 3 (Spring 2024); Satish Nambisan and L. U. O. Yadong, "Think Globally, Innovate Locally," *MIT Sloan Management Review* 63, no. 3 (Spring 2022).
16. Edward E. Lawler and Christopher G. Worley, "Why Boards Need to Change," *MIT Sloan Management Review* 54, no. 1 (2012).
17. Sarah Cliffe and Barbara Hackman Franklin, "The Board View: Directors Must Balance All Interests a Conversation with Corporate Governance Expert Barbara Hackman Franklin by Sarah Cliffe," Editorial Material, *Harvard Business Review* 95, no. 3 (May–Jun 2017).
18. Robert G. Eccles and Tim Youmans, "Why Boards Must Look Beyond Shareholders," *sloanreview.mit.edu*, *MIT Sloan Management Review*, 2015, https://sloanreview.mit.edu/article/why-boards-must-look-beyond-shareholders/.
19. Lynn S. Paine and Suraj Srinivasan, "A Guide to the Big Ideas and Debates in Corporate Governance," *HBR.org*, *Harvard Business Review*, October 14, 2019, 2019, https://hbr.org/2019/10/a-guide-to-the-big-ideas-and-debates-in-corporate-governance.
20. Daniel F. C. Crowley and Robert G. Eccles, "Rescuing ESG from the Culture Wars," *HBR.org*, *Harvard Business Review*, February 09, 2023, https://hbr.org/2023/02/rescuing-esg-from-the-culture-wars.
21. Andrew Winston, "Why Business Leaders Must Resist the Anti-ESG Movement," *HBR.org*, *Harvard Business Review*, April 05, 2023, https://hbr.org/2023/04/why-business-leaders-must-resist-the-anti-esg-movement.
22. Lynn S. Paine, "The Business Roundtable's Stakeholder Pledge, Five Years Later," *HBR.org*, *Harvard Business Review*, August 19, 2024, https://hbr.org/2024/08/the-business-roundtables-stakeholder-pledge-five-years-later.

Chapter 2

Dealing with the dual challenge of the board

The board diamond

Jörg Reinhardt was reflecting on his ten-year tenure as chair of Novartis, a global leader in the pharmaceutical industry. Reinhardt, a healthcare industry veteran with 40 years of experience in various pharmaceutical companies, was named board chair in 2013. Since his appointment, Novartis has faced a decade of significant changes. Competition has intensified, driven by strong pricing pressure on all drugs, patent expirations on certain high-revenue products, industry consolidation through mergers and acquisitions, and a broader shift in large pharmaceutical companies toward innovation and specialty products. In 2018, these trends prompted Novartis to undertake a strategic transformation and appoint a new CEO. Under Vas Narasimhan, the organization refocused its business portfolio by spinning off its eye care division, Alcon, as an independent publicly traded company; selling its 36.5 percent stake in a consumer healthcare joint venture to GlaxoSmithKline (GSK); disposing of its one-third voting stake in rival Roche; and separating its generics and biosimilars division, Sandoz, in 2023. Like many other firms, Novartis also grappled with a more complex operating environment amid the pandemic, the war in Ukraine, and heightened global trade tensions.

As board chair, Reinhardt's mission was not only to guide Novartis through these changes but also to position the company and its board for the future. This called for adjustments across all dimensions of the board. One such area was board

DOI: 10.4324/9781003532200-4

composition, which gradually shifted toward greater diversity and included a higher proportion of younger members, as Reinhardt noted:

> There is a trend towards rejuvenation on boards. Ten years ago, people were over sixty and had their careers behind them. Today, we are hiring professionals, people who are in their fifties, who are tired of being executives but want to be actively involved in two or three boards. We also have two active CEOs, and of course, they have very different schedules, but they can be excellent sparring partners for our CEO. So we try to have a mix of people who play different roles.

The board's ways of working changed as well, with an expanding workload and an ever-increasing number of topics on the agenda. This growth in responsibilities required delegating more items to committees, while simultaneously imposing the need for stricter performance management. For instance, as sustainability had become a high priority in corporate governance, Novartis created a committee focused specifically on sustainability. Reinhardt explained:

> How much time does the board have to spend if you look at all the topics that we have to work through with a level of detail that is meaningful? You can't do it on the full board. It is simply necessary to move them into committees, which then have more time for a single topic.

All these changes also affected Reinhardt's own role as board chair, demanding greater involvement and leadership. He shared:

> The days of the schnapps-drinking, cigar-smoking board chair are over. Expectations have changed massively. Stakeholders today expect quite a different level of involvement and knowledge of what is going on throughout the company at a quite detailed level. And the board needs more leadership to manage the different committees and the relationship with the executive team. But it only works with modern leadership instruments. You have to build around trust and openness.

As the example of Novartis illustrates, creating a modern board cannot rest on a single pillar; rather, it requires a careful configuration of multiple levers to respond to the dual challenge we highlighted in the previous chapter: dealing effectively and efficiently with today's multitude of issues while at the same time preparing for the challenges of tomorrow.

We refer to this configuration of levers as the board diamond (see Figure 2.1). Our board diamond consists of five distinct dimensions: (1) The board's "purpose and role," which defines the tasks the board is taking on and why; (2) who should be on the board ("the people"); (3) "structures and processes" that are central to

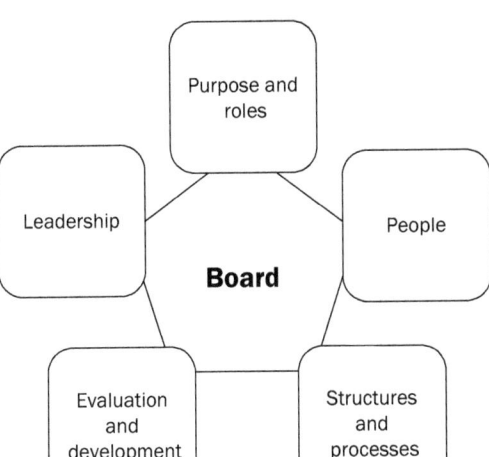

Figure 2.1   The Board Diamond

completing the board tasks; (4) the "board leadership" that defines the role of the board chair and committee chairs; and finally (5) "evaluation and board development" to measure and improve performance and build the necessary skills and tools for tomorrow. None of these dimensions is novel or surprising on its own, and, indeed, the same dimensions could also be applied to the leadership team[1] or other levels of the organization. However, the true insight of the board diamond framework lies in understanding of how each of these five dimensions needs to be fine-tuned to enable the board to excel at the tasks of today and the challenges of tomorrow, and how these dimensions need to be adjusted relative to each other as well as to the specific context of the company.

Purpose and roles

The first step in enabling a board to meet the dual challenge is to clarify its purpose and roles in the organization's strategic apex. In our conversations with board chairs and board members, we encountered very different conceptions of the board's purpose.[2] In particular, executives and CEOs in the companies we studied often held different views on the board's purpose from the board members.

Some boards still see themselves primarily as exclusive clubs of experienced leaders (often former CEOs and CFOs) who serve as wise advisors to the CEO and executive team. Others view their purpose primarily as a mechanism for monitoring and control, chiefly fulfilling externally mandated supervision tasks.

The most advanced boards we encountered view themselves as an integral part of the company's strategic apex, playing multiple roles and adeptly balancing and shifting seamlessly between strategic advice to the CEO and executive team, collaborating with each of them on strategy for the future, and monitoring their actions. This expanded sense of responsibility often involves participation in more tasks than historically associated with a board, and the emphasis on various tasks can shift with the company's changing circumstances and the situation the firm finds itself in. For instance, in times of crisis and rapid change, boards must expand their responsibilities to guide the firm's adaptation and ensure organizational resilience.

To succeed in this modern conception of the board, board chairs and directors need to focus explicitly on balancing immediate priorities and future concerns. A focus on the present requires the board to serve as an effective and efficient monitor governing the company. Increasingly, boards are struggling with focusing their attention on what matters most today, given the breadth of newly emerging issues. As boards face demands to oversee a growing number of topics, they risk diluting their focus and, therefore, risk spreading themselves too thin, thus undermining their effectiveness. This calls for boards to ruthlessly manage their agendas and prioritize strategic issues where they can add the most value, avoid scope creep, and ensure they are not overburdened by compliance and operational matters. By maintaining clarity of roles, delegating operational details to management, and concentrating on strategic guidance, boards can empower management to execute their duties effectively while ensuring appropriate oversight mechanisms are in place.

However, given the fundamental changes in the operating environment that we identified in Chapter 1, boards have a key role in steering the CEO's and executives' focus of attention toward long-term strategy and the purpose of the corporation. In this capacity, the board plays a central advisory and guiding role in strategy making. While boards can play varying roles in the strategy process, the most effective boards foster an open dialogue with management using clear frameworks for strategic input and are focused on sustainable, long-term value creation.

Striking this balance between today and tomorrow also means the board must become a steward of the company's purpose and broader contribution to society. Thomas Thune Andersen, chair at Lloyd's Register Group and VKR Holding, and member of the board at BW Group and IMI plc, underscored this important role of the board:

> One of the things where the board really plays an important role is the purpose of the corporation, the long hairy goal, the societal challenge that you want to address. The board is responsible for trying to ensure that people who work in the company and people outside the company feel that there's a relevance and a purpose in what the company is doing. That is central to the board's work.

Linking the board's purpose and roles with the company's purpose is crucial for building trust and mitigating conflicts among customers, employees, and society.[3] To remain relevant in the future, boards can play a critical role in defining the company's purpose beyond simple profit generation, aligning it with societal challenges and stakeholder expectations. Anne Lange, director at Pernod-Ricard, Orange, and Inditex, noted:

> It used to be that we were successful if we made a profit. What is changing is that companies and their boards are requested to go much beyond that in a world where maintaining the right balance between short-term and long-term requires new arbitrages between performance and robustness. As a board, we are requested to contribute to the good of the shareholders, the employees, and the entire society when sustainability is involved.

Modern boards may also find themselves playing a more active role in public discourse.[4] In doing so, boards must carefully decide how and when to engage in societal debates, balancing advocacy with caution, ensuring that they support social progress without stepping too far beyond their mandate or alienating key stakeholders.

People

The second dimension of our board diamond focuses on who should be on the board, that is, the people dimension of boards. Addressing the dual challenge requires a changing mix of directors and a shift in thinking from viewing the board as a collection of peer experts to seeing it as a structured team. The right mix of individuals is also linked to the board's chosen purpose and roles. Boards need a combination of industry-specific knowledge, strategic thinking, and diverse perspectives to enhance governance quality and provide meaningful strategic guidance. The board's composition should also align with the company's strategic objectives, industry context, and governance requirements.[5] Equipping the board with the necessary expertise needed to address current and future challenges means tailoring its makeup to industry requirements and adapting governance structures to fit an ever-changing company context.

To enable the board to address the new requirements arising from discontinuous strategic change, board design needs to take diversity seriously. For instance, Nicolas Boël, former chair of Solvay, explained:

> One of the key fundamentals to a strong board is to be able to find the right combination of diversity, diversity of experiences, diversity of perspective combined with the same set of core values and the same purpose. Your board members need to be able to bring something different in terms of experience and expertise, but at the same time partake in the same vision that you have.

Although most boards acknowledge the importance of diversity, many struggle to move beyond superficial gestures that fail to shift real power or alter decision-making.[6]

Genuine diversity involves not just bringing different demographics onto the board but also creating an inclusive environment where all directors fully participate and contribute.[7]

Many boards have traditionally worked as a group of independent experts that met relatively rarely and, therefore, did not function as a team. However, modern boards need to function more as cohesive teams that work together closely and leverage the unique strengths of their members to achieve common objectives.[8] Many boards struggle with this due to the infrequency of interaction, lack of mutual trust, and the dominance of some members, all of which serve as obstacles to the creation of a high-performance team.[9] Cultivating a shared purpose, mutual respect, and trust is therefore essential for boards to be able to address the dual challenge of modern governance. This starts with ensuring that directors are there for the right reasons – motivated by genuine service rather than personal benefit – but it also demands regular face-to-face interactions, investing in team-building activities, fostering open dialogue, and a strong facilitating role for the chair.

Our research highlights several key considerations for selecting the right mix of directors. A board needs to balance unique expertise, industry knowledge, and independence; an excessive focus on any one of these dimensions can be problematic. For instance, excessive emphasis on independence can lead to a lack of industry and company knowledge, thereby reducing the board's effectiveness. Also critical in identifying individuals capable of facing the multiple challenges of a modern board role are personality characteristics, alignment of values, and motivations. Boards should seek directors who are curious, courageous, mentally independent, and team-oriented. They should thoroughly assess candidates for personality and values alignment and avoid dominant personalities that hinder collaboration.

Each director should be viewed as part of a larger puzzle consisting of the board chair, the board members, the CEO, and the leadership team: the pieces of the puzzle need to be selected to fit and complement each other and complete the whole picture. A director of a large German corporation explained:

> What you need in the future is really team players who understand the supervisory board as a team, but also understand that you are in the team with the management board. Although you have very different roles, you are all in the same boat. And each of the team players has their role. You are not the referee that is sort of outside, you are responsible for the success of the company, and you are also responsible for driving in the right direction and making it happen.

Finally, to avoid self-perpetuating boards, it's important to refresh membership with new perspectives through transparent selection processes, regularly assess the board's effectiveness, use skills matrices to identify skill gaps, and engage in proactive and forward-looking succession planning.

Structure and processes

The third dimension of the board diamond concerns the structures and processes boards use to accomplish their tasks. As boards take on an expanding array of roles – including those prompted by regulatory requirements – and aim to make the most of directors' expertise, it is no longer feasible to rely on informal, loosely organized approaches.[10] Many boards have either transformed or need to transform into professional entities with clear management structures, well-defined processes, explicit role definitions, and dedicated leadership. Structures and processes also help build resilience, enabling a board to respond quickly to crises and changing conditions.

Professionalization can involve establishing specialized committees, implementing defined processes and protocols, and evolving the chair's role to better coordinate activities and align the board's work with the company's strategic objectives. Moreover, improvements in technology – ranging from virtual meeting platforms to artificial intelligence – affect how boards operate, which means boards must also adopt these tools to stay effective.

Board committees and working groups are crucial for effective governance since they allow focused attention on specific areas, enable leveraging of specialized expertise, and improve efficiency.[11] Joerg Reinhardt, chair of Novartis and member of the board of SwissRe, explained this logic to us:

> For the board, you really have binding time constraints. If you look at all the topics we have to handle, it is necessary to move at least some of them into committees so that you have enough time for the single topic.

That said, committees introduce their own challenges and require a shift in the approach to the functioning of the board. To be effective, committees require careful management to avoid creating in-group-out-group dynamics. An overreliance on committees may also dilute full board oversight.[12] This makes it essential for committees to have clear mandates and roles, a strong committee chair, membership that is thoughtfully selected based on required expertise, and periodical review of each committee's performance and overall purpose by the board, ensuring that committees help rather than hinder governance.

While structures and processes are particularly important for boosting efficiency and effectiveness in addressing current concerns, practices related to open discussion, debate, and decision-making are central to enabling the focus on the future that is needed to balance the forces underlying the board's dual challenge.

In particular, a strong future orientation requires open discussions and constructive conflict. The candid conversations and collaborative problem-solving necessary to address problems that are novel for both the CEO and leadership team and the board require establishing a culture of trust, psychological safety, and collaboration, and behavioral norms that support that culture. Boards need to function as cohesive teams with collective responsibility, operating in an environment where psychological safety allows for open communication. Creating such an environment does not come automatically but requires commitment and work from all board members and leadership from the board chair. It often requires managing egos and the resulting power dynamics. To foster open communication and collaboration, boards should invest in team-building exercises, organize regular social interactions, encourage peer feedback, and emphasize explicit behavioral social norms that encourage directors, as well as the CEO and leadership team, to express uncertainties and lack of knowledge.

To address the discontinuous strategic changes arising from de-globalization, digital technology, and AI, and to incorporate sustainability into the business, boards have to leverage the full range of voices of their members. Integrating diverse perspectives may require more time to reach a consensus, but they tend to yield stronger, more comprehensive decisions. Tea Colaianni, director of SD Worx, Watches of Switzerland, and WiHTL, explained:

> Having diverse perspectives brings richness to the conversation. You look at things from many, many different angles and points of view rather than just one way of looking at things. You look at different facets of the topic. That can bring tension. By definition, people coming from different backgrounds have different perspectives. By nature, they don't think alike. You get less group thinking. However, it takes longer to achieve a consensus because everybody needs to be persuaded. When you've got people who are the same, think the same, and have the same experiences, they just reach a decision more quickly. So it is a trade-off.

The open debate and discussions must also feed into a rigorous decision-making approach[13] that relies on structured processes, adherence to fiduciary duties of loyalty and care,[14] a robust balance between timely decisions and thorough consideration of all issues, and clear communication. Boards need to balance speed and thoroughness, communicating decisions clearly once they are made.

Given the changes in the environment and the board's purpose, role, and composition, boards need to embrace technological advancements like AI for decision support or improved virtual meeting platforms to rethink governance models such as splitting boards or adopting dynamic structures, and experiment with new approaches. Ultimately, boards should systematically review and refine their practices to ensure they remain well-equipped to navigate the future.

Leadership

The fourth dimension of the board diamond concerns the leadership provided by the board chair, lead independent director, and also, increasingly, committee chairs.

For simplicity, we refer broadly to the "board chair," though in some settings – such as the US, where the CEO and board chair may be the same individual, or the UK, where the board chair is non-independent – a lead independent director can play a similar role.

Over time, the role of the board chair has evolved from "primus inter pares" (first among equals) to a proactive leader. Modern chairs actively guide the board, serve as a primary counterpart to the CEO, and manage increasingly complex governance structures to address today's challenges. At the same time, they are called on to provide strategic leadership and engage with stakeholders to ensure the board remains future-focused. This expanded scope and transformation of the role demands a higher time commitment and a wider skill set, including visionary leadership qualities, the ability to act as a strategic partner to the CEO, adaptability to handle multiple responsibilities, and the humility to do it all without seeking personal glory.

Jan Jenisch, then board chair of Holcim, explained:

> The board chair needs to be someone who has enough time and shows enough leadership. Someone who holds preliminary talks with the CEO checks things out and takes the lead on the board. There are a lot of topics where the chair needs to lead. When there are new board members, when you need to renew the board, and when you have to give feedback to the board members, it needs time and leadership. Also, the setting of the board agenda needs leadership. You can fill it all up with bureaucracy. But to be successful, you need the courage to make decisions. To move the company forward, you cannot focus only on the reporting; you need to focus on the future. You need to bring strategic topics to every meeting. As a CEO, you really prefer to have a chair that makes sure the board is aligned in their decisions. Nothing is worse than when you need to go around to sell to every board member again and again.

The most effective chairs see themselves as servant leaders who focus on enabling others, setting the agenda and tone, and promoting a culture of high-performance governance. They orchestrate board dynamics, ensure effective governance, and lead strategic discussions while collaborating closely with the CEO, yet maintaining appropriate oversight and independence. By proactively setting the agenda, influencing the board's culture, and building strong relationships with board members and the senior leadership team, chairs enhance the board's effectiveness and align the board with the company's strategic objectives and purpose.

Given the ever-expanding agenda of the board, board chairs must excel at managing complex governance structures, including committees, advisory boards, and ad hoc groups. Their role is to ensure that these entities function effectively without centralizing too much power or diluting the whole board's oversight capabilities.

They need to balance involvement in committees while remaining impartial, maintaining independence, and avoiding conflicts of interest. Their role further requires addressing information asymmetry between the different players on the board by ensuring a timely and transparent information flow to all directors. Finally, they need to oversee succession planning with a clear, structured approach.

In addition to enabling the efficient and effective governance of the challenges of today, the board chair also plays a pivotal role in focusing the board and the leadership team toward the future. Through agenda setting, steering of board discussion and decision-making, and the interactions with the board, the CEO, and the leadership team at large, the board chair makes certain that sufficient time and resources are used to make the company fit for the challenges of tomorrow. Board chairs do this in different ways. Some board chairs, particularly founders, serve as strategic visionaries, taking a central role in influencing or even outright developing the vision for the future of the organization. Others play the role of facilitator and enabler of the CEO and leadership team in developing their vision while leading the board in providing guidance and critique during strategy development.

A critical component of the chair's role is the relationship with the CEO. The chair and CEO must have distinct but complementary responsibilities and be conscious of how their interaction impacts the rest of the organization. Greg Poux-Guillaume, chairman at Medmix, underscored the importance of avoiding overlaps and conflicts:

> A good chair is somebody who doesn't want to be the CEO. When you have a chair who has not fully made the switch, who still acts as if they want to run the company, you often end up in conflicts and frustration on both sides.

Instead, the chair and CEO should act as the two lynchpins of the strategic apex that balance each other yet collaborate in a close relationship built on trust, open communication, and clear boundaries to ensure both effective governance and strategic alignment. In this relationship, the chair must balance supporting the CEO and acting as a sparring partner while holding the CEO accountable, especially during critical moments, like CEO performance reviews and crisis management. This relationship requires careful navigation to avoid overly adversarial or excessively friendly dynamics that could undermine the board's oversight role or marginalize other directors.

The board chair also plays an essential role in setting the tone and culture of the board by fostering an environment that encourages open dialogue, diverse perspectives, and collaborative decision-making. To do so, chairs often need to manage difficult egos, ensure that less dominant voices are also heard, and promote a culture that acknowledges that in a changing environment, nobody has all the answers. Effective chairs lead by example. They facilitate meaningful discussions, address pressing concerns while maintaining strategic priorities on the agenda, and maintain a productive, forward-looking board atmosphere.

Peter Voser, board chair at ABB, PSA International, and member of the board at IBM, offered two metaphors for this evolving role:

> On the one hand, I view myself as the board's conductor. I make sure that everybody in the diverse group has a chance to speak and contribute, and it's my role to work toward a common decision. I always want the board to stand behind the decision. You need to let the board work to get to this decision, and that's why I call myself a conductor. I often also use the distinction between coach and player from soccer. Mostly, I am the coach on the sideline, but when we cannot make the right decision, I may come onto the field. Then, I will lead differently, much more decisively. I think that the art of a chair is to know when I play the conductor or the coach on the sideline and when I need to play on the field. But even when I play on the field, I am not the one up front trying to be the hero and score the goal, I am more in the midfield, trying to get everybody involved, but make sure that at the end we score the goal, which means we have made a good decision. As the chair, you need to think through your role because you have the power to step in if you want to, but you need to use this power very rarely; otherwise, you kill the discussion culture in the board.

Because the chair's role is evolving, the demands on individual chairs have grown significantly. Meeting both today's needs and tomorrow's aspirations requires a unique combination of personal attributes and skills that adds up to a tall order for any one leader to live up to.[15] Maintaining the focus on the future while managing today effectively and efficiently requires visionary thinking, facilitation skills, emotional intelligence, humility, confidence, and integrity. Effective chairs should be capable of synthesizing complex information, asking insightful questions, and leading from the background without seeking the spotlight. They must possess strong analytical abilities, be adaptable to different CEOs and board dynamics, stay informed about industry trends and governance best practices, and demonstrate commitment and accountability to uphold high ethical standards and act in the company's best interest.

Evaluation and development

The last but by no means least important dimension of the board diamond puts the emphasis on board evaluation and development. In many organizations, boards are the part with the least stringent evaluation and performance management practices. In fact, many board members in our conversations perceived board evaluation as broken and in need of a fundamental overhaul. Stefan Nöken, a member of the board at Vaillant, Vorwerk, and Peri Group, commented:

> In my view, better board evaluation and board development that builds on it are missed opportunities for most boards, both for the board as a

whole and for the individual board member. Feedback is always a personal gift. A lack of board evaluation also affects team dynamics and limits the development of the board as a team. And it also hinders the board regarding the subsequent impact on the company. Continuous improvement is hampered by the fact that evaluation is not taken seriously and not connected to board development.

To address the dual challenges of the modern board, a strong focus on this dimension of the board diamond is required because it is the central mechanism to drive change within the board. Evaluation and performance management are needed to drive efficiency and effectiveness for today's challenges, and a stronger focus on board development and experimentation is needed for boards to be able to make meaningful contributions to addressing the challenges arising from sustainability and strategic discontinuities and become future-oriented.

Board evaluations are often ineffective and serve as mere formalities to meet legal requirements rather than tools for genuine improvement. Directors often hesitate to criticize their peers due to the egalitarian structure of many boards, leading to a lack of meaningful feedback and accountability. Robust performance management in boards needs to start from comprehensive evaluations, such as 360-degree feedback, the inclusion of stakeholders, and external assessments, that assess decision-making effectiveness and link evaluations to tangible consequences in terms of development and board composition. By enhancing detailed performance reporting, seeking management and shareholder input, incorporating external perspectives, and regularly reviewing and learning from past decisions, boards can increase accountability, respond to stakeholder concerns, and continuously improve their governance practices.

Board evaluation needs to be complemented by systematic board development activities. For instance, Luka Mucic, director at Heidelberg Materials, observed:

> From my point of view, training activities are really important. It's not possible to just say, let's set up a committee for the next five years, and then, at some point, the competence will grow automatically. You have to actively invest in competence development for the board.

Surprisingly, many boards still neglect the systematic development of the board as a whole, as well as the continuous education of individual directors.[16] This reluctance to engage in systematic development is critical because to address tomorrow's problems, the solutions of yesterday or today will simply not suffice. Often, cultural barriers such as resistance to training and reluctance to admit knowledge gaps stand in the way.

To achieve a true future orientation and to remain effective in a rapidly changing business environment, boards must foster a culture of continuous learning by making development activities mandatory, encouraging openness to new ideas, implementing strategies like reverse mentoring, and bringing in external experts. But most importantly, they need the will to improve, as Christoph Mohn, chair of the board of German Media giant Bertelsmann, put it:

> Board development hinges on the commitment to improve – questioning processes, scrutinizing decision-making criteria, and continually asking, "What can we do better? Where might we have fallen short? How can we make better decisions, better support management, and fulfill our responsibilities more effectively?"

The final elements of board development are effective succession planning and rigorous onboarding. Many boards do not have a forward-looking approach to replacing directors, leaving gaps when sudden changes occur, which leads to last-minute appointments. Equally important is the integration of new directors through structured induction programs, strategies such as assigning new directors to key committees, and facilitating engagement with the leadership team. This approach ensures that new directors add value more quickly and that the board maintains stability while continually improving its overall performance.

Notes

1. Compare, for instance, Thomas Keil and Marianna Zangrillo, *The Next Leadership Team: How to Select, Build, and Optimize Your Top Team* (London: Routledge, 2021); Marianna Zangrillo, Thomas Keil, and Benedetto Vigna, "Build the Right C-Suite Team for Your Strategy," *MIT Sloan Management Review* 66, no. 1 (2024).
2. For related research see, for instance, Steven Boivie, Michael C. Withers, Scott D. Graffin, and Kevin G. Corley, "Corporate Directors' Implicit Theories of the Roles and Duties of Boards," Strategic Management Journal 42, no. 9 (2021).
3. Witold J. Henisz, "The Value of Corporate Purpose," *HBR.org, Harvard Business Review*, November 20, 2023, https://hbr.org/2023/11/the-value-of-corporate-purpose.
4. Andrea Hagelgans and Lex Suvanto, "How Boards Can Guide Company Strategy on Social Issues," *HBR.org, Harvard Business Review*, December 15, 2022, https://hbr.org/2022/12/how-boards-can-guide-company-strategy-on-social-issues.
5. David Fubini, Suraj Srinivasan, and Patrick Sanguineti, *Board Director Dilemmas: The Tradeoffs of Board Selection*, Case Study: 9-425-023 (Boston, MA: Harvard Business Publishing, September 5, 2024).
6. Boris Groysberg and Deborah Bell, "Dysfunction in the Boardroom," *Harvard Business Review* 91, no. 6 (2013).
7. Randall S. Peterson and Heidi K. Gardner, "Is Your Board Inclusive – or Just Diverse?," *HBR.org, Harvard Business Review*, September 28, 2022, https://hbr.org/2022/09/is-your-board-inclusive-or-just-diverse; Stephanie J. Creary, Janet Foutty, and Kwasi Mitchell, "How Diversity Can Boost Board Effectiveness," *MIT Sloan Management Review* 64, no. 3 (2023).
8. Jordi Canals, *Can the Board of Directors Be an Effective Team?* Case Study: SMN-0709-E (Barcelona: IESE Business School, March 4, 2024).

9. Amy C. Edmondson, *Teaming: How Organizations Learn, Innovate, and Compete in the Knowledge Economy* (San Francisco, CA: John Wiley & Sons, 2012).

10. Chris Thomas, David Kidd, and Claudio Fernandez-Araoz, "Are You Underutilizing Your Board?" *MIT Sloan Management Review* 48, no. 2 (2007).

11. Randall S. Peterson and Pedro Fontes Falcão, "Build a Better Board." *sloanreview.mit. edu. MIT Sloan Management Review* September 26, 2024, https://sloanreview.mit. edu/article/build-a-better-board/.

12. Jay W. Lorsch and Robert C. Clark, "Leading from the Boardroom," *Harvard Business Review* 86, no. 4 (2008).

13. Michael Useem, "How Well-Run Boards Make Decisions," *Harvard Business Review* 84, no. 11 (2006).

14. James Naughton, *Fiduciary Duties and Corporate Disclosure*, Case Study: UVA-C-2484 (Charlottesville, VA: Darden Business Publishing, July 30, 2024).

15. Dennis Carey, Ram Charan, Joseph Griesedieck, and Michael Useem, "8 Questions to Ask before Selecting a New Board Leader," *HBR.org, Harvard Business Review*, January 17, 2023, https://hbr.org/2023/01/8-questions-to-ask-before-selecting-a-new-board-leader.

16. Morela Hernandez, "Game-Changing Strategies for Corporate Boards," *sloanreview. mit.edu, MIT Sloan Management Review*, October 17, 2018, https://sloanreview.mit. edu/article/game-changing-strategies-for-corporate-boards/.

Part II

Key building blocks of effective boards

Chapter 3

Board purpose and the roles of the board

In May 2022, Pauline Van Der Meer Mohr started a new position as the chair of the supervisory board of ASM International, one of the leading players in the global semiconductor industry. Headquartered in Almere, Netherlands, ASM designs and manufactures equipment and materials to produce semiconductor devices, focusing on advanced technology such as atomic layer deposition, epitaxy, chemical vapor deposition, and diffusion processes used in the most advanced semiconductor wafer processing equipment globally.

ASM has enjoyed considerable growth in recent years, spurred by strong demand in areas like advanced logic, memory applications, and increasing reliance on data centers. The company benefited from robust market conditions and a strong strategic positioning within the semiconductor industry. Yet, going forward, the market environment was expected to be difficult despite the exploding demand. To remain competitive, companies like ASM need to work at the leading edge of technology, pushing the envelope of what is physically possible to deliver next-generation equipment. However, the semiconductor equipment segment of the industry has increasingly found itself at the center of political tensions between the US and China, creating uncertainty as to which markets ASM would be able to serve in the future.

In light of these emerging challenges, Van Der Meer Mohr reflected on how the board could continue adding value at ASM. She told us in an interview:

> To me, one of the biggest challenges of any board is to connect the
> long-term perspective we should take with the short-term questions

DOI: 10.4324/9781003532200-6

the company faces today. If I look ahead and think about what will be important for us as companies and boards, one major theme is long-term sustainable value creation. And with sustainability, I mean taking our responsibility for the problems of society seriously. We need to start thinking more about how to define the company's purpose in the context of longer-term sustainability and connect that to the strategy and actions we take today. We need to have a vision that encapsulates our company's responsibility for major problems like climate, biodiversity, and inequality. But as a board, we then need to connect that vision with very detailed questions of what you do here and now. Then there is a myriad of topics we need to deal with regularly, including reporting and compliance topics. You easily end up spending all your time on the past. But what can you do about the past? Clap and applaud. What we need to do is look into the future and look at what's next. And connecting today's problems to that long-term perspective.

Evolving purpose and roles of the board

As the ASM example shows, modern boards play a central role in focusing the firm on dealing with the problems of today while keeping a firm focus on the future. This hasn't always been the case. In the past, boards were mostly exclusive clubs of end-of-career CEOs and executives who joined boards for the status and to retain some connection with the business community and saw their main role mostly in supporting management with minimal critical oversight. These passive boards often failed to demonstrate genuine value, both to outside stakeholders and to the CEO and the top leadership team.

The perception of a passive board has led to a vicious cycle in some organizations. When CEOs see limited value in the board, they often try to keep board oversight to a minimum and do not leverage the potential for advice, making the board even more passive. For instance, a board chair of a large US stock exchange-listed corporation shared an anecdote illustrating this older mindset:

> As a CEO, you get the board you deserve. If you treat the board as a liability, something you need to do for legal reasons, then it will be a passive board; in one board I know of, the CEO told the board outright, "I see no value in any of you. I don't get anything out of you. Just sit here and do the job that the regulation requires you to do. Otherwise, leave me alone." What do you expect the board to do?

In contrast, today's high-performing boards have evolved into central players at the strategic apex of the firm. They collaborate closely with all stakeholders, the CEO, and the top leadership team, to govern the problems of today and address the challenges of tomorrow. It is for this reason that the purpose and roles of the board form the first dimension of the board diamond.

The board's revised purpose is to combine a broad range of advisory, decision-making, and monitoring roles to meet modern governance requirements. Regulators, investors, proxy advisors, and other stakeholders have increased their expectations, pressuring boards to expand their oversight responsibilities to ever-new topics. In times of crisis and rapid change in the geopolitical and technological domains, boards have become a central factor in ensuring organizational resilience, as management teams are overwhelmed by the pace and magnitude of new challenges. By maintaining a future-oriented focus, these boards advise and collaborate with management to craft strategies that address the multiple new changes in technology, regulations, and geopolitics. As the ASM example highlights, this increasingly requires boards to develop a deep understanding of the changes in a geopolitical forcefield and their implications on the future strategies of firms.

In another big shift in their role, some boards have also become stewards for multiple stakeholders. In this role, they work to harmonize corporate actions with numerous diverging stakeholder interests. This requires the board to align the board and company purpose with values and strategies, building trust and reducing conflicts among important stakeholders like customers, employees, and society. However, developing a corporate purpose that creates both societal and shareholder value and driving business practices that are sustainable and financially sound continue to be some of the biggest challenges of today's boards.

Increasing the breadth of the board's roles to deal with the challenges of today

What specific roles does a board need to play to effectively and efficiently manage today's issues while positioning the organization for tomorrow? In many boards, the key roles of the board get summarized into three broad categories. For instance, Jeff Campbell, former vice-chairman and CFO of American Express, former CFO of McKesson and American Airlines, and current director at AON plc, Marathon Petroleum Corp., and Hexcel Corp, pointed out:

> I often try to simplify the role of the board into three areas. One is to hire and fire the CEO. Two is to be an advisor and a sounding board to the CEO and the entire management team on strategy. And the third role involves running a range of governance processes, compliance processes, checks and balances that the board needs to run in order to ensure a smoothly and appropriately functioning public company.

While these broad categories are important,[1] from our research, it is helpful to break them down into a larger set of eight distinct roles that boards may choose to play. These roles are summarized in Figure 3.1.

	Selecting and developing the key people	• Selecting the CEO (and top management team members) • Succession management and talent development
	Ensuring compliance, risk-management and control	• Financial control • Risk management • Compliance and oversight
	Strategy setting	• Setting strategic goals, boundaries, and guard rails for vision and strategy • Identifying and addressing discontinuous strategic change • Supporting and challenging management in the strategy process
	Decision-making	• Influencing and approving key decisions (M&A, divestments, investments) • Improving management's decision quality
	Corporate purpose	• Defining the corporate purpose • Aligning financial and societal impact through integrating sustainability and financial goals • Overseeing alignment of strategy and operations with purpose
	Steering management attention	• Focus on strategy and key priorities • Balancing short-term and long-term orientation
	Setting the tone in the corporation	• Setting key values • Defining the culture
	Shepherding the brand	• Acting as brand steward • Protecting reputation

Figure 3.1   Key Roles of the Modern Board

Key people

Selecting the CEO and overseeing succession planning for key executives has always been among the board's most critical responsibilities[2] because having the right leadership team is essential for navigating complex business environments and achieving strategic objectives. In the words of Joerg Reinhardt, chair of the board of Novartis and board member of SwissRe: "One of the top three topics for the board is personnel planning. Are we happy with the CEO, or do we need to change? Does the management have a good skill set? Do we have everything we need?" Similarly, Doug Baker, lead independent director at Target and member of the board at Merck (MSD), explained: "I think the need to make sure you have the right management team has probably never been higher because their job has probably never been more challenging." Hiring and, if necessary, replacing the CEO can profoundly impact the company's performance and is commonly regarded as one of the most powerful levers the board possesses. Still, boards often fail at this central task.[3]

Boards also add value by participating in the selection of key executives, ensuring that those choices align with strategy, and cultivating a strong bench of potential successors for the CEO. For instance, Don Knauss, director of US-based Kellogg's, McKesson, and Target, explained:

> One thing that's changing is the directors' requirements to spend time with talent. At Target, we'll have directors meet high-potential talent or people who are in the direct line of succession. Board members will

spend a day walking stores with that person, or will spend a day going through a Kellogg manufacturing plant. There's an expectation that board members should have an active role in talent management.

In some companies, boards are increasingly spearheading systematic talent management, including spending time with high-potential employees to understand the talent pipeline, contributing to leadership development, and ensuring robust succession plans are in place. Effective boards should have plans for immediate and long-term succession, with identified candidates ready to step into key roles. Pius Baschera, experienced board member and former board chair of Hilti, elaborated:

> Succession planning starts with the board of directors. For the executive team members and their direct reports, we have a successor ready. And not just someone who has huge potential to be ready in two or three years. For all 30 of them, we have a successor ready that can step in on Monday if something happens on Friday.

Ensuring compliance, risk management, and financial control

A second central governance role of any board is to provide oversight and control on topics such as compliance, risk management, and financial reporting. This responsibility has grown due to new demands from regulators, investors, and proxy advisors. Responding to these growing requirements may lead to neglect of strategy and long-term planning, as these oversight and control tasks consume more and more board time, crowding out strategic discussions from the board agenda. This risk has become more prevalent since many corporations increasingly respond to the emergence of new challenges by assigning responsibility to the board, which in many corporations overextends the board's capacity. Boards, therefore, must prioritize strategic issues and resist pressure to cover every matter in depth and instead focus on areas where their oversight is most critical.

A second risk related to these oversight activities is that boards move from oversight to actively managing operational matters that should be handled by management. One director we interviewed put it bluntly: "The worst thing you can do is have directors that actually think they run the company."

Because directors lack the daily insights management has, they need to be cautious in drawing the boundary between strategic oversight and operations. Doug Baker, board member at retail giant Target and Merck (MSD), summed up:

> Boards play a vital role in governing the company. However, they cannot run the company – it's not their job, and they do not have the information or input needed to do so. They are not there every day. They do not have the needed continuous data input.

Boards, therefore, need to be mindful in drawing the line between strategic issues, where they play a more active role, and operational issues, where their role should be confined to ensuring appropriate oversight. By focusing on strategic guidance, they allow management to execute while providing high-level direction and control.

Strategy

Boards also have always played an important role in strategy.[4] However, the importance of this role has increased with the emergence of multiple crises that require strategic responses, and discontinuous strategic change that forces an increasing number of firms to reinvent themselves. Take the automotive industry, for example, and the emergence of electric vehicles; or the energy sector and the transition to renewable energy and climate change; or the media and entertainment industry and the emergence of streaming services and user-generated content. All face a degree of change that forces the full attention of all players in the strategic apex to work together to develop responses that ensure the viability and success of the company. The geopolitical shift toward de-globalization, protectionism, trade wars, and global bloc formation forces all international companies to rethink their geographic footprint and international strategy.[5] As a result, boards need to play a more important role in strategy than ever before. Thomas Thune Andersen, chair at Lloyd's Register Group and VKR Holding, and member of the board at BW Group and IMI plc, stated:

> One of the things that the board needs to be more involved in is the strategy. What are we going to do in the next three to five years to respond to the changes in our environment and align what we do with the purpose of the organization?

How boards fulfill this role varies widely across countries and even across companies within a country. While some boards mostly rubber-stamp management proposals without active involvement, others supervise and challenge proposed strategies to ensure thorough consideration. For instance, Paul Bulcke, chair of Nestlé, explained:

> You need to have a board that meaningfully understands the company and has the expertise of the externalities facing the company. They need to understand the proposed strategic direction, understand its value potential, and then ask the right questions. What does that mean? Does it address all important issues? They shouldn't try to give answers but ask the right questions that move the strategy and the company forward.

In our view, the most effective boards co-create strategy in a collaborative approach where boards and management iterate during the strategy process, with the board defining targets and guardrails, management driving strategy creation with input of the board, and the board challenging, refining, and approving the final strategy. A collaborative approach like this is most likely to generate the necessary diversity of viewpoints and breadth of perspectives to shape well-rounded strategies, in particular, in the light of strategic discontinuities.

To be a valuable partner in strategy creation, boards need to be clear about their role and the commitments required. They need to invest enough time to fully comprehend industry dynamics and the company's business,[6] foster open and transparent dialogue with management, and develop clear frameworks derived from the company's purpose and focused on sustainable, long-term value creation.[7]

Successful strategy creation requires clarity about the board's and management's contributions.[8] While management is responsible for developing and executing strategy, boards are tasked with advising, providing an external perspective, challenging assumptions, asking critical questions, and ensuring all strategic aspects are thoroughly considered. One board chair we interviewed noted:

> Boards need to be involved in the strategy of the company, setting boundaries, challenging and confirming the strategy. But a board can't create that strategy on its own. The management team has to do that. The board can participate by asking good questions and suggesting things, but ultimately, the management team has to develop the strategy. Once that is done, the board has to continuously test it. So the role of the board is that it should be participating, ensuring that the management team has completely thought about all the issues and opportunities, and then obviously confirming the execution of strategy by the management team.

Finally, in some organizations, we observed that strategic direction is clearly driven by the board. In particular, in organizations like Amazon, Alphabet, Oracle, or, until recently, SAP, where the founders of the company have been or are still on the board, they often continue to control the strategy directly or indirectly. In other companies, an executive chair[9] may accumulate a degree of power that shifts key decisions regarding strategy toward the board, or at least its chair. Such board-led strategy processes may work well when the board and its chair are deeply committed and have both the expertise and time required to drive the company's strategy. However, strategy creation that is predominantly driven by the board may lead to strategies that are disconnected from the operational limitations and current challenges of the organization.[10] It may also reduce the buy-in of the CEO and executive team and therefore lead to problems of implementation.[11]

Decision-making

Typically, boards are also the final decision-maker on important decisions such as investments or M&A. In this role, the board can facilitate sound decision-making by ensuring a rational process is followed and by countering any potential confidence biases of executives.[12] This requires that boards manage the decision-making process by, for example, setting the timetable and milestones for key decisions.

In some of the companies we studied, decision-making has become more collaborative, with the board becoming a sparring partner for the CEO and executive team, rather than simply stamping approval or using their veto. This more collaborative approach hinges on open dialogue and mutual trust with the top leadership team. For instance, Carla Smits-Nusteling, a former board member of Nokia, ASML, and TELE2 AB, explained:

> When I started my board career, the CEO and the executives brought to the board some topics, but also always the answers – this is proposal one, this is proposal two, take your pick. And that was about it. These days, they bring more to the board, their dilemmas and open issues, and then we try to contribute together. Everyone has a different angle and different experience, and we try together to find the best way forward in the dilemmas. I think that's a very positive and motivating change.

Purpose setting

Increasingly, boards have gained an additional critical role that precedes their strategy role: defining the company's purpose beyond profit generation and aligning it with sustainability, broader societal challenges, and the expectations of all stakeholders. Stakeholders increasingly expect companies to contribute to addressing issues like climate change, community well-being, and social justice.[13] Xiaoqun Clever-Steg, director at multiple international corporations, noted:

> For boards, the "social license to operate" has become an increasingly important strategic consideration as stakeholder expectations grow more sophisticated. Businesses must consider their broader contributions to society and how they address societal challenges. However, corporate social responsibility is not a given – it requires resilience and ability to adapt to changes in today's rapidly evolving business environment, where geopolitical tensions reshape the global order and bloc architecture.

Incorporating these concerns into business operations is vital for forging long-term success and building stakeholder trust. This involves articulating a clear company purpose and mission, contributing to sustainable development, and engaging in public discourse on societal issues. A clear purpose provides the foundation to define the company's long-term goals and objectives and a north star toward which the company can orient its strategic decisions. Thomas Thune Andersen, chair at Lloyd's

Register Group and VKR Holding, and member of the board at BW Group and IMI plc, explained:

> As a board, you need to be able to articulate on three or four lines the societal problem that the company wants to be part of solving, and from that flows basically everything else. You can tie everything back to that purpose, giving you the narrative for your strategy work. If the board can get their head around that, it's quite easy for them to support the strategy and each decision that needs to be taken.

Companies are increasingly expected to take positions on political questions like the future of work, environmental sustainability, and diversity and inclusion, and at the same time, face substantial risks when they do so in the current highly politically polarized world. Boards, therefore, must very carefully navigate the extent and manner of this engagement.[14] For instance, Michael Süss, executive chair of OC Oerlikon, argued: "Corporations and their boards need to play a more active role in the public discourse. This is only possible through the participation and involvement of companies and their leadership in the discussion of important topics." At the same time, a director who preferred to remain anonymous in the current political environment highlighted how, with the change of the president in the US, participation in public discourse has fundamentally changed, and voicing dissenting opinions has become risky for boards and their members.

It is for these risks of participation in public discourses that many directors continue to be skeptical of a broader political role of the board as Ming Long, chair of CSIRO and director at Telstra, QBE Insurance (Auspac), and the Committee for Economic Development in Australia (CEDA), explained to us: "I've observed that more traditional governance approaches often emphasize caution around public commentary on current affairs, including topics like diversity and inclusion or climate action, which I believe are critical for future-focused leadership." Taking stances on these issues can bring both risks and rewards, in particular in an increasingly polarized political landscape where changes in political leadership may completely redirect the nature of the political discourse. This can at the moment be observed in the US, where the shift between democrat and republican presidents has created a complete reversal of positions and positions that were mainstream only a year ago now run counter to the agenda of the government and create legal risks for the corporation.

Boards ideally adopt a structured framework, including criteria such as alignment with company values and assessment of stakeholder impact, to decide if and how to engage. A board chair of a large French corporation highlighted the difficult line that large corporations have to strike in their participation in the political discourse:

> Historically, companies in our industry have sounded horrible and lecturing. Today, that would not be well received by the public. We participate in the political discourse, but we mostly try to explain what we do, our decisions, and why we make them. Companies have to be careful

not to confuse their role with the position of an elected politician. We are part of the discourse, but we must walk a thin line and avoid lecturing others about what to do in a democracy.

This approach ensures that the social stances taken by the company are authentic, support business goals, and mitigate reputational risks.[15]

Steering management attention

In modern governance, the CEO and the top leadership team are tasked with running the day-to-day operational business. Given this responsibility, the management team often tends to focus its attention on relatively short-term problems that require solutions here and now. One of the central roles of the board is, therefore, to steer the attention of the CEO and top leadership team toward future and longer-term issues.[16] In other words, where the management team is grounded in the here and now, the board needs to provide a forward-looking perspective as a counterbalance and guide management attention to the future. For many boards, this is not a simple task, since the board also has important responsibilities in ensuring oversight and decision-making that may lead to a shift in its focus on the present or even the past. Boards must consciously strike the right balance and maintain its own focus on the future to be able to guide management.

Setting the tone

Boards strongly influence the organization's culture and core values. Simply put, boards set the tone for overall organizational culture and ethical conduct, and board members' behavior sets examples for the rest of the organization.

Joerg Reinhardt, chair of the board of Novartis and board member of SwissRe, emphasized:

> One of the most important topics is the culture. What kind of culture do I need to create so that people participate and don't just tick boxes and pocket their salaries but really get seriously involved, know that they are needed, that they are heard, and that they have an impact? And that begins from the board but impacts the whole organization." He added: "If you have, let's say, three days of more or less intensive board meetings, cover a lot of topics, then a whole series of management representatives appear there, that quickly adds up to fifty or more senior management members. And every board meeting is also a communication event where you shape the culture. You interact with management; you ask questions, you give feedback, and you voice opinions. All of this naturally also shapes the culture in the company.

By influencing organizational norms, boards ensure that the company's culture supports its strategic objectives and aligns with its purpose and values. Ensuring core values are embedded requires consistent communication and reinforcement. Board interactions with management and employees can play a significant role in fostering a positive and effective organizational culture. For instance, interactions during meetings influence management and shape cultural expectations. Through these actions, boards help embed key values throughout the organization.

Shepherding the brand and reputation

Finally, some board members see themselves as stewards of the corporation's brand and reputation. For instance, Rod Adkins, a board member at United Parcel Service (UPS), PayPal, Grainger, and Avnet, emphasized that the board might act as the brand's steward:

> In my view, the board needs to focus on assisting the management of the company in protecting the brand. The brand should be about trust and integrity, and it is one of the board's tasks to be the brand's steward who protects that.

Ronnie Leten, board chair of Epiroc AB, former chair of Ericsson and Electrolux, and former member of the board of AB SKF, expanded this idea: "The board needs to focus on the meaning and reputation of the brand so that every person in the company can work according to the brand values and support the brand's meaning."

For the board, this implies holding management accountable for ensuring that the corporation's actions are aligned with the brand's values.

Bringing the future back into the board's focus through prioritizing

The extensive range of roles now associated with modern boards does not imply that boards will or even can pay similar attention to all of these roles at all times. Rather, depending on the situation and context, some duties will take precedence over others.

In fact, the large number of roles that modern boards face creates the risk of diluting the board's focus and effectiveness. For instance, Suzanne Thoma, executive chair at fluid engineering company Sulzer, offered a cautionary note:

> I am critical to adding all these new responsibilities to the board. For instance, it is often mentioned that the board should be responsible for cybersecurity. That is, for me, in the wrong direction. The board should

ensure that the management is taking necessary steps, including reporting regarding cybersecurity, but there is no way a board that works on a normal level, even if it meets 10 times a year, which is already a lot, can really make the decisions in such technical areas as cybersecurity. Let me say it more abstractly. I sometimes have the impression that every hot topic, for whatever reason, will be pushed onto the board because the board is the highest in the hierarchy. That has to be rethought because boards simply cannot handle every issue.

To keep future-oriented concerns on the table, boards must carefully manage their agendas to prioritize strategic issues where they can add the most value, avoid scope creep, and ensure they are not overburdened by compliance and operational matters. As many of the chairs and directors we interviewed stressed, overloading the board can impede its ability to add strategic value.

In fact, several interviewees underscored the importance of devoting more time on tomorrow's concerns. Sami Atiya, board member of the Switzerland-based testing, inspection, and certification company SGS SA, shared: "Today, one of the most important tasks of the board is in making your company future-proof, future-resilient."

In summary, the board's role in setting the purpose, creating strategy, aligning decisions with strategy, and, more generally, keeping the management focused on long-term and future-oriented topics has grown in importance. Today, it is as important as the traditional topics of hiring and firing the CEO and the top leadership team, and discharging governance responsibilities regarding compliance, risk management, and financial reporting. Boards that overlook any of these responsibilities risk being unable to handle present challenges or position the company effectively for the future.

Notes

1. Didier Cossin, *High Performance Boards: Improving and Energizing Your Governance* (Chichester: John Wiley & Sons, 2024).
2. Thomas Keil and Marianna Zangrillo, "Don''t Set Your Next CEO up to Fail," *MIT Sloan Management Review* 61, no. 2 (2020); Thomas Keil and Marianna Zangrillo, *The Next CEO: Board and CEO Perspectives for Successful CEO Succession* (London: Routledge, 2021).
3. Robert Hooijberg and Nancy Lane, "How Boards Botch CEO Succession," News Item, *Mit Sloan Management Review* 57, no. 4 (Summer 2016); Keil and Zangrillo, *The Next CEO: Board and CEO Perspectives for Successful CEO Succession*; Dan Ciampa and Adam Bryant, "Power, Influence, and CEO Succession," *Harvard Business Review* 103, no. 7–8 (July–August 2024).
4. Didier Cossin and Estelle Metayer, "How Strategic Is Your Board?," *MIT Sloan Management Review* 56, no. 1 (2014).

5. Michael A. Witt, "Prepare for the U.S. And China to Decouple," Article, *HBR. org*, *Harvard Business Review*, June 26, 2020, https://hbr.org/2020/06/prepare-for-the-u-s-and-china-to-decouple; Steven A. Altman and Caroline R. Bastian, "The State of Globalization in 2023: Data Disproves the Notion That the World Has Become More Regionalized in Recent Years," *HBR.org*, *Harvard Business Review*, July 11, 2023, https://hbr.org/2023/07/the-state-of-globalization-in-2023; Cindy Levy, Shubham Singhal, and Matt Watters, "A Proactive Approach to Navigating Geopolitics Is Essential to Thrive,"www.mckinsey.com. McKinsey & Company, November 12, 2024, https://www.mckinsey.com/capabilities/geopolitics/our-insights/a-proactive-approach-to-navigating-geopolitics-is-essential-to-thrive#/.

6. Dominic Barton and Mark Wiseman, "Where Boards Fall Short," *Harvard Business Review* 93, no. 1 (2015).

7. Guhan Subramanian, "Corporate Governance 2.0," *Harvard Business Review* 93, no. 3 (March 2015).

8. Richard D. Parsons and Marc A. Feigen, "The Boardroom's Quiet Revolution," *Harvard Business Review* 92, no. 3 (2014).

9. Markus Menz, Robert Langan, and Ryan Krause, "Does Your Board Need an Executive Chair?," *HBR.org*, *Harvard Business Review*, November 25, 2022, https://hbr.org/2022/11/does-your-board-need-an-executive-chair.

10. Christian Stadler, Julia Hautz, Kurt Matzler, and Stephan F. von_den_Eichen, *Open Strategy: Mastering Disruption from Outside the C-Suite* (Boston: MIT Press, 2021).

11. Lawrence G. Hrebiniak, *Making Strategy Work: Leading Effective Execution and Change* (Upper Saddle River, NJ: Wharton School Publishing, 2005).

12. Stevo Pavićević, Jerayr Haleblian, and Thomas Keil, "When Do Boards of Directors Contribute to Shareholder Value in Firms Targeted for Acquisition? A Group Information-Processing Perspective," *Organization Science* 34, no. 5 (2023); Stevo Pavićević and Thomas Keil, "The Role of Procedural Rationality in Debiasing Acquisition Decisions of Overconfident CEOs," *Strategic Management Journal* 42, no. 9 (2021).

13. Edward E. Lawler and Christopher G. Worley, "Why Boards Need to Change," *MIT Sloan Management Review* 54, no. 1 (2012).

14. Blair Levin and Larry Downes, "Every Company Needs a Political Strategy Today," *MIT Sloan Management Review* 64, no. 2 (2023).

15. Andrea Hagelgans and Lex Suvanto, "How Boards Can Guide Company Strategy on Social Issues," December 15, 2022, https://hbr.org/2022/12/how-boards-can-guide-company-strategy-on-social-issues.

16. Christopher S. Tuggle, David G. Sirmon, Christopher R. Reutzel, and Leonard Bierman, "Commanding Board of Director Attention: Investigating How Organizational Performance and CEO Duality Affect Board Members' Attention to Monitoring," *Strategic Management Journal* 31, no. 9 (2010).

Chapter 4

Who should be on the board

People, roles, and personalities

Jan Jenisch, Holcim's then board chair, was sitting in the departure lounge at Zurich airport, waiting for his flight to New York. This flight would be one of many flights to the US he had recently taken to build a new board for the spin-off of Holcim's US business.

Swiss-based Holcim had gone through almost a decade of transformation. After its merger with French firm Lafarge in 2015, the company experienced several years of integration and transformation to turn what was a large but underperforming player in the global cement business, one of the world's most notorious CO_2-emitting industries, into a highly profitable and sustainability-focused leader in innovative and sustainable building solutions. In the latest step of this journey that Jenisch had led, first as CEO and now as board chair, Holcim was, at the time of writing,[1] preparing to spin off its USD 11 billion plus US business into a separately listed public company, to capitalize on the full value potential of its positioning as the leading pure-play building solutions company in North America.

As part of the listing process, Jenisch would need to create a board of directors for the new company. This endeavor gave him a rare chance to construct an almost entirely fresh board from scratch. He explained:

> I have the challenging task of putting together a new board. Maybe two or three Holcim board members will join, but in principle, it's a

DOI: 10.4324/9781003532200-7

completely new board. I start with a blank sheet of paper. There are no legacies to take into consideration. You don't have to make any compromises. You can design it from scratch. It is an exciting task.

In building the board, Jenisch was reflecting on what would be the optimal composition to fulfill the various board roles and especially to drive the goals of the company as a leader in innovative and sustainable solutions. He noted:

> There are some boundary conditions I need to consider. You have three mandatory committees for a US-listed company, i.e., Audit, Nomination, and Compensation, and we might do a fourth one, Technology and Sustainability, since it is critical for the success of the company. You need to find people with the right skills for all four. And you want to have some people with CEO experience to support and coach the CEO. And you have requirements for governance, and e.g., diversity. You should have at least 30 percent women on the board, and you need to have underrepresented minorities on the board. We will still have our legal seat in Switzerland, so board members will need to travel to Switzerland for some of the board meetings. Even without issues of legacy, this still creates a lot of external constraints that need to be taken into consideration.

Beyond meeting formal requirements, Jenisch also reflected on the type of board members he wanted to attract to build an active board that would contribute to the company's development and not merely discharge matters of governance compliance. He explained:

> For the new board, I want people who are competent but also committed to the company. Who have a passion for the company and don't treat this just as a hobby. In my view, board members should not be a club of retired people, but board members should be active in executive positions or on other relevant company boards. Board members need to be exposed to current business issues to contribute to the company's success. If not, you know the problems of yesterday but not the problems of today, let alone tomorrow.

Selecting the right people for the board is one of the most critical elements in designing a board that can address the challenges of today and tomorrow, as Kaj-Erik Relander, board member of Louis Dreyfuss Corporation, SES Satellites, and a number of other privately held corporations, noted:

> It starts and ends with people. We can talk about board size, statutes and regulations, governance, and committees. If people don't have the

backbone and integrity, and the right priorities, then governance equals bureaucracy and a lot of paperwork. If you have the structures and processes and good people, then it works.

As the example of Jenisch underlines, even when legacy constraints are minimal, finding the right people to fill specific needs, meet various requirements, and ultimately function as a high-impact board can be daunting. Who should be on the board? And how should they go about finding the right people? This is the focus of the second dimension of our board diamond.

We propose that the choice of board members should start with broader considerations of aligning the board composition with the board's purposes and roles discussed in the previous chapter and with the company's strategic direction and requirements.

Aligning board composition with board purpose and roles, company needs, and strategy

The board's composition should be derived from the roles that the board intends to play. A board focused primarily on oversight and control will require a different blend of skills than one aiming to actively shape strategy or balance financial returns with broader societal impacts. As noted earlier, modern boards are evolving beyond a predominantly oversight-driven model. Increasingly, they are concentrating (or at least balancing) attention on sustainability, multiple stakeholders, and disruptive strategic change. Consequently, boards must seek directors who are not just steeped in past experience but also oriented toward the future, bringing both diversity of perspective and the capacity to think about new paradigms.

A key challenge that every board must resolve is whether the skills and personalities needed for board oversight and compliance can be combined in a single person with the skills supportive of future orientation, innovation, and reinvention of strategy. In other words, does the board need to become larger in response to this change in focus, or can the new skill mix be achieved through a change in directors?

Most directors we interviewed voiced a preference for keeping the board size as small as possible because larger boards make it more difficult to work closely and run the risk of fractionalizing.[2] However, often, the minimum size of the board is driven by regulatory rules, as the Jenisch example highlighted. For instance, in a German or French board, the principle of co-determination mandates that 50 percent of the board seats be filled with employee representatives. US listing rules require specific committees and further require specific skills or experience to chair, for example, the audit committee. In regulated industries like insurance or banking, members with specific profiles need to be chosen for at least some board positions, or a regulator needs to explicitly approve candidates.

Though small boards often make collaboration easier, the increasing number and range of topics that boards need to deal with and the need to balance adding an ever-increasing number of topics related to reporting, compliance, and risk management with a strong focus on the future may necessitate an increase in the board size. If a board's size grows, it must also adjust its structures and processes, a subject we tackle in the next chapter.

One general principle of leadership that is often ignored in board design is that board composition needs to be aligned with the company's strategic challenges, objectives, and the evolution of the industry context.[3] In other words, board composition needs to be, at least to some extent, situational and dynamic.[4] This principle is well-accepted for young ventures where board composition tends to evolve with the growth and evolution of the company and where the board of an early-stage venture looks fundamentally different from the board of a company aiming for an IPO,[5] but it tends to be less common in larger, established organizations that often opt for stability in their board composition. In fact, some of the directors of the mostly large companies we studied advocated for stability on the level of the board disconnected from changes in the company and context. They argued that while frequent changes on the leadership team level are workable, given the full-time commitment of executives, the time it takes to get to know a large company and be effective as a board member through the relatively infrequent board interactions simply leaves little room for regular changes at the board level, as it would preclude members' ability to develop deep, relevant knowledge.

Board composition, in this view, evolves only infrequently or at least slowly, and board members are chosen for their breadth of experience rather than their ability to add value on a specific set of topics. Board members are often viewed as wise women and men who have a wealth of experience and, from that experience and wisdom, can provide a perspective on any contemporary challenges faced by the company, but are not necessarily deep experts on the specific topics that constitute those challenges.

Yet other directors we interviewed highlighted the need for a more dynamic view of board compositions that allows for regular changes, given the evolving operating and strategic environment and challenges faced by the firm. In this perspective, individual board members may join the board for a limited period of time with a clear mandate and focus to help with specific topics, but won't necessarily remain there for long.

This distinction between a static and general versus a dynamic and situational view of board composition also suggests two different ways of designing a board: as an independent governance body or as an integral part of the strategic apex.

The board as an independent governance body

One approach typically linked to the static and general view of the board is to design the board as a completely separate governance body that follows its own logic and is mostly independent of the choices regarding the other players in the strategic apex, that is, the CEO and the leadership team. In this approach, board composition is mainly driven by the needs of governance rules. While this approach provides stability and oversight, it creates the risk of stagnation, self-perpetuation, and ingrained thinking.

The board as part of the strategic apex

The second approach, connected to the dynamic and situational perspective of the board, views all parts of the strategic apex as pieces of a puzzle that need to fit together and adjust to the situation and context.[6] This approach, which we advocate, implies that the board's composition should be designed to complement the strengths and weaknesses of the board chair, CEO, and the leadership team. In this puzzle, the board chair and CEO are the core pieces and should be chosen with fit, complementarity, and balance of power in mind. The members of the leadership team should be chosen to fit the strategic direction, mandate, and leadership team approach of the CEO.[7] Finally, board members should complement the capabilities of the board chair but also fit with the CEO and management team.

The situational and dynamic view of the board that we advocate implies that the composition of the board needs to be adjusted as new, long-term strategic topics enter the board's agenda to ensure the board has the necessary skills to address current and future challenges. For instance, following the increased focus of many firms on ESG, the percentage of Fortune 100 board members with ESG expertise has grown over the past five years.[8]

As companies face multiple crises and discontinuous strategic change, the board's composition needs to reflect the company's changing strategic priorities and challenges. The regular changes to the board that this approach implies not only ensure the board is aligned with the situation but also help to prevent stagnation, self-perpetuation, and ingrained thinking. Of course, this does not imply that the composition board will mirror every change in the environment, but rather, as the pace of change increases, the board will need change experts who can help guide the organization through multiple change processes.

The situational and dynamic view of the board requires that the board as a whole, led by its chair and nominating committee, regularly evaluate the board's effectiveness and alignment with the company's needs. The board must proactively plan for board member turnover to ensure continuity and alignment with strategic goals. To do so, firms can proactively utilize tools like the skills matrix to map required skills and identify gaps in the board's composition. In fact, corporate governance codices in countries such as Australia, Canada, most EU countries, New Zealand, South Africa, the UK, and the US mandate or at least recommend the use of a skills matrix in board member selection but, unfortunately, the tool is often viewed as a formality and used as a tick-box exercise rather than leveraging its benefits and strategic development potential. Mark Joiner, director at QBE AusPa, shared his perspective on improving the skills matrix process:

> We use this skills matrix, but many boards are not doing a good job with it. One of the biggest things that frustrates me about the skills matrix is that, generally, people score themselves. So, because everybody has been through a strategy process, they are all strategists. They are all financial experts. They have all done M&A. That way you do not get much insight from the exercise. You need to go back and take the input from the directors, and pressure test it by reference to their CVs or external references to get a more realistic picture. You need to be forward-looking and identify the skills that will allow us to deal with the issues on the horizon. You do have to be quite forward-looking if you want to be prepared for future change.

Leveraging diversity on the board

Diversity requirements are one topic regarding board composition that has received intense scrutiny and discussion in recent years, and even more so with the recent political change in the US. Similar to the discourse on ESG and sustainability we noted in Chapter 1, the diversity, equity, and inclusion discourse has, in the past years, become highly political,[9] confounding political agenda with what makes good business sense. We focus here on the idea that diversity on the board makes good business sense in many situations[10] and leave the political discourse to others.[11]

Although most boards claim to embrace diversity, the term is often reduced to single demographic indicators like gender, ethnicity, or nationality. Efforts to diversify boards often fall short when vague or too narrow definitions of diversity perpetuate the homogeneity of boards.[12] All too often, therefore, boards struggle to incorporate deeper layers of diversity that reach beyond demographics and observable backgrounds, such as diversity of thought, experience, and perspective, i.e., cognitive diversity.[13]

One reason for the limits to true diversity arises from the nature of board selection. Although many boards have professionalized the selection of board members, there continues to be an elite network that is clubby in nature. For instance, Robert Nicholson, board member at Electro Optic Systems, Port of Melbourne, Alinta Energy, European Australian Business Council, and Baker Heart and Diabetes Institute, explained to us:

> Boards have been a bit clubby. People tend to want to work with people they know and who (subconsciously or otherwise) they feel will think in a similar way to them. They are reluctant to take a risk on someone they

don't know. And that has led to a narrower skill set than many boards need and a lack of diversity of thought.

A director of an Australian stock exchange-listed corporation added a bit more provocatively:

> The Australian director landscape operates like exclusive clubs with invisible gatekeepers. A small cadre of influential directors – both men and established women in the "Golden Skirts" network – control who gets in and what they can say once there. Express too much passion for ESG or challenge conventional thinking too directly, and you could find yourself sidelined. This gatekeeping stifles the diverse perspectives desperately needed at a time of unprecedented change.

While both directors' quotes hail from Australia, the situation is not much different in continental Europe, the UK, or the US, as several directors shared with us in confidence.

Other directors mention that diversity is sometimes treated as a superficial "check-the-box" effort. Several board members told us in confidence that all too often, changes are made only for external appearances and to avoid negative evaluation from proxy advisors, while the power structures and decision-making remain in the hands of individual controlling board members, often founders or former CEOs. While these boards may claim to value diversity, they fail to leverage it effectively.[14] Such superficial initiatives lead to tokenism and fail to alter underlying power structures or influence decision-making processes. Superficial diversity may reduce the quality of the board work.

Internationally, the treatment of the diversity topic has developed in different directions. In Europe, the EU passed a regulation on the representation of women on boards with the aim of increasing the gender balance of boards in 2022.[15] The European Union's Directive on Gender Balance in Corporate Boards requires listed companies across the EU to have either 40 percent of non-executive directors or 33 percent of all board directors (non-executive plus executive directors) from the underrepresented gender by June 2026.

At the same time, in 2025, the US rolled back many regulations regarding diversity, equity, and inclusion (DEI), forcing companies to reconsider diversity initiatives on all levels, including the board. For instance, one director told us in confidence that one of his tasks as the audit and compliance chair in 2025 has been to ensure that no further mention of DEI would be made in filings to comply with the most recent executive orders by the US president.

Boards, therefore, need to critically assess how to comply with differing legislation to avoid shareholder suits or government legal action. This increasingly complex situation makes it even more critical that boards consider the rationale for creating diversity on the board.

In our view, boards should continue to consider the benefits of cognitive diversity on the board. Incorporating different perspectives can significantly improve conversations and decisions, as it helps challenge any entrenched mindsets.[16] For instance, Kathleen Bailey-Lord, board member at AMP, Datacom, St. Vincent's Health Australia, and Janison in Australia, told us:

> The role I play on my boards is to disrupt the thinking by challenging our assumptions. Are our assumptions still serving us well today? Has the context changed? Do we need to fundamentally change our strategy or our business model?

Research on women on boards suggests that female directors can drive more robust accountability, actively seek information, and foster open discussions, reducing competitiveness and encouraging broader perspectives in board discussions. This behavior mitigates "pluralistic ignorance," where individuals hesitate to express doubts that others may share. Overall, women enhance board governance and decision quality, adding depth to discussions and potentially improving corporate outcomes.[17]

Despite efforts to increase gender diversity on boards, female directors often still face exclusion and a lack of influence. Gender diversity brings unique perspectives to the board that drive creativity, but achieving this benefit requires thoughtful recruitment and cultural shifts to fully integrate female directors into board activities.[18] To do so requires more structured work, for instance, through mentorship for female directors.

More generally, leveraging diversity of thought for business results requires not just varied demographics and experiences of the board members but also the fostering of an inclusive environment where all directors can fully participate and contribute. This involves managing power dynamics, ensuring all voices are heard, and balancing diversity with shared core values and purpose.

Effective boards foster inclusive environments that encourage all directors, especially those from underrepresented groups, to participate fully.[19] To leverage diversity in the board, it is also important to address dynamics that may silence members who are less vocal or from underrepresented groups. In diverse boards, it is also important to address stereotypes and biases that hinder the integration of diverse voices.[20]

Generating an inclusive environment may also be important to attract the best diverse talent. Younger professionals and those with specialized skills may be reluctant to join boards that are perceived as stagnant or not inclusive. Thomas Thune Andersen, chair at Lloyd's Register Group and VKR Holding, and board member at BW Group and IMI plc, observed:

> We aim to get new competencies onto the board. Digital, transformational, and innovation capabilities will be key to our business in the future. We also want to deal with key people topics and get a better understanding of politics and stakeholder relations. I have tried to get some younger candidates onto the board, and when I got a 38-year-old

who already had a decent track record and experience with these topics, he told me frankly: "Thank you, but that's not for me. I can't be innovative for an hour between two and three in the afternoon when I've fallen asleep with compliance and governance for four hours before that."

When boards focus on increasing diversity – e.g., international, functional, or experiential – they also need to be mindful of the potential efforts and costs needed to reap the benefits. For instance, there often is an inherent conflict between creating an internationally diverse board and the attempt to create a tight team on the board. Long-distance travel, for example, can prevent deeper relationship-building among board members. Pius Baschera, former chair of the board of Hilti, noted:

> We thought a lot about international diversity on the board. It would be great to have an Asian national on our board, somebody who has experience in Asia and has lived there. But we would like to have this person living in Europe. Why? If a member flies in for a board meeting in the morning and, in the evening, goes on the plane again and leaves, you lose the team aspect. For us, being a team, acting as a team, having trust in each other, and being colleagues with each other are very important. And if you're just flying in six, seven times a year for a day, the connections to the team are pretty loose.

While diversity on the board can bring different perspectives and enhance decision-making, it may also lead to conflicts and delays, and therefore, the role of structured leadership by the board chair and board cultures that embrace differences are essential. Without a set of shared core values and agreement on the company's purpose and mission, diverse boards may disintegrate into dysfunctional groups that are incapable of forming cohesive views on the strategic problems faced by the firm.

Balancing experience, independence, and expertise

Beyond diversity, selecting the right mix of directors involves balancing experience, independence, and expertise. In addition to diverse perspectives, boards need a mix of industry- and company-specific knowledge, novel expertise, and deep strategic thinking to enhance governance quality on today's challenges and strategic guidance for tomorrow's questions. A Nordic board chair commented:

> The board needs to be composed of people bringing the expertise, the knowledge, and experience that is necessary to understand the company, to be able to guide the company, and help the company in the marketplace. To be able to ask the right questions and open the right network for the company.

Creating such a mix requires clear competence requirements derived from the company's purpose, situation, and strategic challenges and priorities.[21]

The need for industry and company experience

However, balancing these elements often leads to tensions and dilemmas, such as choosing between an experienced industry veteran who might lack fresh perspectives or a newcomer who brings deep expertise on a novel topic or new ideas but lacks deep sector knowledge. Different directors resolve these trade-offs in distinct ways. For instance, some directors have a strong preference for deep industry expertise on the board. Riet Cadonau, experienced board chair and director and current director at the Zehnder Group AG, explained:

> It is important that we also have board members who really understand the business and have experience in it, which is rarer than you would expect. Being a former CEO in the industrial sector is not always enough. If someone understands mechanical engineering solutions, they do not automatically understand the industrial services or the system integration business.

On the other hand, when the industry is facing change, deep sector experience can easily become a limitation in finding novel solutions or new directions, and, therefore, directors with different perspectives from outside the industry can be helpful in emphasizing new ideas. Debbie Hewitt, chair of England's Football Association, explained to us:

> Directors with different experience can often bring different perspectives. They can be more curious and will likely challenge the status quo, as they typically don't have a fixed way of defining issues. I think it is the Chair's role to understand if a Board is getting stuck in a pattern of behavior and to ensure that new directors have the space and encouragement to contribute new ideas. What you need is a mix of people.

To resolve these dilemmas in a balanced manner requires that board composition reflects a mix of different profiles and the willingness to make the tensions that may arise from this diverse mix work, as Hewitt continued to explain:

> Whilst new members bring fresh perspectives, it's important that the Board has deep sector experience too. If no one has sector experience, the board may not spot trends quickly enough, could miss opportunities through a lack of knowledge, and is unlikely to respond effectively in a crisis.

Scar tissue and crisis experience

Independent of the degree of industry or role experience, board members should have experience and resilience in dealing with crisis situations, in particular, given today's multi-crisis environment. Several board chairs referred to this with the notion of "scar tissue" that comes from having lived through periods of extreme pressure. Kalidas Madhavpeddi, chair of the Swiss-based mining giant Glencore, put it this way:

> A key requirement for a board member at Glencore is what we call scar tissue, which you build through crisis. For instance, one of our previous board members was sanctioned by the US government because she was a member of a Canadian company that had assets in Cuba. Whilst another was the CEO of a major US bank during the time of the GFC. You need people who have lived through crises so that they won't be paralyzed when a crisis hits and instead immediately start to think about how to fix it.

Board member independence

One topic that became central to most of our conversations on board composition is the question of the independence of board members. There has been long-standing advocacy for independent board chairs and independent board members.[22] Many countries that have issued regulations, or at least recommendations, that boards should be led by an independent chair, should consist mostly or even entirely of independent directors, and proxy advisors continue to emphasize the importance of this issue.

On the surface, the logic is straightforward: Independence is important since it allows the board as a whole to provide objective oversight of the management. For the individual director, it is important since it will enable them to take a stand in the board discussion with fewer fears of negative consequences for them. Stefan Nöken, board member at Vaillant, Vorwerk, and Peri Group, remarked:

> Independence means that I can tackle conflicts on the board because I'm not dependent on this specific board seat. I am financially independent as well as independent in my opinion and in my social status. It's bad for the effectiveness of the board when board members are being chosen because of personal relationships, as this often prevents substantive discussion on contentious issues.

While all board members we spoke to agreed on the importance of board independence for objective oversight, what independence means is not always as easy as,

Doug Baker, lead independent director at Target and member of the board at Merck (MSD), illustrated:

> There are plenty of examples of chairs who are formally independent but are completely in the pocket of the CEO. And then, the CEO places all of their friends on the board. You need clear governance structures and governance principles – rules that the board is following – then you get the independence of the board.

Furthermore, excessive emphasis on independence in the selection of board members can lead to a board that lacks industry and company knowledge, thereby reducing the board's effectiveness. Independent directors who spend limited time and effort on the focus of the firm may lack the depth of understanding needed to advise management that works on company problems day-to-day effectively.

Boards, where only the CEO serves as an insider, can be problematic because independent directors can lack direct understanding or access to internal perspectives, reducing board oversight and hampering strategic decision-making and CEO succession planning.[23] While independent directors are often seen as safeguards against CEO overreach, empirical studies have shown relatively little evidence for a strong relationship between independence and corporate performance. Independent directors may also reduce innovation when they overemphasize compliance and divert focus from strategic guidance. Such an overemphasis can strain relationships with management and limit collaboration between the board and the executive team, which is necessary for innovation.[24]

The problem of independence is particularly pronounced when directors are at the end of their careers with relatively limited incentive to invest time and effort in the company. A board chair, of a US stock exchange-listed corporation, stated this idea provocatively:

> I call those 3G-plus-one board members. They golf; they grandparent; they garden, and then they do one board so that when they are in the country club and someone asks, "What do you do?" They do not feel their professional identity is lost. The longer they are away from their executive role, the less value they bring.

Professional directors

One option to address this may be professional directors who are dedicated professionals with relevant industry expertise and sufficient time to commit to board activities. Professional board members bring dedication and time commitment to their board roles, but to be effective, such directors should either have relevant industry experience or be required to spend more time understanding the industry and company operations.[25] However, professional directors are no panacea for board composition, as some of our interviewees highlighted. Jeff Campbell, former vice chairman and CFO of American Express, former CFO of McKesson and American Airlines, and current director at AON plc, Marathon Petroleum Corp., and Hexcel Corp, explained:

> One problem with professional board members that start their board career very early is that it is challenging to bring someone to oversee management who has not yet had experience of dealing with their own board, and suddenly is expected to understand the role of a board, and to be thoughtful about balancing board and management roles. What does a board do? What does the management team do? What is appropriate oversight? What is getting in the way of management? One of the things that is often hugely misunderstood about the role of board members in large organizations is that one of their most challenging and important tasks is to manage senior, talented people with big egos. And it is hard to do that if you are more junior than they are.

Professional directors might also lack current operational experience or be over-focused on governance processes. As they are not involved in day-to-day business, they may also lose touch with the current problems and the solutions adopted by different companies. Doug Baker, lead independent director at Target and member of the board at Merck (MSD), argued:

> There is a risk that professional directors become quite insular since they are not exposed day-to-day to the economy. If that is the makeup of your board, and you are going into crises like Ukraine and Russia on top of the COVID situation, they might not be able to read the pressures that companies face. They do not have direct feedback from the employees, the customers, or even regulatory institutions or governments on a day-to-day basis. For this reason, you need a mix of people on the board.

A case may, therefore, be made that at least some board members should be inside directors, such as executives or CEOs, or at least former executives or CEOs of the company, who can bring deep insights into company operations that independent members often lack, particularly in complex industries.[26] When the board chair carefully manages these inside directors to avoid them dominating board discussions, they can add significant value to the board as a whole, given their deeper experience with the company's business.

Breadth of expertise – generalists versus specialists

Finally, the question of the breadth of expertise of directors emerged frequently in our conversations. Boards face a choice between appointing specialists to the board, that is, board members with specific expertise, such as AI, ESG, or cybersecurity, or appointing generalists, such as former CEOs or division presidents. A board chair of a Swiss stock-listed company explained:

> I don't see the role of the board as a duplication of executive management. I put another person behind everyone to see if they are doing it right. I understand the board's function as a group of generalists, though strong personalities with maturity and experience. Unlike the executive board, it needs people who can integrate the various viewpoints and functions. Otherwise, you end up in a discussion between experts, for instance, from a former CFO on the board to the current CFO. And you spend 15 minutes talking about a topic that doesn't interest the others at all and may not add that much value. I look for personalities with a broader range of experience and a broad perspective.

Jean-Pierre Clamadieu, chair of French energy company Engie and director of Airbus and TE Connectivity, offered a similar perspective:

> On the board, you need people with experience in leading large organizations and able to make decisions encompassing different viewpoints. I am skeptical about the added value of experts. If you want to increase board awareness on digital transformation, you should bring someone who has this large organization experience but has led a large digital transformation.

However, a case for experts can also be made, particularly in larger boards and when the company faces specific strategic challenges that may benefit from board members with deep expertise who can coach the CEO and executives on particular topics. For instance, Stefan Nöken, a member of the board at Vaillant, Vorwerk, and Peri Group, explained:

> The board should reflect the composition of the company management to some extent in terms of the composition of expertise, and it should also reflect the corporate strategy. Today I need board members who ultimately have the same level of expertise as the executive management. But does every board member necessarily have to be proficient in all domains? In my view, it is similar to an effective management team in a company where individuals who have the necessary depth need to be assigned to the individual domains. They can be a valuable sparring partner and coach for the executive team.

While this choice of generalists versus experts relates to the type of approach to board design, as we discussed above, it also relates to the size of the board. For smaller boards, the choice typically gravitates toward generalists, whereas in larger boards, more often, narrower expertise can be found. However, this choice then has consequences for how the board structure and board process need to be designed, as we will discuss in the next chapter.

Recruiting former or current CEOs and CFOs

The topic of expertise relates to the broader question of what roles board directors should be recruited from. Traditionally, boards have recruited former or current CEOs to coach the sitting CEO, CFOs, and other financial experts to provide financial control.

While former CEOs and executives are easier to hire and have fewer limitations in joining boards, their experience and knowledge become dated more easily. In contrast, current CEOs and executives bring up-to-date knowledge and experience and might also create age diversity on the board. However, they are often severely limited in the time they can contribute. Pius Baschera, experienced board member and former board chair of Hilti, observed:

> When I was CEO, I was on the board of another company. In the beginning, we had six, seven, or even eight meetings. That was no problem. But then we were in a takeover battle, and we had meetings every week, sometimes even twice a week. And I realized how difficult it is to be the CEO of a company while having another board membership.

Another chair advised:

> In a board, it is also important to have spare capacity. If something goes wrong, if there is an attack, an unsolicited offer, or any crisis, many boards fail because people are not available. It is good to have one or at most two people on the board who are still in executive positions themselves and work not just from memory. If you have more than one or two full executives or heavy-weight CEOs, it quickly becomes very academic what they can achieve.

Increasingly, companies also limit the possibilities of executives to join boards. While some companies may not allow executives to hold any board seats, most companies limit executives to one appointment. Furthermore, CEOs and executives themselves have become increasingly reluctant, as Joerg Reinhardt, chair of Novartis and member of the board of SwissRe, explained:

> It is becoming increasingly difficult to get active CEOs interested in boards. A lot of people whom I've spoken to say: "No, my CEO job requires 150 percent of me, and I can't expect my company or myself to do a board role. Maybe I'll do it towards the end of my career, when I'm slowly preparing to join boards as a next step, to try and understand how it works."

Shareholders, employees, and other stakeholders on the board

Another question that many boards face is whether and how stakeholders should be represented on the board. Major shareholders (e.g., anchor shareholders, venture capitalists, or private equity firms) often demand the right to nominate some directors. While these shareholders formally have a fiduciary duty to the company and all shareholders rather than representing a single one, in practice, their position and background often reflect the will of the shareholders who nominated them. The board faces a trade-off in this respect. On the one hand, shareholder-nominated directors could make discussion on the board much easier, as one board chair pointed out:

> Having the representative of an anchor shareholder who holds 25 percent of the shares on the board makes it much easier to make decisions on major strategic initiatives. We can be certain that a major part of the shareholder votes will support this project.

On the other hand, shareholder-nominated board members could dominate the board decision-making and lead to factionalization.

Employee representatives are a second type of stakeholder that is often found on the board. However, there are important differences across countries in this respect. While some countries like Germany and France have a long history of employee representation, it is a rare practice in countries like the US or the UK.

Employee representation can be an opportunity, as Luka Mucic, director at Heidelberg Materials, pointed out:

> Employee representation in Germany, where we have the mandatory co-determination, is an opportunity that other companies do not have. In a supervisory board, there can be trusting cooperation and the will to bring the voice of the workforce into the discussion. It can bring employees from all levels into the board process in a truly open manner and not in the sense of a block formation.

The advantage of employee representatives on the board is that the voice of the employees reaches the decision-making process unfiltered and can influence decision-making. Employee representatives can highlight early warning signals from the organization and make the buy-in for tough decisions from the employees more likely. Markus Beck, vice chair of Deutsche Börse AG, explained:

> The role of the employee representatives is very much appreciated in the supervisory and the management board because the inside view is brought into the discussion. You get unfiltered information on how employees view certain developments. What is critical? What is going

well? The supervisory board and even the management board normally don't get access to this information otherwise.

At the same time, some critical aspects need to be kept in mind when bringing in the employee voice. In general, employee representatives do not have the same level of qualification as other board members. Markus Beck acknowledged:

> Most employee representatives do not have the same qualifications and experiences as shareholder representatives who already have management board experience or sit on other supervisory boards. This means that there can be a fundamental imbalance in the discussion.

He further explained that to counter this imbalance, employee representatives tend to coordinate:

> We always have our internal preparatory meeting as employee representatives before the supervisory board meetings in order to exchange knowledge and coordinate with each other and to agree on what we have to bring into the board meeting. We agree on which points are important to us, how we present them, who presents them, and how we argue. In addition, a possible imbalance can be compensated by a suitable onboarding program for new board members and regular training and workshops, which we practice. The advantages of co-determination therefore far outweigh the disadvantages.

Finally, board chairs need to be cognizant of the difficulties of integrating different profiles and the status differentials that arise when board members with highly varying role backgrounds work together, as we highlighted in our discussion on the inclusion of diverse directors.

Can you have it all? Desirable profiles for the board

From which roles should you recruit your board members? While boards have traditionally focused on former and current CEOs, given the much-expanded scope of the board's responsibilities and the change in topics the board needs to deal with going forward, this source may be too limited going forward. Often, the skills needed for modern boards are found in roles different from those of the CEO or CFO. Boards should consider a wider range of profiles. Below is a partial list of potential backgrounds to consider:

∎ **Former CEOs of other firms**

☐ Generalists who understand the CEO role but may have outsized egos

- **Ex-CEO of the focal firm**

  □ Offers deep institutional knowledge but may resist change or overshadow the current CEO

- **Current CEO**

  □ Has commitment and responsibility, but is it really necessary or optimal to have them as a voting board member?

- **Executives of other firms**

  □ Can bring general managerial insight or specialized expertise in areas like digital, ESG, cybersecurity, etc.

- **Former CFOs or auditors**

  □ Provide critical financial oversight, but might focus narrowly on financials and lean toward risk aversion

- **Industry specialists**

  □ Bring in-depth industry knowledge and a strong grasp of market dynamics

- **CHRO**

  □ People issues and succession planning are vital, but a CHRO can be too narrowly focused if not balanced with broader business acumen

- **Lawyer or general counsel**

  □ Ensures legal and compliance rigor but may steer board discussions into more formalistic or legalistic territory

- **Investor representatives**

  □ Advocate for particular shareholder interests; can create conflict regarding broader fiduciary duties

- **Entrepreneurs**

  □ Spark an entrepreneurial mindset; may find it challenging to adapt to a large, structured company

- **Other**

  □ Military leaders often bring leadership rigor and accountability, but may also introduce bureaucratic tendencies
  □ Academics, NGO leaders, and think-tank representatives might supply cutting-edge thinking, yet lack operational experience
  □ Representatives of critical stakeholders or customers can offer key outside viewpoints

Selecting for personality, values, and motivation

In addition to knowledge, independence, and expertise, the personal characteristics of the board member candidates, the alignment of their values with the board and company values, and their motivation to join the board are central criteria for the selection of board members to ensure effective governance.

Personal characteristics

Directors should exhibit personality traits such as curiosity, inquisitiveness, courage, mental independence, collegiality, and a team-oriented mindset. Board members need to provide oversight, advice, and strategic input. Because board members do not work full-time at the company, they have a strong information disadvantage compared to the CEO and executives. Therefore, a strong eagerness to learn and the ability to ask insightful questions is central to their effectiveness. Kaj-Erik Relander, board member of Louis Dreyfuss Corporation, SES Satellites, and a number of other privately held corporations, explained:

> To be fit for a board role, you need intellectual curiosity about the domain the company is in. If you're in construction chemicals, you have to be interested in that industry. If you're not, you won't be an effective board member. Unless you're interested in the domain, you will not pay enough attention to strategic challenges. And if you do not understand the business initially, which is quite often the case, you need to demonstrate curiosity to learn the business.

We discussed formal independence as a key criterion recommended, or in some countries required, by governance codices and proxy advisors. This notion of independence relates mostly to financial independence. Directors should not be financially dependent on their board remuneration to ensure unbiased judgment and avoid conflicts of interest. However, a second form of independence is equally vital for directors to make unbiased decisions and fulfill their fiduciary duties effectively, namely, mental independence. Board members need the ability to resist groupthink and maintain objectivity to be able to provide effective oversight and give advice in high-pressure situations. To be effective, mental independence needs to be accompanied by the courage to stand up for one's viewpoint, even against the rest of the board members or when the position is uncomfortable. Kaj-Erik Relander pointed out:

> For me, good board members need to have civil courage. If you feel within your role that things are not how they should be, you must be able to speak up. But speaking up is not enough. You need to engage the resources around the table to do something about it. Strong people with this kind of courage and character tend to become better board members than people who don't have that.

Board members also need to exhibit a strong team orientation. Jean-Pierre Clamadieu, chair of French energy company Engie and director of Airbus and TE Connectivity, put it succinctly:

> One key characteristic I expect from every board member is collegiality. You need people who can feel that they want to be part of the team. For the board, you need to have people who want to be part of this group and make decisions jointly. That's really a characteristic which is not so easy to find.

Board members typically have had a long career in executive roles, in which they have had to make and implement individual decisions. Board membership is different from these executive roles because it typically requires influencing through questions rather than commanding through directives. Board members advise and steer management often indirectly, and if the board takes on a decision-maker role, decisions are group decisions. This means board members need to hold their egos in check and work as a group rather than shine as individuals, requiring a strong willingness to collaborate and contribute to collective decision-making processes. Kalidas Madhavpeddi, chair of the Swiss-based mining giant Glencore, put it bluntly:

> There is such a big difference between being a CEO and a board member, and it is such a big transition. In a company, the CEO is at the top of the organization. On a board, your best work is to contribute collectively to a common cause. That does not allow for a big ego. That's why some CEOs make lousy board members.

Overbearing, big-ego directors can hinder collaboration, stifle the ability to leverage diverse perspectives, and reduce the quality of discussion and decision-making. Candidates with overly dominant egos need to be carefully vetted during the selection process. This should, however, not be confused with board members who take contrarian positions with the purpose of creating discussion and looking at all aspects of a problem. Jean-Pierre Clamadieu emphasized this point:

> You don't want to bring people to the board with such a big ego that they won't be able to participate in a collective decision-making process, but it is useful to have contrarians on the board. The fact that some people take a different view is useful for creating a strong discussion and ensuring you look at this subject from every angle. But then you must come together to form a consensus and make a joint decision.

Values

In addition to these personality characteristics, the values of board members also need to align with the board's and the overall company's core values to ensure cohesion and consistent decision-making. If there's a fundamental mismatch in core principles, conflict is almost inevitable. Mark Joiner, director at QBE AusPa, explained:

> It is rather important that people on the board are fairly values-aligned. For instance, I think of business not only in shareholder value terms but also to the benefit of all stakeholders – employees, communities, and future generations. When I interview director candidates, I often get quite explicit about values. I am upfront about what I think is important in the world. It can transform conversations with somebody, either positively or negatively. In my view, it is a good way to separate candidates and bring in people who, despite having a diversity of thinking, share a bedrock of thinking on values.

Asking for diversity on the board can easily be misunderstood to imply that no common value base is needed. However, when board members differ fundamentally in their values, effective board work is close to impossible.

Motivation

Finally, the motivation for joining the board should be a central criterion for selecting board members. Directors should be motivated by the desire to contribute positively to the company and its stakeholders rather than by self-interest. Some interviewees described serving on a board as akin to public service, and board members should commit to a principled perspective, acting in the best interests of shareholders and other stakeholders. Board members who join for personal gain or status often do not act in the best interest of the company, may not dedicate the necessary effort when needed, and could create conflicts of interest and poor governance. Riet Cadonau, experienced board chair and director and current director at the Zehnder Group AG, highlighted this point:

> If someone is financially dependent on a mandate, I don't think they fit on the board. But there is not only financial dependence, but there is also dependence on status. The question of prestige or status is one that I think should be an issue in the recruitment process. If someone is too attached to the status of a mandate, he or she is less likely to express a controversial opinion when required.

Are you fit for this board

For all the status and responsibility that comes with a board seat, prospective directors should be honest with themselves about whether they can truly contribute. Here are five essential questions every candidate should ask:

1. Why do I want to be on this board?
2. What value can I add to this board and the company?

   a. What excites me about this company?
   b. What are the company's key challenges?
   c. What specific skills and expertise do I bring to this board that others don't have?

3. Does this board role conflict with my current roles? How can this conflict be resolved?
4. Do I have the passion for this business to go the extra mile when needed?
5. Do I have the independence to step back from the board in case of conflict?

Search processes for board members

Search processes for board members may take very different forms. Some boards still search mostly through the personal network of the chair or the board members, while other boards engage in highly structured processes to ensure the quality of the process and the outcome of the search. As with the search for a CEO[27] or for leadership team members,[28] the overall trend clearly is toward highly structured processes. Given the changing requirements for boards that also demand new forms of board composition, we advocate for structured and data-driven processes that have the highest likelihood of identifying a sufficient breadth of high-quality candidates and reducing the risk of biased decisions. This process should include at least six steps:

1. Define Strategic opportunities and challenges
2. Involve the right people and resources
3. Define and develop a candidate pool
4. Screen and shortlist candidates
5. Select candidate
6. Onboard the new board member

Define strategic opportunities and challenges, and the resulting needed skills and requirements

The search process should start with defining the needs of the board going forward and assessing the current composition of the board against these needs. Taking a forward-looking perspective, boards should ask several questions.

What are the strategic goals of the company and the specific challenges it faces going forward? Where is the company heading in the next five years? What strategic competencies does the board need to be effective? What do these needs imply for the new skills needed on the board?

As we have argued in our opening chapters, these skills are likely to be different from the past, given the dual challenge of modern boards.

Analyzing the strategic opportunities and challenges allows the board to critically assess the existing skills and experiences of existing board members, ideally based on a structured skills matrix, and identify gaps and blind spots in the current board. Creating such a skills and competency matrix begins with defining what skills are needed and will be critical given the strategic challenges and opportunities faced by the organization. Board members are then mapped against these skills and competencies, and gaps arising from these analyses are taken into consideration in selecting future board members.

Based on the skills identified, the board should define a clear profile for the new board member, including skills, experience, diversity dimensions, and other attributes needed. These attributes need to be aligned with the company's purpose, strategic vision, and major strategic directions the company is considering.

Involve the right people and resources inside and outside the company

The nominating committee should lead the process, but ideally, the board chair or lead independent director (if they are not part of the nominating committee) and all board members should be involved at some stage in the selection process. Independent directors should drive selection through the selection process, which, however, should also involve the CEO to ensure alignment. A board member of multiple European corporations explained:

> No matter if you have a standard nomination committee or any other model to create the board, I think you need to involve the CEO in selecting directors. You need to have a very close dialogue with the CEO based on the most strategic challenges and the type of support and discussions needed in the boardroom. Only then can you decide if the board has the right composition and who may need to be added.

While the nominating committee leads the process, engaging a search firm is advisable to gain access to a broader pool of candidates and ensure there are sufficient resources available for the search process. However, the nominating committee needs to be mindful of the potential biases that search firms bring to these search processes and, therefore, actively steer the process. Carla Smits-Nusteling, a former board member of Nokia, ASML, and TELE2 AB, explained:

What you get from a headhunter depends very much on what you ask them for. If you don't pose the right question, you will get a list of candidates you probably already know yourself, and it's a waste of money. You may only do it because you want to get the documented search process and the outward appearance of a comprehensive process. But if you ask the right questions, it is a different story. If you start with a detailed profile, you may get to see different candidates who are not in your network. But it is a lot of work for the headhunter, and they don't like it because they'd rather present the few names that we know already.

Define and develop a candidate pool in advance

The goal of developing the candidate pool is to develop a diverse pool of potential candidates that fulfill the search criteria as much as possible. While the nominating committee may draw upon the professional network of all directors to search for candidates, at this stage, a search firm can add value by extending the search beyond the personal network of directors. Ideally, the nominating committee works long before the active selection process to develop and qualify candidates for this pool, since, in particular, outstanding board members often find it difficult to win. Christoph Mohn, chair of the board of German Media giant Bertelsmann, explained:

> We look for board members who have excelled in their fields. We seek out strong, dynamic personalities – outstanding performers. If you'll allow a sports analogy, candidates who have played in the Champions League. These types of individuals are hard to find, so we are always on the lookout, even when we don't need a new board member right away. We begin our search years in advance. Finding candidates with the right caliber is incredibly challenging. For example, we recently conducted an exercise where we wanted an active member of an executive team from a top-tier DAX-listed company, preferably from the DAX 30. We ruled out industries that aren't entrepreneurially driven, as they wouldn't be the right fit. After narrowing it down to three potential names, we then had to check if any of them were willing and available. This is why we look for top talent several years ahead of time. There are individuals we won't be able to recruit for five or ten years, but we've already identified them and have them on our radar.

In fact, at times, it may be advisable to anticipate and prepare for the appointment of an outstanding candidate when they become available. Some boards have moved from a succession of disconnected search processes when a board member retires or leaves the board for other reasons, toward a structured talent management process for board members, even though this is more difficult since potential candidates typically are not working for the firm.

Screening and shortlisting the candidates

Candidates should be screened through several rounds of interviews to assess not only their skills and experience but also how their personality would fit with the existing board culture and dynamics. Peter Voser, board chair at ABB, PSA International, and member of the board at IBM, detailed this method:

> I normally do three to four meetings with potential board members. I think any person can play one or two meetings in a more artificial way, but at the third or fourth meeting, the truth will get out. A typical question from my side is always, if others have a different opinion and you are in the minority in a tight vote, how do you deal with that? How do you feel about it? How do you think this would shape your thinking about the other board members and how you would react towards them in the next break you have? That often gives great discussions. I have had many candidates where I was very positive after the first or second meeting, but after discussing this question, something in my stomach would not feel right. I would not have the feeling that they would really compromise in a way that they still remain constructive.

In these interviews, evaluating candidates' ability to contribute strategically, offer independent perspectives, and add value beyond just technical skills is important. Boards should also consider other forms of assessment, such as culture fit assessment or structured exercises, to evaluate the candidates more holistically. These exercises can be particularly valuable when candidates are not well-known to the nominating committee members. Finally, the nominating committee should conduct thorough due diligence, including background checks, to assess the integrity, reputation, and compatibility of the candidates.

What should you ask every director candidate

Creating a complete set of questions for a director interview, independent from the company context, is difficult. However, a comprehensive interview should at least include questions to cover the topic areas below. For each topic, we have defined what you should try to learn about the candidate.

Questions on vision

Strategic vision for the industry
~ic vision for the company

Questions on experience, independence, and expertise

Experience: Relevance for the current company
Crisis: Experience and signs of resilience
Diversity: What new perspective does the candidate bring
Independence: What interest bindings may create conflicts of interest
Expertise: Generalist versus specialist
Expertise: Key technical/commercial/legal skills and their fit with the skills matrix of the board
Generic skills: Analytical capabilities, emotional intelligence, people-orientation

Questions on personal characteristics

Personality: Curiosity, inquisitiveness, courage, financial and mental independence, openness to diverse perspectives, team orientation
Ego: Me or we focus
Future orientation: How strongly is the candidate future-oriented
Key values: Alignment with the board
Motivation to join the board: Stewardship versus status and personal gain

Selecting a candidate

After reducing the candidate pool to a shortlist of candidates, the nominating committee should align with the full board. All board members should interview the final two candidates, and the board should then collectively agree on the best candidate to complement the current board composition, taking the skills matrix and board dynamics into consideration and to enhance overall governance. In some cases, particularly for key appointments such as committee chairs or the board chair, it may be appropriate to seek shareholder input or feedback already before making the final recommendation for the appointment, especially in situations where governance best practices emphasize shareholder engagement. In fact, in many legislations, the final approval for new board members rests with the shareholders in the annual general meeting.

Onboarding the new board member

Once appointed, the new board member should undergo a comprehensive onboarding process. Depending upon their experience and background, a new director may need to spend considerable time to get up to speed on the company and industry. This includes familiarizing them with the company's operations, strategy, financials, corporate governance framework, and other relevant materials. During the onboarding phase, the new board members may need regular coaching and support to ensure they are effectively contributing to the board's work and meeting expectations. We will discuss the topic of onboarding in more detail in Chapter 7 on board evaluation and development.

Forming board members into a team

How "team-like" should boards be? Interestingly, boards are often viewed as a collection of individuals who come together to discuss company topics but do not exhibit the characteristics of a team. In fact, some interviewees raised some doubts about the ability of boards to operate as a team, given that they meet too infrequently compared to many teams in corporations, are often characterized by a lack of mutual trust, and are easily dominated by some board members. The sporadic meetings that characterize board work make it difficult to build strong relationships, while the relative equality among directors can hinder the establishment of clear team roles and dynamics.

However, we argue that modern boards are more effective when the board members are formed into cohesive teams since this allows the board to leverage the diverse strengths of their members to create value in their interactions with the CEO and leadership team. Acting as a team is particularly important for collaborative decision-making. Doing so requires clarity and effort in cultivating a clear board purpose, mutual respect among the members, and dedicated efforts to build trust.[29] Given the infrequency of meetings, explicit efforts in team building during the meetings and the use of informal interactions and social events are often central to strengthening relationships and building a team spirit. A board chair of a large European corporation explained:

> If you want to turn the board into a real team, informal meetings like the dinner the night before the board meeting are, in my opinion, a must. Creating a real group, not only individual people who are sitting next to each other, takes time. If you have meetings only every month or two, it's different than when you're meeting every week, like in an executive committee. You need to take every opportunity, not only the board meeting itself, to work on creating the team.

Board chairs play an essential leadership role in forming boards into a team, as Doug Baker, lead independent director at Target and member of the board at Merck (MSD), explained:

> To create a team spirit in the board, you need leadership. Of course, it starts with bringing people on the board who are there for the company and open to working as a team. But then you also have to create the right

environment. Because if the board is not led in a way that facilitates teamwork, you are not going to get a team.

Board chairs need to foster activities that promote cohesion and understanding among board members. They should define the expectations and responsibilities of different board members. For instance, one board member of a large US stock exchange-listed corporation recounted:

> My chairman told me that I do more work than the rest of the board combined. I chair the audit committee, so I have to deal with internal and external audits, compliance, health and safety, and legal issues. It just is a bigger job. Others who are sitting CEOs are mostly wise people in the room, and the expectation of them is different. Boards are team plays. Not everybody is the batter, not everybody is the pitcher, and not everybody is the catcher. We must understand that we are a team trying to achieve a common objective.

Turning the board into a team also requires a psychologically safe environment where all directors feel comfortable expressing their views, fostering a culture where differing opinions are valued and respected, and implementing mechanisms to manage and resolve conflicts arising from differences in personalities and the potential clashes these create.

How long should a board member stay on the board

A final question related to board composition concerns the length of tenure of individual board members. Many countries have introduced tenure limits by defining them outright or by declaring directors who exceed a tenure limit as no longer independent. In addition, many companies define an age limit for their directors.

Several factors speak against excessive tenure on a board. Over time, the knowledge and expertise of directors will become dated, and therefore, directors may no longer be able to add value to the board. Views may also ossify over time, and long-serving directors may stand in the way of needed change. Debbie Hewitt, chair of England's Football Association, explained:

> I am a great believer in the good governance practice of a set tenure for a board role. In the UK, that is 9 years. While I can think of examples where somebody, after 9 years, is still independent and capable of making a strong contribution to a board, I do think the advantages of a 9-year tenure outweigh the drawbacks. With nine years, you have three years to get to know a business, three years to contribute from a strong knowledge base, and three years to find a successor. After 9 years, there

is a risk that the business has evolved, and your skills don't quite reflect what the business now needs. There is also the risk after 9 years that you'll go "native" and lose the benefit of being independent.

However, these downsides need to be weighed against the benefits of long-serving directors who may reflect the company's institutional memory and may know both the company and industry intimately, thereby complementing directors who come from outside the industry. Furthermore, there is a clear learning curve to becoming effective on a specific company board, as we will discuss in more detail in Chapter 7.

Limits to tenure on the board may also play an important role in increasing the independence of professional directors. Pauline Van der Meer Mohr, chair of the Dutch semiconductor equipment manufacturer ASM, and director of Ahold Delhaize, NN Group, explained:

> When you have directors who have made board memberships a second career, remuneration becomes a topic. And that can reduce their independence. Term limits help with that because if you're dependent on your income for one, two, or three boards, knowing that your term will end and your performance on this board will decide if you get the next board position keeps you independent. You know that if you want to continue doing this, you'll have to go look for another board. You can't just sit back and relax knowing that you can retire on this board.

Related to the question of how long a director should be on a board is the question of when directors should be re-elected. Some companies have opted for staggered re-election, where only a portion of board members are elected each year. Initially seen as a way to promote stability and deter hostile takeovers, staggered boards have been criticized for entrenching management and reducing accountability to shareholders. Research findings on their effectiveness are mixed; while staggered boards may protect young, innovative firms by enabling a focus on long-term goals, they are often associated with reduced shareholder value in mature firms.[30]

The limits to the tenure of board members, combined with when directors should be re-elected, also raise the question of the right level of turnover among board members. Research on the optimal turnover rate[31] finds that moderate turnover – replacing three to four directors every three years – delivers the most substantial shareholder returns. They argue that a moderate level of turnover brings fresh perspectives while preserving continuity. Excessive turnover disrupts stability, while stagnation reduces adaptability. However, the right level of turnover depends on the situation of the company, with structural changes (an IPO, for example, or a going private situation), or strategic changes (such as internationalization or business model transformations) calling for a high rate of turnover to support the change process.

Notes

1. Toward the completion of the manuscript for this book, Holcim announced that Jenisch would step down from the board chair role to lead the new company as CEO and chair. Since these changes were not implemented yet, we decided to present this example from the perspective of Fall 2024.

2. Esha Mendiratta, "Faultlines: Understanding How Board Composition May Influence Team Dynamics and Subgroup Formation in Corporate Boards," in *Research Handbook on Diversity and Corporate Governance*, ed. Sabina Tasheva and Morten Huse (Cheltenham: Edward Elgar Publishing, 2023).

3. For the application of that principle at the level of the leadership team, see Thomas Keil and Marianna Zangrillo, *The Next Leadership Team: How to Select, Build, and Optimize Your Top Team* (London: Routledge, 2023). Many of the same ideas can also be applied on the level of the board.

4. For the idea of a situational approach to board design and behavior see, for instance, Ram Charan, Dennis Carey, and Michael Useem, *Boards That Lead: When to Take Charge, When to Partner, and When to Stay out of the Way* (Boston, MA: Harvard Business Review Press, 2014).

5. Yuval Deutsch and T. W. Ross, "You Are Known by the Directors You Keep: Reputable Directors as a Signaling Mechanism for Young Firms," *Management Science* 49, no. 8 (August 2003); Ekaterina S. Bjørnåli and Magnus Gulbrandsen, "Exploring Board Formation and Evolution of Board Composition in Academic Spin-Offs," *The Journal of Technology Transfer* 35 (2010).

6. For a summary of this situational and dynamic perspective of CEO and top leadership team see our first two books: Thomas Keil and Marianna Zangrillo, *The Next CEO: Board and CEO Perspectives for Successful CEO Succession* (London: Routledge, 2021); Keil and Zangrillo, *The Next Leadership Team*.

7. Keil and Zangrillo, *The Next Leadership Team: How to Select, Build, and Optimize Your Top Team*; Thomas Keil and Marianna Zangrillo, "Why It's Not Enough for Your CEO to Be a Superstar," *Fast Company*, 2023, https://www.fastcompany.com/90909667/why-its-not-enough-for-your-ceo-to-be-a-superstar; Marianna Zangrillo, Thomas Keil, and Benedetto Vigna, "Build the Right C-Suite Team for Your Strategy," *MIT Sloan Management Review* 66, no. 1 (2024): 36–40.

8. Tensie Whelan, "Research: Boards Still Have an ESG Expertise Gap – But They're Improving," *HBR.org*, *Harvard Business Review*, April 18, 2024, https://hbr.org/2024/04/research-boards-still-have-an-esg-expertise-gap-but-theyre-improving.

9. Following several years during which many corporations embraced diversity, equity and inclusion (DEI) initiatives at all levels, including the board of directors, in February 2025, during the final writing stage of this book, the new Trump administration has begun to roll back any DEI initiatives in the public sector and in fact penalizing companies that continue such initiatives. In response and many large private enterprises have begun to also roll back DEI goals and initiatives to comply with public policy and avoid being excluded from public tenders.

10. The effects of diversity on the board on firm behavior and outcomes are a long-standing academic research topic. Overall, the research has identified a number of benefits to diversity. However, as with any topic, there are limits, and situations when diversity provides little benefit or even less diversity may be preferable. For an overview of the research on diversity and some recent examples, see, for instance, Amy J. Hillman, "Board Diversity: Beginning to Unpeel the Onion," *Corporate Governance: An International*

Review 23, no. 2 (2015); Heng An, Carl R. Chen, Qun Wu, and Ting Zhang, "Corporate Innovation: Do Diverse Boards Help?," *Journal of Financial and Quantitative Analysis* 56, no. 1 (2021); Siri Terjesen, Ruth Sealy, and Val Singh, "Women Directors on Corporate Boards: A Review and Research Agenda," *Corporate Governance: An International Review* 17, no. 3 (2009); Renée B. Adams, Jakob De Haan, Siri Terjesen, and Hans Van Ees, "Board Diversity: Moving the Field Forward," *Corporate Governance: An International Review* 23, no. 2 (2015); Walid Ben-Amar, Claude Francoeur, Taïeb Hafsi, and Réal Labelle, "What Makes Better Boards? A Closer Look at Diversity and Ownership," *British Journal of Management* 24, no. 1 (2013); David Larcker and Brian Tayan, *Corporate Governance Matters: A Closer Look at Organizational Choices and Their Consequences,* 3rd ed. (London: Pearson/FT Press, 2020); Paraskevi Katsiampa, Paul B. McGuinness, and Hanxiong Zhang, "The Role of Board Age Diversity in the Performance of Publicly Listed Fintech Entities," *The European Journal of Finance* 30, no. 11 (2024); Mohamed Janahi, Yuval Millo, and Georgios Voulgaris, "Age Diversity and the Monitoring Role of Corporate Boards: Evidence from Banks," *Human Relations* 76, no. 10 (2023); Daniel Ferreira, "Board Diversity," in *Corporate Governance: A Synthesis of Theory, Research, and Practice,* ed. H. Kent Baker and Ronald Anderson (Hoboken, NJ: Wiley, 2010); Corinne Post and Kris Byron, "Women on Boards and Firm Financial Performance: A Meta-Analysis," *Academy of management Journal* 58, no. 5 (2015); Kris Byron and Corinne Post, "Women on Boards of Directors and Corporate Social Performance: A Meta-Analysis," *Corporate Governance: An International Review* 24, no. 4 (2016); Renée B. Adams and Daniel Ferreira, "Women in the Boardroom and Their Impact on Governance and Performance," *Journal of Financial Economics* 94, no. 2 (2009).

11. That hiring practices in boards should be non-discriminatory should be a fairly non-controversial notion. However, this generally agreed notion is often abused to pursue political or power motives, a position that we do not share. In this book, we try to keep these discourses strictly separate.

12. Cynthia E. Clark and Jill A. Brown, "Meet the New Board: Same as the Old Board," *MIT Sloan Management Review* 64, no. 1 (2022): 56–59.

13. Scott E. Page, *The Difference: How the Power of Diversity Creates Better Groups, Firms, Schools, and Society* (Pinceton, NJ: Princeton University Press, 2008).

14. Boris Groysberg and Deborah Bell, "Dysfunction in the Boardroom," *Harvard Business Review* 91, no. 6 (2013): 89–97.

15. https://www.consilium.europa.eu/en/policies/gender-balance-corporate-boards/

16. Jared L. Landaw, *Maximizing the Benefits of Board Diversity: Lessons Learned from Activist Investing*, DN-V11N2 (New York: The Conference Board, June 2020).

17. Margarethe Wiersema and Marie Louise Mors, "How Women Improve Decision-Making on Boards," *HBR.org, Harvard Business Review*, November 17, 2023, https://hbr.org/2023/11/research-how-women-improve-decision-making-on-boards.

18. J. Yo-Jud Cheng and Boris Groysberg, "Gender Diversity at the Board Level Can Mean Innovation Success," *MIT Sloan Management Review* 61, no. 2 (2020).

19. Randall S. Peterson and Heidi K. Gardner, "Is Your Board Inclusive – Or Just Diverse?" *HBR.org, Harvard Business Review*, September 28, 2022, https://hbr.org/2022/09/is-your-board-inclusive-or-just-diverse; Stephanie Creary, Janet Foutty, and Kwasi Mitchell, "How Diversity Can Boost Board Effectiveness," *MIT Sloan Management Review* 64, no. 3 (2023): 1–4.

20. Marta Elvira and Marta Villamor, *Diversity in Boards of Directors: A Synthesis and Review*, Case Study: DPON-0159-E (Barcelona: IESE Publishing, January 31, 2020).

21. David Fubini, Suraj Srinivasan, and Patrick Sanguineti, *Board Director Dilemmas: The Tradeoffs of Board Selection*. Case Study: 9-425-023 (Boston, MA: Harvard Business Publishing, September 5, 2024).

22. Several reviews and metanalyses provide an overview of the research on the effects of board independence. See, for instance, François Neville, Kris Byron, Corinne Post, and Andrew Ward, "Board Independence and Corporate Misconduct: A Cross-National Meta-Analysis," *Journal of Management* 45, no. 6 (2019); Dan R. Dalton, Catherine M. Daily, Alan E. Ellstrand, and Jonathan L. Johnson, "Meta-Analytic Reviews of Board Composition, Leadership Structure, and Financial Performance," *Strategic Management Journal* 19, no. 3 (1998). In addition, see the discussion in Larcker and Tayan, *Corporate Governance Matters: A Closer Look at Organizational Choices and Their Consequences*.

23. Olubunmi Faleye, "The Downside to Full Board Independence," *MIT Sloan Management Review* 58, no. 2 (2017).

24. Olubunmi Faleye, Rani Hoitash, and Udi Hoitash, "The Trouble with Too Much Board Oversight," *MIT Sloan Management Review* 54, no. 3 (2013).

25. Robert C. Pozen, "The Case for Professional Boards," *Harvard Business Review* 88, no. 12 (2010).

26. Bryce Tingle, "The Case for More Company Insiders on Boards," *HBR.org*, *Harvard Business Review*, September 30, 2024, https://hbr.org/2024/09/the-case-for-more-company-insiders-on-boards?

27. Keil and Zangrillo, *The Next CEO: Board and CEO Perspectives for Successful CEO Succession*.

28. Keil and Zangrillo, *The Next Leadership Team: How to Select, Build, and Optimize Your Top Team*.

29. Jordi Canals, *Can the Board of Directors Be an Effective Team?* Case Study: SMN-0709-E (Barcelona: IESE Business School, March 4, 2024).

30. Lynn S. Paine and Will Hurwitz, *Brief Note on Staggered Boards*, Case Study: 9-323-040 (Boston, MA: Harvard Business Publishing, December 2022 (Revised May 2024)).

31. George M. Anderson and David Chun, "How Much Board Turnover Is Best?" Editorial Material, *Harvard Business Review* 92, no. 4 (April 2014).

Chapter 5

Structures and processes in modern boards

Many companies fail to fully leverage the skills and expertise of their boards, even when they have highly qualified directors.[1] How can boards put their members to work most effectively to address the purpose and different roles of the board that we discussed in the previous two chapters, and thereby meet the modern board's dual mandate of tackling the problems of today and the challenges of tomorrow? This is where structures and processes come into play as the essential third dimension of the board diamond.

A look at ABB and its chair, Peter Voser, provides a first glimpse at the function of these structures and processes. Voser has been the board chair of Swiss-Swedish electrical engineering giant ABB since 2015. He joined ABB from Royal Dutch Shell, where he had been CEO from 2009 to 2013. In addition to his CEO experience, he has been a board member at international blue-chip companies such as Aegon, IBM, Roche, Temasek, and UBS.

During his tenure as chair at ABB, Voser has led the company through one of the most dynamic periods of its over 140-year history. That period spanned not only the COVID pandemic and the Ukraine-Russia war but also a significant organizational and strategic transformation. ABB has evolved from a highly diversified yet tightly integrated organization, widely recognized as the inventor of the matrix organization, to a company concentrated on a narrower range of businesses, managed in a decentralized way. Alongside this major strategic shift, ABB also underwent two CEO changes, and Voser took on the role of interim CEO for a year.

The changes at ABB have affected not just the CEO and leadership team and the operating model, but the board has also changed dramatically under Voser's

DOI: 10.4324/9781003532200-8

leadership, driven by the same dual challenge that is the heart of this book. As Voser explained:

> Investors and other stakeholders expect so much more from the board regarding the steering, monitoring, and also guiding of the management in the right direction. The board needs to be not just an information receiver but a strategic partner who can challenge and work with the management. The other thing that has also clearly changed is the involvement of the board in setting, discussing, monitoring, and challenging the strategy. These two trends have profound effects on the way you need to structure and run the board.

To address this dual challenge, Voser emphasized that changing a board's composition, as highlighted in the previous chapter, is insufficient. Instead, boards need to consider how to utilize both board structure and board processes to translate their increasingly diverse membership into meaningful action.

Voser explained:

> At ABB, we clearly split the board meetings into strategic work, operational performance reviews, and what you might call compliance topics. Given the increasing list of responsibilities, we have to move more issues to the committees and give them much more accountability and trust. We do that to create more time for the full board to focus on strategy. It is, however, important to understand that although the committees prepare the work, in the end, it is still the full board that's on the hook. You need deep trust in the work of the committees, and their reporting back to the main board is an extremely important part of the board meeting.

Yet delegating additional topics to committees has required ABB's board to adjust its approach when introducing them to the full board. Voser continued:

> For each board meeting, I sit together with committee chairs, and we brief each other, look at overlaps of issues, and identify what we need to get the board really involved in. This needs more planning, more coordination, and a little bit more active steering and management by the chair. You combine more accountability of the committees with active alignment so that we can have the right risk discussion at the board level.

Finally, the way the full board operates had to be modified given the larger number of responsibilities, the increased attention on strategy, and the changes Voser made to board composition and structure. He elaborated:

> Given the broader range of topics we deal with, the board has become much more diverse than it used to be in the past. And that forces you

to think about how you manage the board meetings and how you make decisions. You cannot steer a company or help the CEO to develop it if the board discussions are all over the place and you don't arrive at decisions. You need the board members to contribute different perspectives, but you need them to compromise in the end. For that, everybody in this diverse group has to have a chance to say and contribute, but you also need to work toward a common decision that the board can stand behind.

It is precisely this interplay between board structure and significant board processes and practices, such as agenda setting, discussion, and decision-making, that constitutes the central theme of this chapter.

Changing structures, processes, and practices of modern boards – the need for ambidexterity

Boards have evolved from informal, weakly facilitated groups of peers into professional organizations characterized by structure, processes, dedicated leadership, and defined roles. Historically, boards operated as loosely organized groups with minimal structures, relying on the collective wisdom of peers. Ironically, the body at the top of the organization that is tasked with overseeing effective organization and management often has itself been the least structured and managed group in the whole organization.

Today, the best boards function professionally, employing clearly defined structures and processes, standard practices and behavioral norms, and clearly defined leadership roles to fulfill their broader mandates and responsibilities effectively.

This professionalization is required because of the expanded scope of the board's purpose, roles, and responsibilities, increased regulatory and stakeholder demands, and increased need for involvement in strategy setting arising from the discontinuous changes in the geopolitical and technological environment and the increased importance of sustainability.

As we noted in Chapter 1, modern boards face a dual challenge, now overseeing a wider range of issues related to reporting, risk management, and compliance, to name only a few. Increased legal and regulatory requirements and additional stakeholder demands necessitate more formal and documented processes to respond to the compliance demands of modern governance. The increased workload accompanying these added responsibilities forces boards to become more efficient and effective in how they address them.

However, the business environment has also become much more complex and uncertain, given the multi-crisis environment, discontinuous strategic change related to the geopolitical environment and technology, and the need to integrate sustainability into the core business meaningfully. In response to this shift, boards need to substantially strengthen their ability to contribute to the firm's strategy and become more agile and resilient in managing change.

A key challenge in responding to these new demands is that structures, processes, and practices that are geared toward effectively handling the expanded scope of today's problem are often not equally suitable for supporting a strong focus on tomorrow and the open debate and discussion that is needed for novel strategy creation. From long-standing research on organizational ambidexterity,[2] we know that structuring organizations to handle existing tasks efficiently typically requires very different approaches than those that foster creative exploration of new solutions. This tension is equally present at the board level.

To resolve this tension, boards need to design their structures and processes for ambidexterity, which we discuss in this chapter, while the leadership demands that arise will be discussed in the next chapter. First, boards can adopt structures such as mandatory and voluntary committees, ad hoc working groups, and advisory boards to shift some responsibilities away from the full board, enabling a more in-depth focus by a differently composed group of people. Secondly, these structures should be complemented by clear processes and practices around board meetings, including meeting calendars, the meeting agenda, materials, and information systems. Finally, board meeting practices around discussion and decision-making are central for achieving ambidexterity at the board level.

Board structures and their management

Throughout our research, we encountered a trend that many boards are discussing how to move more work into committees. Board committees play a crucial role in modern governance[3] by allowing focused attention on specific areas, preparing decisions, and leveraging specialized expertise.[4] Carla Smits-Nusteling, a former board member of Nokia, ASML, and TELE2 AB, remarked:

> In all the boards I am a member of, we push as much as we can into the committees. Committees like an audit committee or risk committee handle a lot of the routine things and free up time for the full board to focus on strategy.

Two roles of committees

Committees can play two main roles in modern governance. On the one hand, they are an important driver of board efficiency and effectiveness, as they can be utilized to work through topics related to compliance or reporting with focus and depth, thereby freeing the full board's time for other topics. Mandatory committees – that are related to, for example, audit, risk, or remuneration, depending upon the legislation – often fulfill this role by dedicating themselves to conducting routine work, which allows the full board to focus more attention on its other key responsibilities.

On the other hand, committees can play an important second role in assisting the full board on future-oriented topics such as geopolitical change, discontinuous technological innovations, the development of new business models, or sustainability. The creation of voluntary committees (covering, for instance, strategy, sustainability, or technology) may help boards shift from a reactive approach to problems to a proactive approach, which enables a forward-looking and strategic perspective. For instance, establishing board technology committees can be instrumental in proactively exploring emerging technology trends rather than simply reacting to emerging threats.[5] Innovation-focused committees like P&G's Innovation and Technology Committee can work closely with CEOs to explore emerging technologies and industry or market shifts. When boards engage through such committees more directly in strategic innovation, they may offer valuable external perspectives and strengthen the company's adaptive capabilities, helping to sustain future orientation and long-term growth and survival.[6]

In line with our ambidexterity argument, these two roles of committees, however, imply a different role and focus for the committees and, therefore, also imply different practices and management approaches. While committees focused on compliance and reporting are designed to move most of the work to committee level, with the board playing an oversight and approval role, committees created for future-oriented topics are more deeply integrated with both management and the full board, acting as an extended resource, with the full board continuing to lead discussions and decisions. Crucially, both types of committees should be taken into consideration in order to address the full breadth of roles of the modern board we discussed above.

Mandatory (past- and present-oriented) committees

Committees, such as those focused on audit, risk, governance, and compliance, should not be viewed solely as a necessary evil – mandated by regulatory requirements in many jurisdictions – but as a lever for board effectiveness. Committees can provide deeper engagement and more focused oversight on these topics than the full board and also allow for the participation of outside experts without them occupying a full board seat. Mark Joiner, director at QBE AusPa, explained:

> One way of leveraging the committees is that you can bring specialists in as members of the committees, but not directors of the company. That allows you, a) to leverage their expertise, but b) to pressure test them and consider whether you would like them in the succession plan for the main board.

Such use of committees to provide depth and focus requires boards to regularly revisit the mandate of the committees, to adjust them to the changing business environment and to address emerging topics. Adaptation to a changing set of requirements needs to be balanced with the risk of "mission creep," where an ever-wider set of issues in a single committee dilutes the focus of the committee and overloads its members. For instance, while the audit committee's scope has broadened significantly over time,[7] in some organizations, this expansion has diluted its core mandate by turning it into a default repository for all compliance-related matters.

Optional (future-oriented) committees

With respect to future-oriented committees, strategy and sustainability committees have in the past played a critical role. Strategy committees allow the board to shift even more focus on strategic issues and long-term planning. Anne Lange, director at Pernod-Ricard, Orange, and Inditex, commented:

> I'm a great fan of the strategy committee. The problem is that the agenda of boards has become so detailed that you don't have the time to discuss the strategy properly with sufficient depth. Having a strategy committee can help to address this. A place where non-executive directors have an open dialogue with the chairman and management to say, "We should reinvest more in that topic." "We should re-analyze our geographical footprint." "We should reform our supply chain." Those kinds of issues have to be discussed by the strategy committee.

However, strategy committees can present a double-edged sword for boards since they also risk isolating strategy development from the full board, potentially leading to misalignment or worse, reducing the involvement of all directors in strategy work.[8] It is, therefore, particularly important to think about what role such a committee should play in strategy development relative to the board as a whole and how its work is embedded in the overall strategy process of the firm. In their strategy work, ideally, boards will iterate between the work of the full board, the strategy committee, and the leadership team.

A similar discourse has taken place regarding the topic of sustainability. The debate has centered on the question of whether sustainability considerations should be tackled by the board or handled by a dedicated committee. Luka Mucic, a member of the board at Heidelberg Materials, explained:

> You have to look at sustainability from the board's point of view, which includes setting management focus and incentives towards sustainable success in the core business and continues with investment decisions. That means that not only the financial result but also the sustainability footprint must be a criterion in the decision-making process. Creating a sustainability committee makes sense to discuss the impact of sustainable transformation challenges on the portfolio and the company's overarching strategy in sufficient depth. That's why we decided to form a separate

sustainability committee at Heidelberg Materials. Looking at it more broadly, a sustainability committee can maintain a dialogue with the management board at a higher frequency, as it bundles competence and understanding of the topic. Irrespective of this, I believe there is a need to provide the entire board with a sufficient basis for understanding, for example, through suitable training measures to ensure ownership of the topic. Everybody needs to understand where the levers of sustainability are. It is also a question for the board as a whole.

However, sustainability should ultimately be viewed, like corporate strategy, as the responsibility of the full board. Pauline Van der Meer Mohr, chair of the Dutch semiconductor equipment manufacturer ASM and director of Ahold Delhaize, NN Group, emphasized:

> You would like sustainability to be a responsibility for the full board just as strategy is. Sustainability should be part and parcel of your strategy process, and it should be at the core of all activities. But depending on where you are in your maturity cycle, in your thinking on sustainability, you may want to create a focused committee first before you accept it as a broader board responsibility.

To gain the benefits of committees, the board must assign directors to committees based on their expertise. A stronger reliance on committees needs to be accompanied by processes, practices, and management to realize the potential advantages of committees. Joerg Reinhardt, chair of Novartis and member of the board of SwissRe, explained:

> If you split the responsibilities up and move them to committees, it creates new challenges. It needs more management. You have to make sure that there is no duplication of effort and that the committees are not covering the same topic twice, which means you have to coordinate and you have to agree with the committees on what their primary goals are, what they have to talk about, how deeply they discuss the matter, and who they invite. You need to work harder with the committee chairs to ensure this coordination. It almost creates a management team in the board itself.

In other words, effective management of board committees starts with the definition of clear mandates and roles and the definition of the scope and responsibilities. However, Suzanne Thoma, executive chair of Sulzer, underscored that it is equally important to be explicit about the limits of the committee: "It is important to remember that the committee is preparing for the board and it's not making decisions. That must be the prerogative of the full board."

Committees must also be carefully integrated into the broader board work to avoid creating insider-outsider dynamics. Without that integration, committees may create a two-tiered board structure where some directors are more informed or influential than others, potentially leading to resentment or disengagement of those directors on the outside. Regular, inclusive reporting to the entire board is critical. Doug Baker, lead independent director at Target and member of the board at Merck (MSD), noted:

> Committee chairs and the lead directors should not end up with different legal liability. They may end up with different access to information just because of the frequency of their interactions with the company. But you really need to fight the tendency to create a two-tiered board. You really need to work hard so that you have a board where everybody's voice matters.

An increasing number of committees also elevates the importance of the role of committee chairs. Alongside the board chair, committee chairs ensure alignment, communication, and oversight to avert overlap and promote synergy. Jeff Campbell, former vice chairman and CFO of American Express, former CFO of McKesson and American Airlines, and current director at AON plc, Marathon Petroleum Corp., and Hexcel Corp, explained:

> We use the committees, or just the committee chairs, when there are issues that are either more urgent or more challenging. That's where the regulatory and other demands are the greatest. I do not see the full board involved in those new challenges. I see the committee chairs working with the management team, trying to figure out how to make sure we are checking all the boxes that we need to tick nowadays.

Board committees cannot solve all the challenges confronting today's boards. In fact, in some situations, overreliance on committees can result in the whole board losing sight of critical issues, particularly if significant decisions are prepared at the committee level without adequate involvement of the whole board, only to be rubber-stamped by the board. For instance, management succession is often delegated to a committee that deals with personnel matters, yet succession planning should be one, if not the most important, task of the board, and therefore, the full board should be involved at least in critical stages, as we noted in the previous chapter. Stefan Nöken, a member of the board at Vaillant, Vorwerk, and Peri Group, emphasized:

> Succession planning for the company management does not belong in a committee. It is one of the core responsibilities of the board. The entire board must know the first and second management levels personally and

form an opinion in order to remain involved in the succession process. This cannot be delegated to a committee.

At the very least, committees need to be complemented by directors who take an active role in fostering dialogue on strategy, sustainable growth, engaging in succession planning, and, in general, supporting future-oriented initiatives, even when they are not committee members.

Temporary committees and ad hoc working groups

Committees, due to their formal role in board governance, are at times too inflexible to address the diverse problems that boards must handle. Another viable solution to the problem of work allocation and how to ensure sufficient focus on all the different responsibilities of the board could be to create temporary committees or ad hoc working groups that allow at least some of the board members to dedicate more time and attention to specific issues.

Take, for instance, strategy setting, where we identified the need to provide focus and resources to strategy creation without the board losing sight of other key topics. In such a set-up, the full board sets the mandate and the guardrails for the strategy work and also plays a regular role in the decision-making for the overall strategy. However, during the strategy development phase, a smaller group of board members may participate more intensely in the strategy work, acting as a sparring partner for the executive team based on a mandate given by the full board. In such an ad hoc working group, external members who are experts on the specific industry of the firm or the strategic topics to be discussed can complement the board members. This allows a higher frequency of interaction than the full board can achieve, and the addition of external expertise without isolating the board from the overall process. One board member of a large European stock exchange-listed corporation explained:

> A good example of a temporary committee is the China strategy committee that we had last year. It was a temporary committee that only existed for about one and a half years. The executive board wanted to start a new approach to the business in China. Our company was contemplating a joint venture and wanted to understand what the business in China would look like in five to ten years. We established a temporary committee that worked intensely with the executive board. We helped the management board develop the strategy and implement it. But it was no longer needed after one-and-a-half years, so we stopped it.

Boards should show flexibility to use mechanisms like temporary or informal committees, ad hoc work groups, or advisory bodies that are either explicitly set up as temporary vehicles or are not a formal part of the board, to provide the necessary resources and focus without removing responsibility from the board. These mechanisms are not only able to draw on different voices but may also allow for different modes of working. For instance, Kathleen Bailey-Lord, chair at ed-tech company Janison and member of the boards at Datacom, AMP, and St Vincent's Health Australia, explained to us:

> On some boards, we have got ad hoc working groups which are deliberately out of the formal governance system. They are forums where a couple of directors and a few members of the management team are working on a problem together as peers and without the constraints of the formal board mechanisms. Then, it goes back into the formal governance system, usually to a committee for a more formal conversation. The committee then makes some sort of recommendation or conclusion or prepares a couple of scenarios that finally get discussed in the full board.

Ad hoc groups are more flexible than formal committees, which, in most legislations, need the approval of the annual general meeting (AGM) of the shareholders. They can be constituted more rapidly, work intensely (often in parallel to the existing committee structure), and be dissolved more easily once their task is completed.

Advisory boards

An alternative is to create advisory boards that bring in external perspectives and expertise without being part of the formal board structure. Such advisory boards can be more flexible and do not face the same regulatory constraints. For instance, one board chair of a large European financial services company explained:

> You need to hear from people that are free thinkers, that can give you an outside perspective, but you cannot have these on the board in a highly regulated industry. In our advisory board, we have seven or eight members coming from all over the planet, Asia, the US, Europe, Africa, and Latin America, and they bring a different perspective. But we cannot have them on the board where you have to take responsibility for financial decisions, decisions on solvency, address regulatory compliance, and so on and so forth. The regulatory constraints simply do not allow that.

Board secretaries and other board resources

Boards should also utilize resources such as board secretaries or a board office as support for themselves and their committees. However, given the importance of its work, in many companies, the board has surprisingly few resources directly under its control. If there is a board secretary, the individuals holding this role usually have a legal background and support the board chair in terms of process and structures, providing the chair with an efficient infrastructure. A board office can go further by offering analysis and advice on detailed topics. Shaun Coles, global director of governance at Santander, explained:

> The existence of a dedicated set of professionals who understand governance in practice and act as an effective conduit between the leadership team and the board is absolutely essential. The ability to provide counsel, to challenge the highest cadre, to advise the board, and, on occasion, to stand up and give opinions in difficult situations where maybe those opinions are not always the ones everybody wants to hear.

Board meetings

While changes to the use and construction of committees, ad hoc working groups, and advisory boards are an important structural mechanism to enable boards to respond to the dual challenges of modern governance, board meetings – the key instrument of most boards – also need to be reimagined, redesigned, and aligned with this new committee structure. Board meetings must address the increasing scope of topics by efficiently leveraging the work of the committees and, at the same time, provide sufficient time and focus on more open, future-oriented discussion on how to reinvent the company, its strategy, and business model in the light of fundamental global shifts in the political and economic arena, technological discontinuities like AI, and the shift toward multiple stakeholders and sustainability. Often, these two challenges create opposing demands for the design of board meetings. For instance, while the increase in topics focusing on the present requires more time to report the work of management and committees, future orientation focuses require board meetings that allow for open-ended discussion.

To adapt, boards may need to reevaluate how frequently they meet, how these meetings are structured (including length, virtual versus physical formats, formal versus informal components), how the agenda is set, what materials are shared, and the behavioral norms for meetings and other related meeting practices.

Board meeting frequency and calendar

Many boards have increased the frequency of their meetings in response to the heavier workload. Board meeting frequency is important to ensure the board has sufficient time and attention for information processing.[9] In the past, boards may have met as rarely as four to six times a year, but many additional meetings have been added to their calendars, and the frequency of regular board meetings is up to ten meetings per year in some companies. In the face of major acquisitions, a takeover bot by another company, or when an activist investor targets the company, this number may be much higher. However, there is a natural limit to further increasing this frequency. Given that board roles are part-time positions and, in some countries, not particularly well compensated for the responsibilities involved, or when compared with the compensation of executive team members, increasing board meetings further is difficult, unrealistic, and even infeasible without fundamental changes to how a board position is conceptualized and compensated. Boards, therefore, need to rethink how to use their meetings as effectively as possible.

Many boards have also changed the yearly calendar of their meetings, introducing dedicated meetings for some topics such as strategy, sustainability, or succession planning in addition to the meetings related to financial reporting, which follow the flow of the financial year. Setting a yearly calendar in advance, at least for some topics, has the advantage that these issues are regularly on the board's agenda and receive attention, rather than having to compete for time with other topics. However, at the same time, boards need to retain flexibility to bring urgent matters to the agenda with short notice in response to changes in the business and its environment, sometimes as late as the evening before the meeting.

Carla Smits-Nusteling, a former board member of Nokia, ASML, and TELE2 AB, explained:

> Sometimes we adjust the board agenda right before the meeting. You read through all the pre-reads, and a concern or a big question starts forming in your mind, but then you have to wait for a day and a half before you can raise it under agenda topic 25, when it really might merit discussion up-front because of its importance. I try to check with other board members and, if a few people agree, we change the agenda.

Length and structure of board meetings

Not only have board meetings become more frequent, but their length has also extended, at least in some of the companies we studied. In larger companies, meetings of the full board may run a whole day and typically are preceded by committee meetings, which means board members may spend up to three days in both. While longer meetings imply a substantial time commitment for the board members, they also allow for a mixture of formal meetings and informal events such as board dinners, social activities, and visits to company sites. Informal activities like this make turning a board into a team easier and may provide directors with opportunities to get to know the company better. Longer meetings may also allow for more open-ended strategy discussions or deep dives into specific strategic topics that are more difficult to tackle when time is too constrained. Longer board meetings also make it easier for the board to meet in different configurations, for instance, by incorporating executive sessions without the CEO and leadership team members present.

Naturally, there are disadvantages, and these must be carefully balanced against the advantages. Long board meetings need to be carefully planned to ensure that the board retains the right energy level to work productively. Ten or twelve-hour marathon meetings easily lead to fatigue and extended periods of low energy, in particular when members fly in from different continents as Sami Atiya, a board member of the Switzerland-based testing, inspection and certification company SGS SA, noted: "When you have an international board with people joining from the US and Asia you can't run a ten-hour board meeting. It is just not possible. People don't have the energy to contribute."

It is also clear that the design of board meetings needs to be aligned with choices regarding board composition and the structure of board committees. It is not very realistic, for instance, to attract executives from another continent if they are expected to attend up to ten meetings a year, and each meeting is two to three days long. With travel time on top, each meeting could then easily take a full week out of the schedule of a busy executive.

Physical and virtual formats

In the past, board meetings were held almost universally in person. However, since the global pandemic, many boards have also introduced virtual and hybrid meetings to the board calendar. Such virtual meetings allow boards to respond far faster to emerging events and allow members to cut back on travel, thereby allowing an increase in the frequency of meetings, an important mechanism to improve the board's contribution to key decisions and evolving strategy topics.[10]

However, virtual board meetings often require extra effort to maintain engagement, and many of the board members we interviewed expressed skepticism that a board could be run mostly virtually in the long run. A board chair of a US stock exchange-listed corporation told us:

> Face-to-face meetings are key. You can see the difference between board meetings that you attend remotely and the meetings that you attend physically. There is a lot more action, a lot more decisions, and a lot more discussions when we are physically in the same room than when we are in videoconference. People who speak in the videoconference don't speak that much when they are physically present. People who are the leaders of the discussion in physical meetings may be very quiet when the meeting is held as a videoconference.

Since boards convene less frequently than executive teams and board members do not necessarily interact outside of board meetings, in-person meetings are essential for fostering richer interactions, deeper relationships, and livelier and deeper debates. To balance the advantages and disadvantages of both physical and virtual meetings, many companies have created mixed formats where some meetings are held in person, while others take place virtually. Committee work in particular, which often requires more frequent and in-depth engagement of sub-groups, has to a large degree moved to virtual meetings in many of the boards we studied.

While a mixture of in-person and virtual meetings is relatively easy, hybrid meetings (with some members attending physically and others virtually) are often more problematic since they can lead to different degrees of participation from those attending virtually. The reason for this is often to do with the fact that effective virtual meetings must be structured differently from in-person meetings and, therefore, a hybrid format runs the risk of being ineffective for one of the two groups or even both. Nonetheless, such hybrid formats have become the norm in many organizations, especially in boards with international members. Sami Atiya, a member of the board of SGS, explained:

> Many boards work in hybrid mode. If you want to have people from different continents, you cannot be rigid on in-person attendance. But we do insist on having at least two physical meetings, because there's value in it. But the rest is virtual. The physical meetings need to have a certain purpose. They tend to be strategy meetings, where you invite, for example, business heads, because they can sense and feel the business and understand the people. In many cases, the board doesn't know the individuals under the CEO very well, and there's a big value in spending the whole day together. So, for the strategy meetings, it's not only content; it's also people. Creativity increases when you sit in the same room. But I don't see any disadvantage of not being in the room for a lot of the other work.

Boards must adopt a strategic perspective on meeting planning to ensure the effectiveness of this crucial process.

Formal and informal components of board meetings

One would think that the most important board work gets done in formal meetings. However, for a board to effectively work as a team, trust, respect, and psychological safety are essential, and given that board members do not interact daily outside the board meetings, informal components of board meetings are even more critical than in other organizational teams to create the foundations of board effectiveness. Greg Poux-Guillaume, a chairman at Swiss-based Medmix, noted:

> For the board, you have to define the formal interactions, the bodies in which decisions are made, and how they are documented. That is, of course, important, but it's incomplete. What is often missing in this view is all the informal discussions that can get people aligned, get people to think, and challenge. Those are hard to do in a formal board meeting when there's an agenda, people have lives at the end of the day, and many don't like to disagree publicly. So you need to add mechanisms so that people can interact informally.

This challenge implies that despite board meetings' time and agenda pressures, boards must set aside sufficient time for informal interactions before, during, and after the meeting. Jean-Pierre Clamadieu, chair of French energy company Engie and director of Airbus and TE Connectivity, told us:

> Informal interactions have an important role to play for the board. They create this sense of belonging to a team. For example, when you have a situation where board members call each other ahead of a board meeting to share some questions or some views on a given subject. That can be quite a useful process. Of course, it cannot lead to pre-decision, but these interactions will make the formal meeting at the committee or at the board meeting richer and more effective.

Discussions in informal settings can encourage candid discourse and idea-sharing that may not take place during the formal part of meetings. Some of these interactions may be limited to the board only, but some should also involve the leadership team. In particular, to fulfill the board's increased role in strategy, a robust platform for the often-difficult debates on strategic choices requires strong trust between the board and the leadership team that can best be created through a combination of formal and informal interactions. Carla Smits-Nusteling, a former board member of Nokia, ASML, and TELE2 AB, explained:

> When we have a board meeting, the previous day will always have the committee meetings. That evening we go out for dinner. The board members, the CEO, and the CFO. It's completely informal without an agenda. We start with an hour of drinks to get out of the formalities. Then we just sit and eat and talk about dilemmas for the company. Simply put, what keeps the CEO and the CFO busy? What keeps any one of us busy related to the company? In my view, when you can create that trusted atmosphere, those dinners are the most effective mechanism for the board outside of the formal board meetings with their agenda.

However, boards also need to be mindful of the potential risks of too high a reliance on informal interactions around the board meetings because such conversations can be used to side-step the board's due process. Andreas Umbach, former board chair of Swiss-based SIG Group AG, cautioned:

> You have to understand that there also is a risk with informal interactions. Decision-making becomes such an iterative process. For instance, I used to call each individual after every board meeting or in advance. But you have to be careful. You risk being perceived as not trying to get them up to speed on the topic or provide them with the information required, but rather as trying to influence them. I am very careful not to

give others the impression that I am trying to steer them in any direction. That's a real dilemma. If I don't do it, they say: "Hey, I'd like to talk to you, I need more information." And if I do, it feels a bit Machiavellian, like I've got all my puppets on a string, and I'm controlling what comes out of the board meeting. And I don't think there is a simple answer to finding the right balance.

The double-edged sword of informal interactions outside the boardroom

The topic of informal interactions on the board also extends to the interactions between board members and the leadership team or other stakeholders. While in some organizations, board members, other than the board chair or committee chairs (who have natural touch points with certain members of the leadership team), limit their interactions to each other, and limit their interactions with the leadership team strictly to formal board meetings, other boards utilize a variety of informal interaction mechanisms to facilitate a tight integration of the board members and the leadership team on future-oriented topics.

Tight interaction can provide a number of distinct benefits:

- In-depth learning by the board members.
- More frequent information for directors.
- Leveraging director expertise for advice and coaching of management.
- Building a strong board and leadership culture through more regular interaction.
- In-depth work on future-oriented topics.

However, these advantages need to be weighed against several risks and costs of too close involvement:

- Too deep operational involvement by the board.
- Reduced oversight ability of operationally involved directors.
- Risk of politics.

We advocate that a strongly future-oriented board should also engage with the leadership team outside of formal board meetings, but they should follow three main ground rules:

Transparency: Openly sharing information to avoid misunderstandings.
Balance: Directors must navigate the tension between oversight and advisory roles.
Oversight: The board chair and CEO should be fully aware of all interactions.

Board meeting agenda

Good board meetings start with a well-thought-out agenda. In most companies we examined, the board agenda is designed by the board chair in collaboration with the CEO, though individual board members can influence it.

It is all too common for board agendas to become cluttered by mandatory reporting and compliance topics or routine items from the board's annual calendar, which can stifle forward-looking conversations. Therefore, it is particularly important to strike a balance between such mandatory topics and a more open, forward-looking discussion on strategy and emerging strategic issues when designing the board agenda.

Strictly allocating time per agenda item, relying on committee preparation for detailed topics, establishing strong behavioral norms around agenda discipline, and ensuring the board chair takes an active role all help keep the meeting focused.

Finally, it is essential to prioritize issues correctly to ensure an effective use of time. If important topics are placed at the bottom of the agenda, it is a little surprising when the board is unable to allocate sufficient time to them.

Supporting materials

In addition to a clear agenda, well-structured board materials are critical to enabling thorough preparation and focused discussion. An essential challenge of most boards is the information advantage that management holds over the board. This information asymmetry can lead to situations where the board is unable to provide value because directors do not sufficiently understand the issues at hand. High-quality materials provided in advance are therefore crucial. In many companies, boards still get overwhelmed by the magnitude of materials, and substantive time is wasted presenting these materials before any discussion can begin. The best boards we examined cut back on this by spending time and effort on preparing well-thought-out material for the board and minimizing one-way presentations by the leadership team or CEO.

To increase effectiveness, materials for the board need to be timely, compact, and largely self-explanatory so that the boardroom conversation can proceed immediately to Q&A and debate rather than time being wasted on presenting information that board members could have read before the meeting. Because, by and large, board members have become more diligent in preparing for board meetings, the nature and quality of the material today often determines how well-prepared a board member can be. Jean-Pierre Clamadieu, chair of French energy company Engie and director of Airbus and TE Connectivity, explained to us:

> The quality and brevity of the material shared with the board is important. If you send a 1,000-page file for a six or seven-hour board meeting, it's not effective. You are drowning your board in information, but it's

not quality information. I am a strong believer in simple material. Most subjects could be summarized in five pages plus a few attachments with a very clear Executive Summary on the first page.

Ensuring high-caliber board materials often falls to the CEO, board chair, or board secretary, who may step in to refine and unify the documents. For instance, Greg Poux-Guillaume, chairman at Swiss-based Medmix, described how he took on this role while serving as CEO of Sulzer:

> One of my biggest contributions when I was CEO of Sulzer was to improve the quality of the board material. All the documents had to be ready ahead of time and first went to me for editing. The deadline for getting the documents to me was three days before the documents were put to the board, and I edited all the documents. What I mean by editing is that I got people to clarify their messages. "What does this slide say? Why is it useful? What's the message? If you can't tell me the message, and if it's the same message as in your three slides before, choose one slide." So the whole process was about paring it down and making sure that the important stuff actually came out, and that there was a storyline.

In other boards we studied, the chair or a board secretary played the same role. Ideally, the board chair, CEO, and board secretary will work together to ensure the material meets the board's needs. In doing so, they also need to balance the needs of the board with the need of the management teams not to be overburdened with information requests.

With ever-improving technology, AI can increasingly be helpful in condensing the material in a format that allows board members to prepare better and reduce information sharing in the meeting. For instance, a recent company update can be turned by AI into a brief podcast that provides as much information as a management presentation, but can be listened to in advance and frees time for the discussion with the CEO and leadership team. Still, many boards are reluctant to adopt these technologies and the novel formats they can provide. For instance, a board chair of a large European corporation remarked: "People want to have information live. When do you stop these highlights? Things happen daily, and board members want to know exactly what happened until last night."

Given the role of the board to challenge, advise, and monitor management, it should not rely solely on the information provided by management. Some authors advocate for reducing board reliance on management-provided information by establishing independent information channels to reduce the information asymmetry between management and the board.[11] While board members often have only limited access to outside information sources, AI can become increasingly useful and help reduce information asymmetry.

Behavioral norms and other related practices

Ultimately, board meeting effectiveness depends a great deal on the behavioral norms that govern the board. Boardrooms need to be places where directors feel psychologically safe and able to express dissenting perspectives without fear of backlash. Establishing such an environment begins with the selection of directors, as we discussed in Chapter 4, but requires explicit focus and effort from the board as a whole and leadership from the board chair in establishing mutual respect and trust among directors. For instance, a board member of multiple European corporations explained to us:

> One of the most powerful mechanisms to create psychological safety between the board and the management is when a director on the board admits that the board itself made a mistake. Admitting that at this juncture, we could have made this decision, but we did not see it. How should we now fix it?' Then, the management understands that it is not always about the higher level evaluating the lower level. People make mistakes, and we learn from them, and that is fine. The board also needs to show that.

These behavioral norms not only affect how well a board functions but can also set the tone for the leadership team and the entire organization. An unforgiving culture in the boardroom will trickle down the organization. In contrast, directors and leadership team members who acknowledge errors and focus on constructive resolution foster a culture of learning and improvement that can set the tone and inspire the whole company.

Decision-making

For many important decisions, boards are the final decision-makers, or at least they need to approve the leadership team's decisions. However, as we already noted, the board members often have a severe information disadvantage compared to the executives and are under time pressure in these decisions, given the meeting schedule. This makes a principles-based approach to decision-making vital.[12] Principles for effective board decision-making include structured decision processes, clear responsibilities, and decision protocols. These are supported by well-defined decision-making roles that enable the board to focus on strategic priorities and avoid ad hoc choices. Clear governance frameworks help directors maintain strategic oversight, improve the CEO's and leadership team's accountability, and ensure critical decisions align with long-term organizational goals.[13]

Effective decision-making in boards hinges on adherence to directors' fiduciary duties, clear communication, behavioral norms, decision-making style, the ability to balance speed with thorough consideration, and the willingness to leave conflicts and disagreements behind.

Fiduciary duties

In their decision-making, directors need to focus on their fiduciary duties – in particular, the duties of loyalty and care. The duty of loyalty requires acting in the company's best interests and avoiding conflicts of interest, whereas the duty of care requires informed decisions made after appropriate diligence and reflection. Properly executing these duties is essential for preserving trust and ensuring transparent governance. Failure to meet these obligations can result in legal consequences and erode investor confidence.[14]

Communication

Directors frequently grapple with communication barriers in the boardroom, which arise from the tension between monitoring and advising management. In many cases, directors speak indirectly or avoid conflict to maintain harmony, which can lead to misunderstandings or missed opportunities. Executive sessions and proactive in-meeting leadership can help alleviate these issues.[15]

How tough should board debates be?

Board meetings often serve as the crucible where strategic initiatives meet their first real test. But how vigorous should that examination be, and how critical should board members get? On one hand, it's the board's responsibility to challenge and refine leadership's plans. On the other hand, boards are increasingly co-creators of strategy, raising the question: "How do you combine a collaborative role with the need for rigorous oversight?" Below are four guiding principles to help strike that balance.

1. **The content: stress-test every plan.** The board's job isn't just to "greenlight" proposals. Instead, it should probe and pressure-test each initiative, offering fresh perspectives that push leadership to think bigger and spot potential pitfalls early. These discussions must be *solution-oriented* – identifying issues without proposing ways to address them does little good. A well-run stress test doesn't simply expose weaknesses; it strengthens the final plan.
2. **The style: practice tough love.** Critical discussions are vital to improving strategy and developing leadership talent. A board that's too gentle risks rubber-stamping undercooked ideas. At the same time, an overly aggressive stance can shut down dialogue and strain relationships. Think of it as *tough love*: hold high standards for the quality of plans but remain supportive of the people who develop them.

3. **The roles: separate strategy creation from strategy challenge.** Many boards now play a more hands-on role in shaping strategy, especially during periods of strategic upheaval. But when board members are involved in creating strategy, others must step back and adopt the challenger role to ensure objectivity. This dual approach – some members innovating and others scrutinizing – prevents groupthink and leads to more robust plans.

4. **Reminder: remember that no one has a crystal ball.** Regardless of board members' seniority or the management team's informational edge, the future is inherently uncertain. Neither side "knows it all." Success comes from combining the board's broader experience with the leadership team's frontline insights. When both parties respect the inherent uncertainty and remain open to each other's expertise, they're more likely to craft strategies that stand the test of time.

Behavioral norms

The board's behavioral norms related to trust, respect, and psychological safety, as we discussed in the previous section, are particularly important for the board's decision-making.[16] Directors need to be able to engage in critical discussions in important decisions enabling different viewpoints to be voiced because inclusion of diverse viewpoints and respectful debate of different positions leads to more robust decision-making. Setting clear expectations for director behavior thereby facilitates building a culture of trust among directors and enables the candid conversations, constructive conflict, and problem-solving needed for high-quality decisions.

Decision-making style

Boards differ widely in their decision-making style. Some boards will only take a decision once a unanimous view has emerged on an issue. Others feel comfortable to vote after discussion and, in case of a tie, have the board chair act as a tie-breaker. The decision-making approach often reflects the expectations of large shareholders, the board's culture, and the board chair's preferences.

Decisiveness and speed versus depth of consideration

In their choice of decision-making style, the boards need to resolve an important tension. On the one hand, they need to be decisive. Stefan Nöken, a member of the board at Vaillant, Vorwerk, and Peri Group, noted:

> Sometimes boards are not decisive enough to make decisions. If the board doesn't yet feel comfortable with a decision yet, the executive

team is often sent into a loop to gather more information. All too often, investing another three months doesn't make the decision much better. We would be well advised to get our act together and take a position in one way or the other in a timely manner.

In particular, routine operational decisions, but also responses to crisis situations, require expeditious and timely decision-making. As such, discussions need to be steered to a decision, and at times, a decision may need to be made even if no unanimous consensus has emerged.

On the other hand, boards need to make decisions that commit the organization in the long term and are made under high levels of uncertainty, and, therefore, need to ensure that strategic decisions are well-considered and unbiased.[17] Such strategic decisions require that diverse voices on the board be brought into the decision process. Incorporating different viewpoints, however, may require more time to reach an agreement, but such discussion contributes to more comprehensive and higher-quality decisions. Tea Colaianni, director of SD Worx, Watches of Switzerland, and WiHTL, explained:

> For me, the most important factor for good decisions is whether we have considered all the different factors. Have we considered all the risks? Have we included different perspectives in the conversation? It might take longer, and it might bring tension. But I think that it is a positive thing. Having a healthy debate ensures that you have thought about issues more deeply and more comprehensively. Because when you put your decisions out there, there are lots of different stakeholders that look at these decisions, and they will challenge them.

For decision quality, especially in relation to long-term strategic decisions, it is also important to ensure heterogeneity of the information considered and sufficient elaboration of all information.[18] It is these decisions where boards particularly need to focus on ensuring that directors receive relevant, concise, and timely information to enhance their ability to make informed decisions. To accomplish this, boards should seek information beyond what management provides, including from other organizational levels and external sources. Kaj-Erik Relander, board member of Louis Dreyfuss Corporation, SES Satellites, and a number of other privately held corporations, explained to us:

> Boards should seek input from the organization. Make sure also that the ambitious young people from the organization talk to them about what they think is the right thing to do without fear. The CEO should be willing to take that risk rather than filter all information. The best

environment is where the board is exposed to different kinds of thoughts. The worst thing is if there is thought control by the top management, and that you find a lot.

Taken together, boards need to balance the requirement for prompt decisions with the benefits of an inclusive, reflective, and robust debate. The specifics of an issue and the company's circumstances help determine which approach is most appropriate.

Keeping disagreements in the boardroom

Irrespective of the decision-making style and how boards resolve the tradeoff between speed and depth of consideration, boards should adhere to a simple principle after a decision has been made: Whatever disagreement there has been in the board room stays in the board room. Ian Carter, board chair of Watches of Switzerland Group PLC and Eataly, explained:

> We agreed on a clear rule for final decision-making for our board. When we are in the boardroom and the doors are closed, anything is up for discussion. Of course, the right tone is very important – no personal agendas. We discuss and argue different points of view, but at the core of our process is that we are here to genuinely improve the decision-making for the benefit of our teams, the shareholders, and our Company. Once we agree on our decisions, the expectation is that everybody will stay behind those decisions. Once we leave the boardroom, everybody speaks as one. It doesn't matter whether you or I disagree with the consensus, the majority; we're all on the same page that this is the decision, and we demonstrate that externally. It is important for the organization and everyone around to see us aligned outside the boardroom.

Taking disagreements outside the boardroom is often the first sign that a board is dysfunctional and not able to fulfill its roles. Such boards need strong intervention from the board chair and often require rebuilding of both the board and its processes and practices.

Countering decision biases in board decision-making

Board decisions often fall prey to a variety of decision biases. To ensure their decisions are as unbiased as possible, boards can utilize four process levers related to preparation, board materials and their presentation, discussion rules, and decision rules.

Some simple points to consider regarding each of these levers are summarized in Figure 5.1.

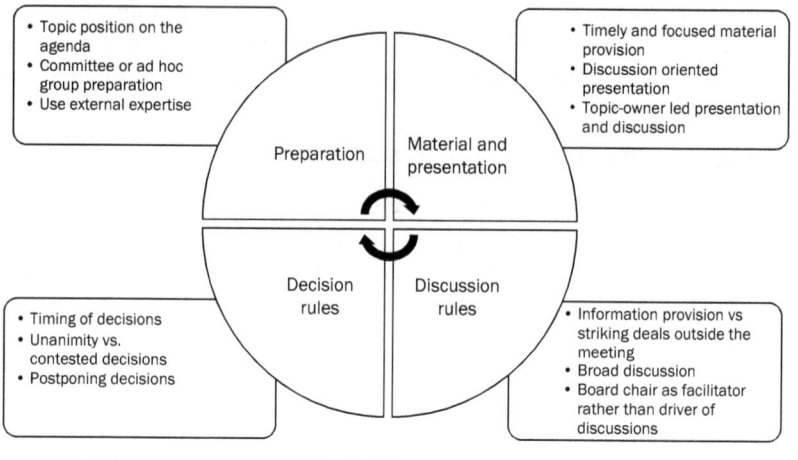

Figure 5.1   Countering Biases in Board Decision-Making

Notes

1. Chris Thomas, David Kidd, and Claudio Fernandez-Araoz, "Are You Underutilizing Your Board?" *MIT Sloan Management Review* 48, no. 2 (2007): 71–76.
2. Charles A. O'Reilly and Michael L. Tushman, "The Ambidextrous Organisation," *Harvard Business Review* 82, no. 4 (Apr 2004); Scott D. Anthony, Clark G. Gilbert, and Mark W. Johnson, *Dual Transformation: How to Reposition Today's Business While Creating the Future* (Boston, MA: Harvard Business Review Press, 2017); Charles A. O'Reilly III and Michael L. Tushman, *Lead and Disrupt: How to Solve the Innovator's Dilemma*, 2nd ed. (Palo Alto, CA: Stanford Business Books, 2021).
3. Randall S. Peterson and Pedro Fontes Falcão, "Build a Better Board," *sloanreview.mit. edu. MIT Sloan Management Review* September 26, 2024, https://sloanreview.mit.edu/article/build-a-better-board/.
4. Kalin D. Kolev, David B. Wangrow, Vincent L. Barker III, and Donald J. Schepker, "Board Committees in Corporate Governance: A Cross-Disciplinary Review and Agenda for the Future," *Journal of Management Studies* 56, no. 6 (2019).
5. Tarun Khanna, Mary C. Beckerle, and Nabil Y. Sakkab, "Boards Need a New Approach to Technology," *Harvard Business Review* 103, no. 9–10 (September–October 2024).
6. Michael Useem, Dennis Carey, and Ram Charan, "How Boards Can Innovate," *HBR.org, Harvard Business Review*, May 21, 2014, https://hbr.org/2014/05/how-boards-can-innovate.
7. H. David Sherman, Dennis Carey, and Robert Brust, "The Audit Committee's New Agenda," *Harvard Business Review* 87, no. 6 (2009).

8. Jay William Lorsch and Robert C. Clark, "Leading from the Boardroom," *Harvard Business Review* 86, no. 4 (2008): 104–111.
9. Stevo Pavićević, Jerayr Haleblian, and Thomas Keil, "When Do Boards of Directors Contribute to Shareholder Value in Firms Targeted for Acquisition? A Group Information-Processing Perspective," *Organization Science* 34, no. 5 (2023): 1759–1776.
10. Pavićević, Haleblian, and Keil, "When Do Boards of Directors Contribute to Shareholder Value in Firms Targeted for Acquisition? A Group Information-Processing Perspective."
11. Robert J. Thomas, Michael Schrage, Joshua B. Bellin, and George Marcotte, "How Boards Can Be Better – A Manifesto," *MIT Sloan Management Review* 50, no. 2 (2009).
12. Michael Useem, "How Well-Run Boards Make Decisions," *Harvard Business Review* 84, no. 11 (2006): 130–138.
13. Stevo Pavićević and Thomas Keil, "Research: How Boards Can Increase CEO Accountability," *HBR.org, Harvard Business Review*, February 4, 2025, https://hbr.org/2025/02/research-how-boards-can-increase-ceo-accountability.
14. James Naughton, *Fiduciary Duties and Corporate Disclosure*. Case Study: UVA-C-2484 (Charlottesville, VA: Darden Business Publishing, July 30, 2024).
15. Katharina Pick, "Can You Hear Me Now?," *Harvard Business Review* 86, no. 8 (2008).
16. Holly J. Gregory and Sidley Austin LLP, "Establishing Norms for Director Behavior to Enhance Board Culture and Effectiveness," *corpgov.law.harvard.edu, Harvard Law School Forum on Corporate Governance*, November 8, 2022, https://corpgov.law.harvard.edu/2022/11/08/establishing-norms-for-director-behavior-to-enhance-board-culture-and-effectiveness/.
17. Ryan Krause, Michael C. Withers, and Mary J. Waller, "Reducing Bias through Board Decision-Making: An Information-Processing Model of Board Decision Synergy," *Academy of Management Review* (2024), forthcoming. https://doi.org/10.5465/amr.2022.0271; Stevo Pavićević, Thomas Keil, and Gerry McNamara, "Debiasing the Literature on Executive Decision-Making Biases," *Academy of Management Annals* (2025), forthcoming. https://doi.org/10.5465/annals.2022.0152.
18. Krause, Withers, and Waller, "Reducing Bias through Board Decision-Making: an Information-Processing Model of Board Decision Synergy."

Chapter 6

Leading the board

The board chair or lead independent director

As we highlighted in previous chapters, the transformation of the board's purpose and roles, its composition, structures, processes, and practices requires a different type of board leadership: the fourth dimension of our board diamond. Today's board leaders look and act very differently from their predecessors, play different roles, and shoulder fundamentally new responsibilities.

Debbie Hewitt, MBE, is a prime example of how modern chairs define and play their role. In 2021, Hewitt made history when she became the first-ever chairwoman of The Football Association, the governing body of English football, thereby occupying one of the most visible positions in international professional sports. She has held executive positions across multiple industries and has been a board member and board chair in more than ten private and public corporations. At the time of writing, she is also chair of the board of Visa Europe, the European arm of the globally recognized payments business, and The BGL Group, a digital distributor of insurance and household financial services, which owns brands including comparethemarket.com.

In our conversation, Hewitt reflected on the role of a modern board chair. She explained:

> The chief executive runs the business, and the chair runs the board. I do not think businesses are necessarily successful because of a board. It takes a lot more than a good board to make a business successful. But they will not be successful if they do not have a good board, and a board needs an effective chair to optimize its contribution.

DOI: 10.4324/9781003532200-9

What does it mean to be an effective chair? According to Hewitt, part of "running the board" involves setting the right tone:

> The chair sets the tone through and for the people who are sitting around the board table. Because the chair ultimately recruits and develops those people. The chair also sets the tone by determining what is on the board's agenda. The agenda reflects what the board will spend its time on, and that in itself will determine what they influence. The chair has to determine the key things that are important enough for the agenda. The chair also sets the tone in the way the board evaluates itself. In my opinion, effective chairs embrace, encourage, and contribute to rigorous board evaluations and make sure that the insights are high quality and the recommendations for improvement are debated and implemented.

She further elaborated:

> You can sense the quality of a board chair by listening to a board discussion. To what extent does the chair dominate? To what extent does the chair ask good questions? To what extent does the chair open up or close down debate at the right point? How does the chair frame a question that the board is about to debate? What context does the chair set? The chair really plays an important role in setting the tone of the discussion.

By contrast, Hewitt described weaker chairs who dominate conversations and overlook the importance of feedback:

> If I think about the less effective chairs that I have come across, there is sometimes a sense that they have "done" their executive bit, and now they are beyond reproach. They have strong opinions, but they do not always provide leadership. They do not consistently give appraisals of board directors. Why? Possibly because they feel that once someone becomes a director, it is no longer necessary. And they often do not take feedback themselves. But for the board to be successful, all directors, including the chair, need feedback.

Hewitt's examples paint a picture of a chair as a strong orchestrator and facilitator. To play that role, board chairs must excel at asking the right questions rather than simply providing answers, as Hewitt explained:

> What makes me equipped to be the chair of the FA? It is the fact that I have learned how to ask questions and that I am deeply interested in understanding how the organization works. That is part curiosity, part interest, and part having different business models to be able to make

comparisons with. It is also the experience of working in different organizations, appreciating different ways of doing things. It is the breadth of experience that I think ultimately allows me to be more adaptable and less likely to fall into a rut by adopting one approach.

But asking questions is not enough. Modern board chairs also need to proactively assume accountability, as Hewitt emphasized:

I think one of the most important characteristics of a chair is the willingness to take accountability. And particularly the resilience that is required to fully take accountability. Being a chair is not always easy. The chair needs to have a strong sense of accountability and show resilience.

Finally, Hewitt noted the need to blend strong people skills with analytical abilities:

It is really important that a chair can sort and sift through an immense amount of data and zoom in on the two or three things that really matter. They have to have a strong analytical capability. But the best chairs can also use their instincts, too, knowing the difference between when they are relying on fact or their own opinion. There is an important difference. People skills are crucial. The ability to engage and empathize with others, build relationships, and show good judgment around people. These may be seen as softer skills, but they are an essential part of being a good chair.

The transformation of the board chair role

It's important to note that the chair's role varies by country – something we'll explore in more depth in Chapter 10. In many places, the board has been traditionally conceptualized as a group of peers, with the board chair serving as a formal head of the group, but not necessarily providing strong leadership. A classic example of this model is the traditional model of governance in US boards, where the power in the corporation rests with the CEO, who often also holds the role of board chair. In such scenarios, the lead independent director or an independent chair holds limited power. For instance, a lead independent director of a US stock exchange-listed corporation illustrated this dynamic:

I have been lead director. I had extra responsibilities, but my voice did not carry any more clout in the discussions than anybody else's voice. And in fact, I was probably quieter as a lead director than I am when I am not a lead director because I really did not want to influence the discussion unduly.

Another director of a US stock exchange-listed corporation echoed these sentiments:

> The worst thing you can do is to have lead independent directors or an independent board chair who thinks they run the company. There needs to be absolute clarity about who runs the show, and it is the CEO. That's why I am not a big proponent of the independent chair. I do not think that it creates a better company. But I think if you have a combined chairman and CEO, and you have a lead director, that lead director really can represent the board in communicating directly to the CEO. In my mind, that can work very effectively.

Driven by the changes in the business environment and the demands on boards, however, the role of the board chair or lead independent director has evolved from the relatively passive "primus inter pares" (first among equals) who simply presides over meetings to a proactive leader who manages and leads the board and serves as a key counterpart to the CEO. Johannes Huth, a former partner at private equity firm KKR, senior independent director of Coty Inc., and director at Axel Springer, noted:

> Being a chair has become a very time-intensive task. You have to actively manage and lead the board and prepare for board meetings well in order to be able to make decisions. As chair, you are also in regular contact with the management team, certainly every other week, if not every week. So it's a completely different level of work than in the past. It is also qualitatively different. You have to manage it so that you get as much out of the board as possible. That means you also have to involve the people, ideally at an early stage through committees, and give them tasks so that they are used effectively. After all, they are on the board because they can help the company in some way, and it is your task to use them accordingly. It is a really intensive management task.

In light of the dual challenges of modern governance, today's board chairs need to provide strategic leadership, facilitate effective governance, and manage complex board structures.

This broader definition of the board chair role and the enhanced set of tasks require a much higher time commitment of today's board's chairs, as Riet Cadonau, experienced board chair and director and current director at the Zehnder Group AG, explained:

> The days when a board chair spent a few hours every two weeks dealing with the company are over. If you want to be close to management, close to the board and close to the market at the same time, I think that's a half-time job. I'm talking about medium-sized companies with a turnover of up to four or five billion. For even larger companies, I think

that's a full-time job and there's not much room for other important professional activities.

In line with this trend, independent board chairs have become more common than they used to be,[1] and an increasing number of companies have experimented with executive chair positions.[2]

Board chair as a leader

To be effective in today's business environment, the chair needs to actively lead the board rather than simply presiding over meetings. A board member of multiple European corporations explained:

> In my view, the role of the chair has changed a lot over the last five to ten years. Back then, I saw people who were appointed as chairs because they were the wisest people in the room and had the most extensive sector expertise. Today, you ask, is the chair the right facilitator? Is the chair someone who knows how to conclude things and get people to speak up? When the time is right, make the bold decision and communicate to the management team what bold decisions the board has made. I also think that the strong leadership dimension in the chair role is new.

Today's chairs can enable others on the board to be effective through servant leadership. The chair's behavior and leadership style set the tone for board interactions and overall governance practices, fostering a productive board culture. Conni Jonnson, founder of the Swedish private equity firm EQT, explained: "As board chair, you are the team leader, like a captain in the soccer team. Not the smartest, not the one who talks the most, but the one who gets the best out of all the different board members."

Modern chairs need to be effective in managing board dynamics, leading strategic discussions, and ensuring effective decision-making. Successful board leadership is built on trust, open communication, and the ability to synthesize diverse perspectives, ensuring strategic alignment across the board and company leadership.[3]

Today's board chairs also have to transform their boards to play the novel roles that an increasing scope of board tasks has created, and focus the board's attention firmly on the future. They have to drive the board toward addressing the emerging strategic discontinuities and the continued challenge of sustainability, thereby future-proofing the corporation. Pauline Van der Meer Mohr, chair of the Dutch semiconductor equipment manufacturer ASM and director of Ahold Delhaize, NN Group, put it this way:

> I see it as my role as a chair to lead the board first and foremost, not to lead the company. To create the right opportunities for the right

conversations to be had. I'm not going to tell the CEO how he should lead his company, but I am going to create opportunities for the conversations that we need to have around the company's strategic direction. I think it's definitely a role for the board chair to create an opportunity to talk about global trends and how they will affect the strategy. And by helping the board ask the right questions. Board leadership is about creating opportunities, creating the space, and asking the right questions that enable management to rethink their strategy and make the ship change course.

Finally, in many companies leadership by the board chair also means that the chair acts as an essential contact for various stakeholders inside and outside the company as Luka Mucic, a member of the board of Heidelberg Materials, noted:

> There has been a long-standing governance discussion in Germany about whether the supervisory board, the chairman of the supervisory board in particular, should engage in direct dialog with investors. And if so, on which topics? It is a difficult subject because the primacy of the management board to talk about strategy and the like is, of course, also an important consideration. You have to be careful not to step over the boundaries here. However, I believe in the value of such dialog situations, to address questions of governance and questions of the externally perceived functioning of the supervisory board. To face the feedback and also some form of evaluation. It's a bit painful from time to time, in particular when it's not the portfolio managers but also the governance analysts who make different considerations, but a supervisory board has to face this. That's why I'm a big advocate of such regular meetings.

Managing board structures

Board chairs now oversee a more complex board structure that includes multiple committees, advisory boards, and ad hoc groups; steering, coordinating, and integrating them into the activities of the full board. These structures help the board address compliance and reporting demands while also staying focused on larger strategic questions. The complex governance structure that results needs leadership and management from the board chair. A board member of a Swiss-based public company neatly summarized the connection between leadership and structure: "For a successful board, you need leadership and structure. Leadership without structure can, but most often does not, work well. Structure without leadership skills and personality certainly does not work."

Chairs must ensure that the committees function effectively without centralizing too much authority or weakening the board's oversight role. This often includes overseeing the work of various committees, ensuring alignment with the board's objectives, and coordinating between different groups to prevent siloed operations.

The chair also must balance their own involvement in committees while maintaining independence and avoiding overconcentration of power and conflicts of interest. This raises questions, for instance, on whether the chair should lead or participate in key committees like the nomination committee, or focus on working with the committee chairs.

The central challenge in managing the committee structure is to address information asymmetry between the chair, the board, and management by ensuring the timely and transparent flow of information. A board member of a Swiss-based public firm explained to us:

> You need a strong information architecture. How does the chair do briefings for the board of directors? How do you address the information asymmetry between management, the board chair, and the directors? Do you use reports, do you use presentations, and do you use calls with committee chairs or individual members? It depends on the structure of the board and the leadership abilities of the chair.

Setting the agenda, tone, and culture of the board

Beyond the chair's managerial responsibilities, modern board leadership also involves shaping the board's agenda, tone, and culture, particularly to help the board play a more central role in addressing strategic discontinuities and sustainability challenges.

Modern chairs set the board agenda in consultation with the CEO rather than merely approving management-prepared agendas, as Rod Adkins, board member at United Parcel Service (UPS), PayPal, Grainger, and Avnet, explained:

> The board chair and the lead director should be the ones to help set the tone and the agenda with both the board and with management. Often, the CEO on the management team puts the board agenda together, and the chair shows up and orchestrates the meeting. I think the role requires more than that. The board chair needs to be very engaged with the CEO and the various members of the board. The board chair should set the tone of the board meetings, and they should be in charge of the board meetings and set the agenda. You can always use the management team and their staff in terms of administrative support, but the board chair should be setting the agenda and tone of the board meetings.

Board chairs should focus the agenda of the board firmly on the future. This involves determining, together with the CEO, what items take priority on the agenda while addressing pressing concerns raised by directors. Kalidas Madhavpeddi, chair of the

Swiss-based mining giant Glencore, highlighted the importance of prioritizing issues with significant impact:

> The debate on the board has to be proportional to the gravitas of the issue. But human nature is that there are some subjects that we can debate forever and not find a solution. I think that's where a good chairman really can make a difference by focusing the time and attention of the board on where it matters the most.

Chairs should foster an environment that encourages open dialogue, diverse perspectives, and collaborative decision-making. This includes setting an example of openness and inclusivity. Kathleen Bailey-Lord, chair at ed-tech company Janison and member of the board at Datacom, AMP, and St. Vincent's Health Australia explained:

> Board chairs need to be very inclusive leaders; they need to know how to create psychologically safe space in the boardroom and they need to lean into positions different to their own to get the best out from the board. They have to create these safe spaces and then keep building them so that people truly contribute. It is not enough just to ask people for their opinions when they are around the table. What I have observed is that even if a chair asks to hear from every voice, not every voice will speak their truth until they're really certain that it is genuinely a psychologically safe environment. Otherwise, they may or may not say what they really think; they might say a bit of what they think but will edit it to fit in with everyone else.

In practice, that means creating space for everyone's input, especially from those directors who are less vocal. During meetings, modern chairs should focus on creating opportunities for meaningful discussions by ensuring all directors have opportunities to contribute, and prevent some individuals from dominating the conversation, monopolizing the discussion, or undermining collaboration. Ian Carter, chair of Watches of Switzerland plc, described it this way:

> In my view, diversity and difference of thought based on different experiences are central to a high-performance board. Each board member should feel comfortable challenging anyone else's point of view. My job as chair is to create an atmosphere to allow that openness to flourish so that nobody holds back on expressing their views and, more importantly, is able to express them in the right way and thus improve overall decision-making. We all appreciate we're all having the discussion for the right reason, which is to make the company better.

Ensuring that all voices are being heard on the board may require not just facilitating the conversation during board meetings but also providing feedback to the different board members. For instance, Mark Joiner, director at QBE AusPa, explained:

> As chair, I have tried to support diversity of thought. I have encountered instances where people undervalue their own contribution, for instance, because they are not financially experienced. We may have a very financially deep conversation, and they may feel intimidated. So, after board meetings, I often go back to people telling them that their points were really valuable and helped us appreciate all angles on the topic. Just reinforcing that they are adding value rather than feeling increasingly intimidated and shrinking back.

At the same time, good board chairs are mindful that directors differ in style and demeanor. Every board includes individuals with distinct backgrounds and personalities, and, therefore, also needs to be led differently.[4] It is part of the chair's responsibility to guide all board members effectively and maintain a productive decision-making environment. Understanding the differences in specific behavioral traits and how they influence directors' engagement in board discussions helps board chairs to direct board dynamics more effectively and ensure smoother decision-making.

To promote an open discussion culture, modern board chairs encourage directors to admit when they don't know something. Debbie Hewitt, chair of England's Football Association, offered an example of how chairs should encourage transparency and acknowledge uncertainty:

> *It is important for* the chair to create a culture where directors feel comfortable to admit when they don't have an answer. Often, when directors join a board, they have had a successful executive career, and they sense an expectation that they should have all the answers. The chair plays a key role in getting directors to talk openly about where they have gaps in their knowledge.

The same openness should extend to the CEO and leadership team as Andreas Umbach, former board chair of Swiss-based SIG Group AG, emphasized:

> CEOs are strong personalities, and they are usually very strong communicators. As chair, I will say to the CEO: "Please be clear when your statements are based on one hundred percent of hard facts, for example, from a financial report. Please also say where you have made a conclusion, because fact A, fact B, and fact F together add up to that. And please have the courage to tell us when you are just speculating. We need to know when you are in speculation mode."… The problem is that CEOs often believe that they have everything under control and

don't dare to ask if they are unsure. I need to create a risk-free board environment for management where they have the courage to ask and to be wrong. Nobody is perfect. Use the expertise and experience on the board, and it will not be used against you.

Handling difficult board members

Managing difficult board members is a particularly delicate aspect of the chair's leadership role. Board members might be poorly prepared, try to dominate the airtime, undermine other board members or management, and, over time, poison the atmosphere. The board structure implies that board chairs need to handle these individuals. For instance, Don Knauss, director of US-based Kellogg's, McKesson, and Target, explained:

> In my role as chair or lead director, I've certainly had to counsel directors and say you're being ineffective in this way. And that ineffectiveness usually involves a director misunderstanding the difference between running the operation and providing oversight. You have to have those conversations. Otherwise, you're not a very effective chair or lead director.

To improve the effectiveness of directors, modern chairs provide constructive feedback and coaching during and after meetings. Suzanne Thoma, executive chair of Sulzer, shared how she addresses overly dominant members:

> There are several things you can do if you have very dominant board members. First, you don't want this person on a committee where you really need to do good work and collaborate with each other. You must address the issue by talking to them one-to-one. If that does not help, you must have an open discussion in the board about the topic, but be aware of the risk that they might lose face, so don't just do that out of the blue. Prepare for it. I have had one case on a board where someone with a very successful executive career had a lot of experience and made valuable contributions, but was not interested in learning from others. The problem is they hinder the others from making their valuable contributions.

Because board members are near-peers, the chair needs a certain level of diplomacy. One board chair noted in confidence:

> Some board members are so careless that it's obvious from their first question that they have not read the material. ... But you can't expose them in front of the whole team because then it becomes a matter of

pride. ... They aren't inclined to back down either but will fight, simply on principle, to conceal their lack of preparation.

If direct feedback does not lead to a change in behavior, the chair could remove an underperforming board member by involving the nomination committee. Some companies might use the board evaluation process to make this more transparent; however, this can be a double-edged sword and lead to unintended consequences, as Carla Smits-Nusteling, a former board member of Nokia, ASML, and TELE2 AB, observed:

> In one board I served, they put in the annual evaluation that you could score each other from zero to ten. ... It was very effective, pretty blunt, and direct, but it helped remove some dysfunctional directors. But it also created a different dynamic because some of my board colleagues said they didn't feel safe with this system, so they started to self-censor what they would say.

Managing conflict and politics in the boardroom

Corporate boardrooms are places where big egos often collide. Boardrooms frequently bring together individuals with substantial egos, from CEOs working long hours to directors explicitly recruited to challenge and oversee management. This dynamic can create tension that the board chair must channel into productive debate rather than let it dissolve into personal conflict or politics.

The best board chairs keep a close eye on the subtleties of boardroom dynamics to spot signs of emerging factions. They are mindful of the egos in the leadership team and the board, and the potential power differentials and group dynamics these create.

Board chairs want the board to stress test the leadership team's ideas. Yet, they need to ensure that debates remain focused on the subject matter and ideas rather than deteriorating into clashes of personality and personal battles. Addressing interpersonal issues constructively is essential to maintaining a healthy board environment.

Effective board chairs are also careful about the formation of alliances in the board that can potentially turn a discussion of ideas into a power struggle between different groups. Such conflicts are particularly problematic when they extend beyond the boardroom, when stakeholders take advantage of the factions in the board to manipulate decisions, for example, or when board members lean on specific stakeholders to help them pursue their own agenda.

To head off disputes, the board needs a culture that values open information sharing, early identification of disagreements, and prompt resolution. By confronting problems head-on rather than ignoring them, chairs foster a positive environment that keeps the focus on strategic and governance concerns.

The chair-CEO relationship

A cornerstone of any effective chair is a well-balanced relationship with the CEO, one marked by trust, clear communication, and well-defined boundaries, to provide direction, advice, and ensure adequate oversight and alignment with the company's strategic objectives. Strong chairs work closely with the CEO, managing the board while the CEO manages the company. The chair acts as the CEO's sparring partner and coach, supporting the CEO but also holding them accountable. Striking the right balance is essential: an adversarial relationship can lead to power struggles, while one that is too friendly can sideline and render the rest of the board ineffective. As one board chair cautioned:

> If the CEO and the chairman join forces on too many matters, then the rest of the board doesn't stand a chance. A lot of mischief happens in companies if the chairman and the CEO are too united and make decisions between themselves. The rest of the board quickly becomes relegated to the role of observer.

The chair's approach should build trust through consistency, empathy, and transparency so that the board can hold the CEO accountable in a supportive way.[5] For instance, Andreas Umbach, former chair of Swiss-based SIG Group AG, explained his style:

> The interaction with the CEO is really important. I adapt my style a little to that of the CEO. Some people are more structured and like to have a jour fixe and a list of topics. Other CEOs feel the need to talk to me about individual topics. I combine a formal, structured approach with informal conversations. ... If you only rely on the official information on the board and in the documents, you miss out on a lot.

The effectiveness of the CEO-board chair relationship often hinges on key interactions that either build trust or create tensions. Critical moments such as selecting a CEO, performance reviews, and crisis management are critical junctures where clear communication and alignment form the foundation for success.

Early on, the board chair and the CEO should define clear roles that avoid overlaps, confusion, and conflicts. In particular, board chairs are well advised to avoid acting as de facto CEO, which almost always leads to frustration, tension, and conflict. For example, when former CEOs – particularly founders – transition to board chair, the boundaries between the roles can easily become blurred, and the chair must stay focused on maintaining the agreed-upon separation of duties.

The chair and the CEO should agree on clear task responsibilities. All too often, responsibilities are defined too vaguely, leading to misunderstandings and conflict. The precise definition of responsibilities is also central to enabling the board chair to hold a CEO accountable.[6]

It is equally essential for the chair to maintain a healthy degree of pressure so that board-approved initiatives are actually implemented. In the absence of this pressure, the CEO and management team may not be as responsible to the board as is needed to be effective. One director of a large European corporation explained how their board's chair was overly focused on preserving harmony, which led to subpar execution. Board materials were frequently late and not of the quality needed for good board discourse. Also, recommendations by the board were not implemented properly. In the words of that director: "Because it has no consequences, everything is done with 80 percent effort. If what I achieve with 80 percent suffices, why should I put in more effort?"

Board chairs should also drive transparent performance evaluations of the CEO. Board chairs and, even more so, lead independent directors often shy away from candid discussions about CEO performance when the CEO is present, fearing that such discussions may undermine the CEO's authority, standing, or morale. This lack of transparency leaves underperforming CEOs in the dark about where they stand and gives them limited opportunity to address perceived performance issues. Regular and transparent reviews create an opportunity for open dialogue, making performance evaluations a routine practice rather than a sign of trouble and fostering a learning-oriented culture.

Finally, board chairs should engage in early and decisive intervention when performance problems emerge. When problems linger on for too long without this intervention, they often escalate. Board chairs who delay decisive action risk deeper organizational crises and lost opportunities for course correction. Early intervention allows board chairs to coach the CEO to resolve issues and get back on track, rather than waiting for dismissal to be the only option left. When it becomes clear that the CEO is either unable or unwilling to resolve underperformance, board chairs should initiate decisive action, including dismissal, to prevent further damage.

Personal attributes and skills required for effective board chairs

The new role of the board chair demands a unique combination of personal attributes and skills that may be difficult to find in a single individual.[7] Today's board chairs must combine leadership skills, personal humility, analytical thinking, and strong interpersonal awareness.

The best board chairs we have encountered are strategic visionaries who possess the leadership skills necessary to accomplish tasks through facilitating others and are able to steer a group of high-powered individuals effectively. They serve as a counterweight to a forceful CEO and keep their own egos in check. In doing so, they need to be comfortable with multiple roles and responsibilities and be willing to lead the board without seeking the spotlight, but rather lead from the background.

The best board chairs often act as "servant leaders," creating psychologically safe environments where all directors feel comfortable contributing. They have a strong sense of accountability for the board's performance and the company's governance and prioritize the board's and the company's needs over personal recognition, enabling others to contribute effectively. Strong board chairs need to possess a steady ethical compass to uphold governance principles even when facing resistance.

On a personal level, effective board chairs blend analytical prowess with good people skills, balance humility with confidence, and demonstrate an eagerness for learning.

Selecting the right chair is one of the most critical decisions a corporation makes. Traditional norms sometimes favor promoting a former CEO to the chair role, but that path can be problematic if it's treated as a default move.

In deciding whether to appoint the former CEO as board chair, several considerations need to be taken into account. First, the transition from CEO to chair is often difficult. Johannes Huth, a former partner at private equity firm KKR, senior independent director of Coty Inc., and director at Axel Springer, underscored this difficulty:

> The transition from active CEO to board chair is often difficult. The chair is no longer the CEO. And it is difficult for many CEOs to make this leap. You have to let the CEO make the decisions and can no longer do it yourself. That's why I always say that board experience is very important, ... realizing that you can no longer implement things yourself and you need to leave that to someone else.

Secondly, while the former CEO no doubt has deep knowledge of the company and can provide expertise, as chair, they may hold back the board for several reasons. A board member of multiple European corporations explained:

> If I need to decide if the former CEO can become chair, I need to understand if that person would allow for mistakes. ... If it is a person who is protective, defensive, and not allowing that type of discussion, I would be very hesitant to promote such a person to the board level.

Finally, if the former CEO becomes board chair, it also makes it more difficult for the current CEO to introduce strategic changes to the board. Andreas Joehle, former CEO and now a partner at the private equity firm Ufenau Capital Partners and board member, noted the practical difficulties for a new CEO when the previous CEO becomes chair:

> When the former CEO is still around, things can feel a little different. It can be a bit harder for the new CEO to say, "Hey, we are struggling with this decision you made when you were in charge, and we'd love to change it."

In short, a thorough, objective process is essential for appointing a chair – one driven by the nominating committee and the full board and informed by stakeholders. A board member of multiple European corporations pointed out:

> It is important that you conduct a really thorough assessment before you appoint the chair. The same way you would assess a CEO candidate. A thorough assessment, a lot of interviews, and a profile analysis. What type of person is this? What type of leadership does that person provide? How did they carry out their prior job? References from other boards, discussions with CEOs who work with them. A very thorough analysis. I think this doesn't often happen. You would rather appoint someone with the longest CV and the deepest industry expertise, and think that person will do the trick. That person could be a very good expert to have on the board, but maybe not as chair.

Qualities of the ideal board chair

The qualities of a board chair can be summarized in five dimensions: Leadership qualities, personal traits, analytical and interpersonal skills, commitment and accountability, and adaptability.

Leadership qualities:

Strong leader who can keep ego in check.
Visionary thinking that guides the board's long-term strategy.
Facilitation skills for productive discussion and collaboration.
Management skills that coordinate committees and working groups.

Personal traits:

Humility: Willingness to admit mistakes and not seek the spotlight.
Confidence: Capable of counterbalancing a powerful CEO.
Integrity: Upholds high ethical standards and acts in the company's best interest.
Comfortable leading from behind the scenes and staying out of the spotlight.

Analytical and interpersonal skills:

Ability to synthesize complex information and focus on key issues.
Aptitude for asking insightful questions that drive deeper understanding and better decisions.
Strong interpersonal skills to engage a diverse board.
Emotional intelligence to read and manage interpersonal and group dynamics.

Commitment and accountability:

Recognizes the significant time and effort the role demands.

Accepts accountability for the board's performance and the company's governance.

Adaptability:

Adjusts leadership style to match different CEOs and board dynamics.

Stays informed about industry trends and governance best practices.

Dealing with dysfunctional board chairs

Just as chairs can lead effectively, they can also become overly dominant or even dysfunctional. In these cases, the board or its nomination committee needs to take the initiative to coach the board chair. For instance, one board member noted in confidence:

> [Name] is such a strong personality and drives the business so hard, and also drives the board to align with the business. But sometimes, he does need to be pushed back. ... There are some occasions where the chairman has something in his head and wants to drive it, and then the board has to stand up and push back.

When feedback doesn't work or the chair refuses to adjust, the board may need to take steps to change the board chair. One board member who preferred to remain anonymous remarked:

> As a board member, you need the courage, perhaps also the independence, to say: "That's enough." You need to understand when it is time to intervene. We had this situation. We first discussed it in a small group. Eventually, we had to say, it is either him or us. And I think you have to have the courage to do that.

A full-blown "revolt" against the chair is rare, partly because it carries significant reputational risks. Additionally, in many jurisdictions, removing a chair against their will can be legally complex. One board member described a process involving multiple steps:

To remove a board chair, you need stages of escalation. It starts with openly addressing the problems at a very early stage. If you can do that somehow, then I think you can probably resolve many conflicts in a relatively professional way at the start. And if not, you need to escalate further. In one situation I was involved in, we first spoke to the chair but couldn't resolve the issue. Then we spoke to the chair of the audit committee and said, "Do you agree we can't go on like this?" Since he agreed, we raised it as a risk factor in the audit committee. Then, we took it to the chair of the nomination committee. Again, we asked, "How do you see it? Is this behavior crossing red lines, or is it still professionally acceptable?" The committee chair agreed that it wasn't professional. There were one or two members who said: "I see it the same way, but it's not really my business." However, a common understanding gradually emerged that we had a responsibility as a board. Out of loyalty to the shareholders, the company, and the employees. Since we were the majority, we decided that we would have to raise this discussion openly with the full board. It then became a bit emotional, so it wasn't easy. What I have learned from this is that it's best if you can play the escalation stages cleanly, i.e., first, I discuss it professionally and objectively with the committee chairs and then take it to the full board. Eventually, you will take it to a vote of no confidence. It has to be factual and avoid emotions as much as possible. You cannot just say, "Your leadership isn't working." The idea is to approach the chair via different escalation levels in order to allow them to make a change or make a decision at each stage. This allows the chair to ask the question of trust and to step back if needed without losing face.

The need for such drastic changes also highlights the limits of structure and process, as Greg Poux-Guillaume, chairman at Swiss-based Medmix, explained:

At the end of the day, it all comes back to the selection of the chair. You can't make people be something they're not by process. You have to be clear from the beginning who your chair is, who your CEO is, and what kind of personalities you are getting on board. If you have a chair who is a dictator, who doesn't discuss and doesn't debate, they are not going to play the chair role; he will try to play the CEO role. You can throw all the processes in the world at that person, but you are simply rearranging deckchairs on the Titanic.

Notes

1. Jerilyn W. Coles and William S. Hesterly, "Independence of the Chairman and Board Composition: Firm Choices and Shareholder Value," *Journal of Management* 26, no. 2 (2000); Ryan Krause, "Being the CEO's Boss: An Examination of Board Chair Orientations," *Strategic Management Journal* 38, no. 3 (2017); Ryan Krause, Matthew Semadeni, and Michael C. Withers, "That Special Someone: When the Board Views Its Chair as a Resource," *Strategic Management Journal* 37, no. 9 (September 2016).

2. Markus Menz, Robert Langan, and Ryan Krause, "Does Your Board Need an Executive Chair?" *HBR.org, Harvard Business Review*, November 25, 2022, https://hbr.org/2022/11/does-your-board-need-an-executive-chair.

3. Dennis Carey, Ram Charan, Joseph Griesedieck, and Michael Useem, "8 Questions to Ask before Selecting a New Board Leader," *HBR.org, Harvard Business Review*, January 17, 2023, https://hbr.org/2023/01/8-questions-to-ask-before-selecting-a-new-board-leader.

4. Randall S. Peterson and Pedro Fontes Falcão, "6 Kinds of Board Members – And How to Influence," *HBR.org, Harvard Business Review*, December 20, 2023, https://hbr.org/2023/12/6-kinds-of-board-members-and-how-to-influence-them.

5. George Anderson, James M. Citrin, Cassandra Frangos, and Zachary Morfín, "5 Moments That Make or Break a CEO-Board Chair Relationship," *HBR.org, Harvard Business Review*, August 23, 2024, https://hbr.org/2024/08/5-moments-that-make-or-break-a-ceo-board-chair-relationship.

6. Stevo Pavićević and Thomas Keil, "Research: How Boards Can Increase CEO Accountability," *HBR.org, Harvard Business Review*, February 4, 2025, https://hbr.org/2025/02/research-how-boards-can-increase-ceo-accountability.

7. For an insightful discussion of the criteria for selecting a board chair see Chapter 5 of Ram Charan, Dennis Carey, and Michael Useem, *Boards That Lead: When to Take Charge, When to Partner, and When to Stay out of the Way* (Boston, MA: Harvard Business Review Press, 2014).

Chapter 7

Board evaluation and development

During our conversation, Rod Adkins reflected on his work as board chair at Avnet, a US-based, publicly listed electronic components distributor. Adkins joined Avent's board in 2015 and was elected board chair in 2018. He had an impressive career at IBM, where he spent over 30 years and ultimately became the first African American to serve as a senior vice president in the company's history. In his various executive roles – including senior vice president of the Systems and Technology Group and later Corporate Strategy – he oversaw significant product groups, technological innovations, and strategic initiatives. Adkins retired from IBM in 2014.

He became highly sought-after for board positions, applying his deep corporate governance and innovation expertise to multiple organizations. Adkins has served on PPL Corporation, Pitney Bowes, and PeopleClick Inc. boards, in addition to various not-for-profit organizations. At the time of writing, as well as Avnet, he also serves on United Parcel Service (UPS), PayPal, and WW Grainger boards.

Adkins offered us his insights on the difficulties of implementing effective performance management at the board level. He noted:

> The challenge with performance management for public boards is that all directors are peers and re-elected each year by the shareholders. One of the board members ends up being the chair or the lead director, but for the most part, it is a peer structure. Frankly, this can make performance management challenging. How do you have an effective performance management process that works for a structure that is, by design, a group of equals?

DOI: 10.4324/9781003532200-10

Adkins also underscored how bringing outside perspectives can help:

> I use an external third party to help do the annual assessments every other year, because it helps address dealing with some nuances in giving constructive feedback to colleagues. This allows directors to have a different, more open conversation about how we think about the board's performance. How do we think about our own performance, the performance as a group, and how do we think about the performance of our colleagues? With that third-party assessment, you get richer input in terms of the true performance of the board. A better assessment of the roles that your various colleagues are playing. It tends to be a little bit more critical, in terms of how you evaluate yourself, depending on the effectiveness of that third-party assessor.

However, regular assessment of the board is not enough if it is not translated into action and does not lead to development activities on the board. Not every board is ready to confront the results of its evaluations, as Adkins remarked:

> The big challenge with effective assessment is to enforce what is coming out of it. If the performance is not there, then there should be some form of action with the director, ranging from a conversation about behavioral change to suggesting this might not be the right board for them. But now, although many have endorsed, I am unsure if every board member has embraced the notion that your performance on the board matters.

In addition to using board evaluations as a tool to identify and address problems, Adkins stressed the broader importance of the general development of the board as a group and of each director. He explained:

> I firmly believe that boards and individual directors must embrace continuous education. Some boards do a good job saying, "Every year, a director should invest in education. There are several approaches, including using some available resources to focus on a new topic area. For example, take a course with the National Association of Corporate Directors (NACD) on boardroom and committee trends or take a course at a university offering board education, looking at the trends and directions in the industry. Every director should be encouraged to stay up to speed within their domain. Still, at the same time, they also try to understand some of the changes that might be affecting the company as we advance and what these imply in terms of the skills needed in the future. Self-evaluation is a useful tool. In one board I'm on, the self-evaluation questionnaire asks very pointed

questions regarding how we think we are keeping up with the latest market trends and providing guidance in some new areas. This creates some healthy pressure to be current on what is happening with topics like AI, for example, and how AI is being applied to various business processes.

While support for – or pressure on – directors to upskill, their game is an important factor, Adkins was adamant that the ultimate responsibility for growth and development lies with each director: "In my view, each director owns their continued development. As a director, you should not occupy these jobs if you are not staying relevant."

In addition to director development, Adkins also highlighted the need for systematic succession management to keep boards aligned with shifting market requirements. He observed that many boards are unprepared:

> Many boards are challenged in how they constantly refresh and replenish their directors. They do not have effective succession planning for directors. That is why all boards should have a skills matrix where you constantly update your skills to see where you are strong and where you have gaps. And then, you can look for new directors to fill in some gaps when a director retires or leaves the board. You fill in those gaps whenever there are opportunities to bring in new directors.

The core challenges and opportunities that Adkins identifies – performance management, board development, and succession planning – are the focus of this chapter. They also represent the fifth and final building block of the board diamond, which is aimed at helping boards address the dual challenge of modern governance and future-proof themselves.

Why performance management is broken in many boards

Under most governance codices and in many legislations, boards must conduct some form of evaluation, often a self-evaluation. When done well, these evaluations strengthen a board's ability to guide corporate strategy, balance oversight with the right level of support for leadership, and address potential shortcomings such as underperforming or inattentive directors.[1] A rigorous self-evaluation process can also improve board dynamics (e.g., by identifying "trophy directors" who rarely contribute), enhance strategic discussions, and even potentially reduce liability insurance costs over time.[2] Board evaluations can indeed boost board effectiveness and drive stronger corporate performance, provided the evaluation system is fit for its intended purpose.[3]

However, many of these evaluations amount to little more than a tick-box exercise, carried out solely to meet legal requirements or appease stakeholders. They lack genuine engagement or any real intention by the board to use the results to improve practices. A board chair with experience in large UK and US corporations explained:

> I believe that the board evaluation process is broken in many companies in both the US and the UK. It essentially doesn't exist in substance because the board is so self-referential, and management doesn't want to take on any issues with the board either. And even if you get a third-party lawyer or consultant to do the work, it is barely worth the paper it's written on. As a company, we would not accept this anywhere else in our organization. It is kind of bizarre that we don't set the same process up for the boards that we do further down into the organization.

Reflecting this tendency to overlook board evaluations, there has been little systematic academic research on the topic. Practitioner-focused resources are also comparatively limited.[4]

A few fundamental issues drive this problem. First, many boards fail to articulate clear goals for themselves. It is quite paradoxical that the very entity responsible for the organization achieving its goals often does not set explicit, measurable targets for its own performance. Also, the structure of boards frequently gets in the way of effective board evaluation. Boards are essentially peer structures, which makes many directors hesitant to provide honest and frank feedback or critique of their colleagues. Moreover, boards often have no institutional mechanism or individual charged to enforce performance management based on the evaluation. Institutional mechanisms such as annual shareholder meetings or reviews of proxy advisors are too far removed from the day-to-day reality of the board to be useful in this role. Board chairs, meanwhile, are often hesitant to take on the responsibility of ensuring performance management consequences, and without the board chair's strong commitment to using the board evaluation as a management tool, the evaluation often remains a symbolic exercise without consequence.

As well as not being taken sufficiently seriously, board evaluation is often not sufficiently comprehensive and focuses on the wrong questions, as a board chair explained:

> My critique of most board evaluation systems is that we tend to evaluate how we perform as a board in the meeting. Are we using our time effectively, as opposed to, are we making the right decisions? Are we getting the right outcomes? It's the same for the compensation committee. We look at how the committee meeting is run and how efficient the meeting is, when we should be looking at how well our decisions around compensation are working. Are we getting the outcomes we expect? Are we paying for the right outcomes?

Jeff Campbell, former vice chairman and CFO of American Express, former CFO of McKesson and American Airlines, and current director at AON plc, Marathon Petroleum Corp., and Hexcel Corp, made a similar point about the lack of retrospective assessment of board decisions:

> I do not think we spend as much time as we should periodically stepping back and saying let us reflect as a board on the last couple of years' worth of decisions that we really had to debate and how do we feel about them in hindsight? I do not see us doing a lot of that, and I think that it would probably lead to better decisions if we did. Every company I have been a part of has a process that will allow you to review the last three years' worth of acquisitions. Do that periodically and derive lessons. What was good? What was bad? What should we do differently? We simply do not have a similar process for the board.

Finally, board evaluation is often not transparent to shareholders who ultimately decide whether board members remain in their roles. A board chair of a large European corporation explained:

> There is also the problem that investors have no idea who the board members really are and what they do on the board. You go to the website and see the names of the board members. But when the company is struggling, or failing, or not delivering, it's very hard for external people, for investors, even professional investors to say, "Well, these are the people on the board who are the right ones for solving the issue and these are the people who are not," and therefore external people can decide the board doesn't work and needs fixing, and then what they will do is they will start voting against the chair and blindly voting against everybody. But it's never targeted because they don't have the right information. That information only exists within the board.

The enhanced requirements for boards and the changes in the operating environments of many companies that we discussed in the opening of the book make it more and more important for boards to engage in constant development and, to do so, they need to implement systematic and credible performance management systems that tie comprehensive, transparent, and meaningful evaluations to tangible changes in how the board is composed, structured, and how it operates. A board member of multiple European corporations captured this urgency:

> You need to increase the board's temperature by talking about board effectiveness in a very open manner. As well as evaluating the management team, you need to evaluate the board. I think we have just seen the start of it there. You need to develop as a board member and be as

tough towards yourself as a director and a board member as you would be when hiring or firing the CEO and the rest of the management team. That is how I think it needs to develop.

A more robust and transparent board evaluation – one that goes beyond minimal legal requirements – can help hold boards accountable for both their actions and their development. It can also support continuous, systematic development at the individual and team levels, and it can feed into succession planning to ensure boards remain aligned with the challenges ahead.

Improving board evaluation through comprehensiveness, transparency, and accountability

Improving the comprehensiveness and transparency of board evaluation and accountability within the board and to external stakeholders is essential for effective governance and as a basis for continuous board development and succession planning. The comprehensiveness of the board evaluation reflects the breadth of topics being evaluated. Board evaluations should consider the performance of individual board members, different board structures – such as committees or advisory boards – and the board as a whole. Evaluation ideally will combine quantitative and qualitative components. Don Knauss, director of US-based Kellogg's, McKesson, and Target, shared an example:

> We will do an annual board survey where we cover the four topics our investors care most about: board composition, strategy & risk oversight, executive compensation, and shareholder rights. I asked every director to rate the board's performance in those four areas. I will then follow up with one-on-one conversations with each director to ensure I've captured all their feedback on the board's performance. From that survey and those one-on-one conversations, we develop an annual action plan on the areas the board will focus on for continuous improvement.

Evaluations need to look at both effectiveness and efficiency, identifying what has worked well, what could be improved, and how lessons from past decisions – successful or not – can shape future decision-making.

Comprehensiveness

The comprehensiveness of board evaluations can be improved through 360-degree feedback that incorporates input from executive management, shareholders, and possibly other stakeholders to gain a full perspective on board performance. Greg Poux-Guillaume, a chairman at Swiss-based Medmix, noted: "One of the tools I like to use is a 360-degree review. You don't have to make it public, but you can use it to have a good conversation. It creates some facts that can facilitate the conversation."

Seeking feedback from the CEO, leadership team, or investors enables the board to understand how its actions are perceived and where enhancements are needed. For instance, CEOs often desire a more constructive challenge and strategic engagement and bemoan the lack of risk tolerance from boards because they feel that directors may prioritize personal interests, such as continued service or avoiding conflict, leading them to favor risk-averse decisions.[5]

Understanding the board as a part of the strategic apex of the corporation rather than a disconnected oversight body implies the need to take such bidirectional feedback for mutual improvement, as Luka Mucic, a member of the board of Heidelberg Materials, noted:

> I am a big fan of bidirectional feedback. I think we, as supervisory board members, are also required to offer the individual members of the management board open feedback and coaching, not just in the institutionalized form of a supervisory board meeting. We recently introduced this at SAP, for example, by assigning individual members of the supervisory board to individual members of the executive board to give them regular feedback outside of the tight corset of meetings. To give more honest and sometimes more direct and open feedback. The same should happen in the other direction by regularly asking the individual members of the management board, the chairman of the management board, and the entire board to reflect on how helpful they perceive the work of the supervisory board to be. To convey to them that there is a serious interest in receiving critical feedback.

Transparency

Transparency often involves thorough disclosures about board activities, the evaluation process, and director contributions. This may include engaging with shareholders or other stakeholders, like NGOs, to understand their concerns and expectations regarding board performance.

Transparency can be improved through systematic reporting of board activities. This includes providing shareholders and other stakeholders with better insights into board performance and individual director contributions. A board chair of a large European corporation explained:

> You could have the executive committee grading the board members and report the results. That creates some attention. It has its own issues. You have to be nice to people. It forces you to tone things down. So, it

creates its own biases. But you have to create a system that highlights to the outside world what's working and what's not working in a board because today investors have no visibility.

Given that board evaluations often suffer from a reluctance of the directors to provide negative feedback to a board chair whom they perceive as a peer, comprehensiveness and transparency also can be improved by engaging in external assessments that use independent advisors to conduct evaluations to create more objective insights and facilitate honest feedback. Johannes Huth, former partner at private equity firm KKR, senior independent director of Coty Inc., and director at Axel Springer, explained:

> The self-assessment that is required nowadays can be done in two ways. One can just say: "We have to do it! Let's all fill out a questionnaire, and then we'll be good for another five years." Or it can be used intensively as a development tool. With the better boards, this means that someone is commissioned to interview all the board members, not just send out a questionnaire, but also to talk to them. That a summary is then drawn up from this that clearly identifies we could perhaps do better.

An interesting model in this respect is the system of Sweden, in which board evaluation is conducted by a nominating committee that consists mostly of representatives of the largest shareholders and, therefore, is fairly independent of the board. Conni Jonnson, founder of the Swedish private equity firm EQT, summarized the cornerstones of this system:

> The way it works up here is that normally we have the board meetings, or the AGMs, here in the spring. Then, during the fall, the chairman's office, together with the shareholder coverage office, reviews the shareholder list. And then they take the biggest shareholders, if it's four or five, depending on how many you would like to have in the nomination committee, and you ask them whom they would like to appoint to the nomination committee. The only one from the company that is on the nomination committee is normally the chair of the board, but he's the only one. The nomination committee does the appraisal for the board, and then it's reported and discussed in the nomination committee as input for the proposal of the board slate at the next AGM.

Improving board evaluation in many boards also requires a cultural change, as Rod Adkins suggests in the example at the beginning of this chapter. Boards need to develop behavioral norms that encourage directors to provide constructive feedback to each other to improve team dynamics.

Improving board evaluations is fundamentally a leadership task, and as a result, the board chair plays a central role. The quality of the evaluation often stands and falls with the will of the board chair to utilize board evaluation as a transparent and objective tool for board performance management.

Accountability

Accountability means acting on evaluation results to align the board with future requirements. Boards should be prepared to change processes, adjust structures, or even alter director remuneration, re-nomination, and continuation if called for by evaluation findings.

Improving the quality of the board evaluation is of little use if it is not translated into actions and board accountability. Board accountability can be improved by linking evaluations to changes in board processes and practices, as well as director remuneration, re-nomination, and continuation on the board.

Taking accountability seriously also implies listening to shareholder votes as important feedback. Shareholder votes on directors can be viewed as indicators of performance and legitimacy, and boards should take corrective measures when facing significant shareholder dissent or feedback. Jan Jenisch, former chair of the board of Swiss-based Holcim, suggested:

> An important aspect where the board has to take a stand is the voting result at the Annual General Meeting. When I stood for election as board chair while still CEO, the support of the shareholders was important for me. The proposal that the board of directors had made did not correspond to the recommendations of the proxy advisors. But the board had the courage to make this decision. It was important to me that the shareholder supports this. Otherwise, I would be violating shareholder interests. If I had not been elected with at least 80 percent, I would not have had the legitimacy to do this job. I'm amazed at how some companies ignore this a little. Whether it is the vote on the climate report, the remuneration policy, or the directors, the shareholder ultimately should have the final say, not the board of directors.

The need for continuous board development

Board evaluation and action based on these evaluations is only the first step to future-proofing the board. In a rapidly changing landscape, boards need to invest in systematic and continuous development at both the collective level and for individual directors. For boards to take a more strategic role by setting long-term vision and direction requires investing in continuous education for directors, emphasizing the importance of foresight and agility to respond to unexpected challenges.[6]

Yet many boards still fail to provide enough structured resources for director development, leaving training and education mostly up to individuals. For instance, many boards still invest surprisingly few resources in the training and development of the board.

Barriers to board development

Cultural and behavioral barriers, such as resistance to training and reluctance to admit knowledge gaps, hinder effective development. Seasoned directors in particular may view training as unnecessary, believing that their experience suffices, or are uncomfortable acknowledging areas where they lack expertise, impeding their learning. Debbie Hewitt, chair of England's Football Association, explained: "Training is often overlooked by boards. Directors can assume that training is not for them. I am very keen to understand the training needs of the boards; it's about continual professional development."

This can be particularly detrimental in areas such as digital transformation, artificial intelligence, cybersecurity, and sustainability, which are both new and fast developing and, therefore, require directors to keep their knowledge up to date. To address these gaps, boards should begin by establishing a culture that values continuous learning, openness to new ideas, frank dialogue, a willingness to acknowledge knowledge gaps, and investment in training and development activities. As Hewitt put it:

> For board development to work, you need that the board openly accepts it does not know everything, that it is curious about finding out different ways of learning, and that it is open to acknowledging where the weaknesses might be.

Strategies to overcome development barriers

Boards should engage in a number of tangible strategies to overcome the barriers to development. These include mandatory, or at least strong encouragement of, training programs for all directors. While the needs may differ from director to director, an important mechanism is to make some development activities mandatory. Debbie Hewitt shared an example:

> I'd be disappointed if any director opted out of training that the board identified we needed. By participating in the training, directors not only learn new skills but they can also coach their peers in areas where they are experts.' So everyone participates, whether you are being trained or doing the training. In many regulated businesses, you cannot get access to email or board papers if you have not done your regulatory training. It is obligatory.

In some boards, directors are asked to report their training activities regularly, creating a degree of peer pressure. For instance, one board member of a US stock exchange-listed corporation explained to us:

> Every quarter, we get a note right after the quarter end, that says, "please send us a list of all the training that you did in the last quarter." That creates peer pressure because it then gets put in the board papers. Here is what we did as a group and what everyone did individually.

Another strategy is to regularly bring in external experts – economists, sociologists, or technologists, for example – to share insights during board meetings, especially during informal sessions such as board dinners or board retreats. Anne Lange, director at Pernod-Ricard, Orange, and Inditex, emphasized:

> As a board, we need to understand our world, and it's very important to regularly inject sociology and geopolitics in our reflections. I'm not recommending developing such debates during the board meeting. We don't have the time for that, but I think that for a given company, it's a duty to educate the board on the social and political trends that affect the business because it's impossible for one single person to be aware of all of them. They are paramount to understanding the business.

For topics such as sustainability, digitalization, or AI, younger members of the organization may be well-positioned to provide guidance to directors. Therefore, some boards also experiment with different forms of reverse mentoring where younger or less senior organizational members mentor directors to provide fresh perspectives. For instance, Thomas Thune Andersen, chair at Lloyd's Register Group and VKR Holding, and member of the board at BW Group and IMI plc, explained:

> I've instigated that somebody mentors me from within the organization. And that is typically people much younger, much further down the organization. It takes a little while for them to get comfortable doing it because here I sit as a chair, and they're in a junior role. However, having created that trust, it has been extremely useful for me to understand whether the purpose permeates all the way through the organization. What are the values, and how does the younger generation actually get inspired? What are some of the tools they use? I do not know how Facebook and those things work because I'm such an old-fashioned person. But I learned a lot from them and gained a new understanding. I think that would be a very important tool for each board member to be exposed to.

More advanced organizations also use the skills matrix to define development needs for their directors and may provide training opportunities to develop additional skills and competencies to address gaps.

Turning the board into a high-performing team

As boards grapple with strategic discontinuities, sustainability concerns, and other forward-looking challenges, they need to function more like a high-performance team. One area where continuous development is critical is the board's approach to building a high-performance team at the board level. This requires trust, openness, and psychological safety for directors to voice their opinions and challenge each other. Traditional boards have struggled to do so due to the more intermittent interactions and the absence of team development activities in the busy board meeting schedule. Modern boards need to invest in team-building exercises and social interactions, and create an environment where directors feel comfortable expressing uncertainties and providing feedback.

To turn boards from a group of disconnected individuals into a strong team, boards need to invest the time and resources to organize retreats, workshops, and facilitated sessions focused on team building and strategic discussions. In addition to these dedicated activities, boards should also leverage dinners, social events connected to the meetings, and other informal opportunities to engage in activities that build relationships and enhance trust. A board chair shared with us an effective exercise to build trust in the board:

> You have to build trust amongst the board members. The board doesn't meet often enough to be a true team, but you can take a lot of the team-building approaches to the board level and make the board more effective. In one of the boards I am on, the CEO spent a dinner going around the board saying, "Tell us one thing about yourself that no one else would know. And then tell us the most impactful thing that happened to you in your life." It was mind-blowing what we learned about each other that evening. The diversity of experience in the backgrounds was amazing. That gave all of us a much better appreciation for each other. And that was followed up with other events, so we got to know each other better. That made us a more effective board because it helped us understand each other better. So when we saw someone operating a certain way, we came at it from a perspective of trust as opposed to distrust, assumed a positive intent as opposed to assuming this person is just trying to railroad this topic through.

Toward continuity in board development

Board chairs should emphasize the importance of continuous professional development and set directors' expectations accordingly. They play a central role in creating a culture of continuous development by acting as role models through their own openness to learning and by actively encouraging directors to embrace development opportunities.

To ensure the continuity of board development activities, it is also useful to build these explicitly into the board schedule. This could take, for instance, the format of a regular short private (executive) session after board meetings to reflect on effectiveness and discuss improvements. For instance, a board member of a large European corporation noted:

> We always have a private session right after the meeting, where we discuss how we as the board of directors have acted over the last three, four, or five hours when we've had the meeting. Where we can reflect on topics that are critical and ask if we have handled them well or not, and reflect on whether the management has understood the message we wanted to provide. It's always a question of verifying, just among the board members, if we have done a good job as a team. We also ask ourselves whether we've slipped too deeply into some detail or what we should perhaps do differently.

The role of individual directors

Although we see important development potential in systematizing director and board development at the board level, this does not imply that the role of individual directors in this would be reduced. Directors need to take responsibility for personal development, stay updated on industry trends, and generally be open to new ideas. In particular, individual directors should also reflect on past decisions and be willing to admit mistakes in a spirit of continuous improvement. One board member of a US stock exchange-listed corporation explained:

> As individual members of the board of directors, we also have an important responsibility in developing the board onwards. After every meeting, you can say to the board chair or other members: "I didn't think that was good. You should have left that alone. Because you saw that the other person was overburdened." This type of feedback works. And I think that's important. That it doesn't just remain in the room, but that you discuss it and develop the discussion culture based on it.

Board succession management

The final pillar of board evaluation and development is a systematic approach to succession management at the board level. Effective succession planning and onboarding of new directors are critical to keeping a board dynamic and high performing.

In some jurisdictions, rotation of committee chairs and directors is mandated, which calls for thoughtful, proactive planning. Yet many boards lack a clear plan for the future needs of the board or a pipeline of qualified candidates and do not plan adequately for rotation or retirement. Boards often do not have a forward-looking skills map or a well-developed pipeline of candidates, let alone a proactive approach to identifying and testing future directors, leading to last-minute appointments as Rod Adkins, board member at United Parcel Service (UPS), PayPal, Grainger, and Avnet, cautioned: "Many boards are challenged in terms of how do you constantly refresh and replenish your directors? How do you have effective succession planning for directors?"

In addition to identifying skills needed and potential directors, boards need to improve how they onboard new directors to leverage their skills more rapidly. Given that board work is not full-time, it may take considerable time before a director gets to know a complex company sufficiently to bring their full value. Views on the length of time it needs to be effective as a board member differ substantively. While some board chairs expect new members to be effective after a year, others estimate the time needed to be closer to three years, in particular in large, complex organizations. Peter Voser, board chair at ABB, PSA International, and member of the board at IBM, explained this logic for his organization:

> Most European companies have five to six board meetings. That means every two and a half months, you get together. Do you really think that the board members still have everything present between those two meetings? No. For a significant percentage of the content, they start not from zero, but clearly will need to refresh the company's knowledge during the meeting. In a business like ABB, we run 19 divisions, and each of these divisions is a sizable global business. Just to understand one of them, it takes some time. So, you need to structure the induction training very well and bring the people to the factories, but you also need to structure your board meeting in a way that they really have a chance to learn over time. So, at every board meeting, we bring two out of the 19 businesses for a two-hour deep dive, a complete strategic, operational, and financial discussion on how this business actually works. So we need roughly two years to go around the shop. That means it needs at least two years before they have a detailed understanding of the various divisions, and I would say three years before they understand the entire global company with its dynamic strategic business developments. That's why, for me, nine years on a board is just a very good number because then you can contribute quite significantly over time. For specialists, it could be different. They could also be only three to four years of membership because then we really want to know exactly what is needed for the strategic thinking in the area we want a specialist.

Accelerating that learning curve is in the board's best interest, especially where term limits exist. Rigorous onboarding can shorten the time needed for a new director to become effective. Shaun Coles, global director of governance at Santander, highlighted the critical nature of this planning:

> The discipline of succession planning at the board level is critical. This is probably one of the areas that we've invested the most in, ensuring that we have an exceptional understanding of the non-executive director or potential non-executive director population across any skillset/, market, and/or geography. In Spain, the board audit chair can only serve for four years, and then they have to rotate for a minimum of a year before they can come back and do that role again. Planning something like that in terms of ensuring that you have an appropriate internal director on the board is important because assuming the chair role of a committee on day one is not optimal at all. Ensuring that you're planning ahead of the game is critical right through to key roles like the lead independent director, which plays an absolutely critical role in terms of checks and balances and a role within the organization as well as for investors. Having a rigorous discipline on succession is one of the key elements to ensuring that you avoid either a cliff event or scrambling around for directors at the last minute, which is suboptimal in many respects.

The best boards use structured induction programs that help new directors understand the company's operations, culture, and strategic priorities. Coles explained: "It can take time for a non-executive to embed themselves well and to become truly effective. There's a familiarization program that has to happen. I think the rigor around induction, onboarding programs, and ongoing training is really important."

A solid onboarding program goes beyond the standard orientation session. It should include opportunities for new directors to engage with management, tour facilities or key operations, and participate in deep dives into different segments of the business. Sami Atiya, board member of the Switzerland-based testing, inspection, and certification company SGS SA, commented:

> At the beginning, you need to invest time to get to know the business better. It's this dilemma that you don't want to be involved in the operations, but at the same time, you have to understand the business. For me, it is an area where boards and their new directors need to spend more time.

Committee assignments can play an important role. For instance, assigning new directors to key committees, like the audit committee, can be an approach to accelerate their learning and integration. From this chapter's opening example, Rod Adkins explained:

> There is a learning curve when you join a board, and it could be easily two to three years, depending on the company and the industry. That is one reason why all of my new directors at Avnet, where I am chair, need to start on the audit committee. It is the committee where you will learn the most about the company quickly. You start on the audit committee independently of having a financial, risk management, or process management background. The goal is to quickly get that director to a level where they are as productive as possible.

Further, boards can facilitate direct interaction between directors and management outside formal meetings. Adkins continued:

> The other thing I do is director and management engagement as much as possible. Because when you think about the amount of time we spend with management in the boardroom, that is not enough time to get to know the leadership team. Through more management engagement, directors get a deeper appreciation of the company's leadership, which can help them understand business performance and succession planning.

Finally, deep dives into different business units during meetings to educate directors are particularly valuable to new directors. Since many directors do not have experience in a specific industry, bringing them up to speed on the industry the firm is in is important, as Kaj-Erik Relander, board member of Louis Dreyfuss Corporation, SES Satellites, and a number of other privately held corporations, stressed:

> You can't have a substantive discussion on strategy unless you have some idea of what the industry is actually all about. What is important in this industry? What is not? What does good look like? Where's the competition? I don't think boards focus enough on this for new directors. The board and the company should spend more time educating the newly joining board members on what this industry is. There is an educational agenda.

Four questions for designing effective board evaluations[7]

Who performs the evaluation

Evaluations can take the form of an evaluation by the *board chair*, a *self-evaluation* by the board members, an evaluation by the *nomination committee* (consisting of internal and possibly external members, an evaluation by an *external party*, and a *360-degree* evaluation including board members, the leadership team, and key stakeholders. Each option has distinct advantages and disadvantages related to comprehensiveness, objectivity, transparency, and required effort.

What is being evaluated

The evaluation may focus on *skills* of the board and how well they align with future needs, effectiveness, and efficiency of different *board processes* (e.g., meeting preparation, board meeting, committee work) or the quality of different *board outcomes* (e.g., quality of board decisions).

For whom the evaluation is intended

Board evaluations can be purely for the board's *internal use* to inform and develop board practices; they can be designed to be *shared selectively*, for instance, with the leadership team to improve the work of the strategic apex, or they can be utilized as a communication tool with different *stakeholders* (e.g., proxy advisors, shareholders, employees), or they can be designed to allow shareholders to evaluate the board. The intended audience shapes which aspects of board activity receive emphasis.

How the evaluation is carried out

Depending upon the answer to the other three questions, board evaluations may involve the use of *questionnaires, in-depth interviews* with board members and stakeholders, and the *analysis of past decisions*. Equally important is the process for translating findings into tangible *board changes* – potentially involving board composition, committee structure and composition, board processes and practices, and even remuneration of board members. Ideally, board evaluations should also be tied to *development actions* at both the individual and collective levels, such as director training and efforts to reinforce or reshape board culture.

By approaching evaluation, development, and succession planning systematically, boards can become more than just oversight bodies. They can evolve into agile, future-oriented teams capable of guiding their organizations through increasingly complex challenges.

Notes

1. Laurence J. Stybel and Maryanne Peabody, "How Should Board Directors Evaluate Themselves?," *MIT Sloan Management Review* 47, no. 1 (2005).
2. Stybel and Peabody, "How Should Board Directors Evaluate Themselves?"

3. Alessandro Minichilli, Jonas Gabrielsson, and Morten Huse, "Board Evaluations: Making a Fit between the Purpose and the System," *Corporate Governance: An International Review* 15, no. 4 (2007).

4. Jakob Stengel, "Board Succession, Evaluation, and Recruitment: A Global Perspective," in *The Handbook of Board Governance*, ed. Richard Leblanc (Hoboken, NJ: Wiley 2020); Martin Hilb, *New Corporate Governance: Successful Board Management Tools*, 5th ed. (Heidelberg: Springer, 2016).

5. Jeffrey Sonnenfeld, Melanie Kusin, and Elise Walton, "What CEOs Really Think of Their Boards," *Harvard Business Review* 91, no. 4 (2013).

6. Hernandez Game-Changing Strategies for Corporate Boards.

7. For literature on how to design board evaluation see for instance, Alessandro Minichilli, Alessandro Gabrielsson, and Morten Huse, "Board Evaluations: Making a Fit between the Purpose and the System," *Corporate Governance: An International Review* 15, no. 4 (2007); Stybel and Peabody, "How Should Board Directors Evaluate Themselves?"; Stengel, "Board Succession, Evaluation, and Recruitment: A Global Perspective."; Hilb, *New Corporate Governance: Successful Board Management Tools*.

Part III

One size does not fit all

Adapting boards for different contexts

Chapter 8

Board design for private versus publicly listed corporations

Christoph Franz was reflecting on a recent board meeting that focused on how Roche, the Swiss-based pharma giant, could take its sustainability commitments to the next level. Franz has served as board chair of Roche since 2014, following a career in the aviation industry that included CEO of Swiss International Air Lines (2004–2009), deputy CEO of Lufthansa (2009–2011), and finally CEO of Lufthansa (2011–2014). In addition to Roche, Franz has served and continues to serve on the boards of Chugai Pharmaceutical (2017-present), Zurich Insurance (2014–present), Stadler Rail AG (2019–present), and Artemis Holding (2024–present).

Under his stewardship, Roche has continued to expand its global footprint in the pharmaceuticals and diagnostics industries, advanced its personalized healthcare offerings, and maintained strong research and development investments. His tenure has not only been credited with helping Roche sustain its status as a leader in innovation and patient-focused healthcare solutions but also with advancing Roche's global reputation for its sustainability and Environmental, Social, and Governance (ESG) performance. Roche has consistently ranked among the top companies in the pharmaceutical sector for responsible business practices, including in the Dow Jones Sustainability Index.

In our conversation, Franz emphasized how Roche's family-controlled ownership model helps sustain its focus on responsible business practices:

> It's a special situation here at Roche. Firstly, because we are still majority family-owned, in this case the Hoffmann-Oeri family, which has had a

DOI: 10.4324/9781003532200-12

historically very special representative in the person of Luc Hoffmann, who was not only one of the major co-owners and board members but was also someone who placed the topic of nature very much in the foreground in his professional life. An ornithologist by training, he made efforts to preserve the Camargue as a nature park by buying land there and then persuaded the French state to turn it into a regional park. The Camargue, as it exists today, would not exist in this form without him. Based on this experience, he later became one of the co-founders of the World Wildlife Fund (WWF), or World Wildlife Fund for Nature, and made the issue of nature conservation and biodiversity his core concern. And, of course, this also left its mark on his work on the board of directors, with the consequence that Roche was one of the very first companies to set up a Corporate Governance and Sustainability Committee. So, sustainability is not something that has only been around for the last two, three, or even ten years, but has been with us for well over 20 years. And in this committee, we deal with matters of sustainability regularly and very systematically, several times a year, in a wide variety of dimensions.

Franz continued:

And sustainability is not something we just talk about; we also define and measure very concrete goals. At the last board meeting, we took another look at the 25 years of SHE, our Safety, Health, and Environment department, and reviewed what we have achieved. We have reduced chemical waste by 94 percent. We've reduced organic compounds in wastewater by 60 percent, and we've reduced CO_2 produced by ourselves and our suppliers by 80 percent. Organic air pollutants by 87 percent. Same with industrial accidents and energy consumption. Sustainability has been a strategic topic for us for over two decades now.

As discussed in earlier chapters, sustainability is one of the emerging challenges facing many boards. However, as Roche illustrates, it's not something that is new for every company, nor will all boards find it equally difficult or easy to integrate into their governance processes.

More generally, the dual challenge of modern boards – balancing a broader range of topics today with a strong focus on a strategic vision for tomorrow – will manifest differently across various companies depending upon their situation and context. The board diamond will need to be configured differently to suit each organization's unique circumstances. How these challenges take shape, and which responses are feasible, depends on a set of enablers and constraints: ownership, the institutional environment, and the strategic situation the company faces.

In this chapter, we explore the first constraint, the firm's ownership structure. We focus on differences across publicly versus privately owned companies and will distinguish further between widely held, family- or founder-controlled, and private-equity-controlled companies. Each ownership form creates specific allowances and constraints that influence every dimension of the board diamond.

Influence of ownership structure on governance and board design

A company's ownership – whether the general public, an individual or a family, or a private investment organization – has far-reaching effects on governance and board design and thereby shapes the success of the company, as a Nordic board chair noted:

> If an owner is a family or an institution, it can easily destroy a good company if they do not create the right board. The owner's role is to ensure that the company has the relevant board and then set up a clear, understandable, and good governance structure to allow it to function effectively. Because a great board can be completely worthless if the governance isn't clear.

Whether a company is publicly traded on a stock exchange or privately held by individuals or institutions has important implications for the corporate governance rules that apply to the company. Different types of owners, such as founders, families, venture capital or private equity firms, or professional investors such as pension funds, also differ in their expectations, goals, time horizon, and willingness and ability to play an active role in the governance in general and the board in particular.

For simplicity, we focus on comparing three broad groups of owners: family- or founder-controlled firms, private-equity-controlled companies, and widely held public companies (Table 8.1). Representatives of each group often claim superiority for their type of ownership,[1] but we emphasize the implications of each for board design and functionality and highlight the advantages and disadvantages of each model. Rather than one being superior in all situations, we see that boards from each ownership type can learn from the other ownership types[2] to build on their strength while addressing the unique challenges and vulnerabilities for governance that each model poses.

Family- and founder-controlled firms

Some of the world's largest public corporations – including such household names as ABB, Bosch, Ford, LVMH, Meta, Roche, Tesla, Volkswagen, and Walmart – remain at least partially under founder or family control.[3] This control can persist regardless of whether the firm is privately or publicly held, and often, a majority of votes can be secured with less than the majority of shares owned.

Our conversations suggest that family- and founder-controlled firms can offer the best and worst of governance, depending on how family and founder involvement

Table 8.1 Board work in different ownership structures

Governance Model	Advantages	Disadvantages
Family- or founder-controlled	■ Long-term orientation through family or founder ■ Concentrated investor provides owner strategy and oversight ■ Relatively fast decision through concentrated ownership	■ Family issues spill into the business ■ Challenging to align the family on a strategy ■ Challenging to implement the needed strategy change against the family or founder ■ Lack of transparency
PE-controlled	■ Professional investor with a clear strategy ■ Reduced information and compliance requirements compared to public firms ■ Often strong incentives for board members	■ PE partners sideline the rest of board ■ Narrow focus on financial results ■ Often lack of diverse perspectives on the board ■ Lack of transparency
Widely held public	■ Public status requires transparency ■ Allows for diverse perspectives ■ Naturally incorporates all stakeholders	■ Heavy information and compliance requirements ■ Lack of oversight of the board ■ Little direction and support for the board ■ Board members often lack clear incentives

is managed. In these companies, founder and family values and interests can deeply influence strategic decisions, corporate culture, and priorities like sustainability. Families (and, at times, founders) may act as passive owners, investors, stewards, governors, or active operators; each role requires different engagement with the board and executive management.

On the positive side, family- and founder-controlled companies can focus on long-term value creation and sustainability, integrating strong values into the company's purpose and vision. On the negative side, however, family conflict and succession issues can spill over into the business and founders can dominate decision-making on the board. In the worst cases, family or founder control may also come at the expense of other shareholders when they view the firm as their personal asset. Conflicts like those within the Porsche-Piech family at Volkswagen AG or the Swarovski family illustrate how family conflict can spill over to the board, and the resulting board-level discord can hamper strategic decision-making. In both instances, differences in view and personal animosities led to board-level conflicts that paralyzed and endangered the company. A key step to avoiding many of these problems is to create role clarity for the family and to emphasize professional management to prevent nepotism and overstepping of boundaries between family and firm.

Private-equity-controlled firms

Private-equity (PE)-controlled firms are a second type of company where ownership is centralized, which has important implications for governance and board design. Although most PE firms focus on privately held companies, as the name suggests, and may take a public firm they acquire private, some large PE funds, such as KKR or EQT, have gone further by controlling stakes in publicly held firms. With few exceptions, PE firms focus primarily on financial returns, rarely adopting a broader perspective.

Most PE firms hold their investments for five to seven years. More recently, PE firms have started to adapt approaches with longer holding periods, but this is the exception rather than the rule. Generally, the strategy is to grow the portfolio company and improve financial performance so that the firm can be sold to another PE fund, an industrial buyer, or via IPO. Christian Trümpler from Partners Group put it this way:

> PE investors have a strategic approach that starts from the idea that as the institutional owner, with the expertise that we bring in, with the capital that we bring in, we can achieve a strategic transformation with this investment and take this company from A to B and deliver added value. That means the companies on average have to grow twice as fast as they would without us. When you put leverage on these companies, that is just the economic logic behind it. You have to deliver an ambitious growth plan and at the same time generate cash to service your debt. This puts pressure on the system. It creates a dynamic of its own across all levels of governance. You need know-how on how to scale companies, but you also need this PE know-how, because this leveraged buyout dynamic has its very own rules.

In PE-controlled firms, the PE firm's representatives are on the board and typically tend to dominate the board. In fact, in many PE-held companies, the board may serve as a formality that mostly just rubber stamps the decisions made by the firm. However, in better-run PE-controlled companies, the company incentivizes a board of experienced directors who usually have significant personal investments ("skin in the game"), aligning their interests with the firm's financial performance, which leads to a more robust engagement. Erik Huggers, board member at Hexagon and several other privately owned companies and former board member of ProSieben, explained:

> The PE model works best when the chairperson, CEO, and deal team partner meet frequently, have clear objectives, and consistently measure progress against a defined value-creation plan. When a problem arises,

like technology issues, everyone – board members, the CTO, the chair, and the PE partner – joins forces, rolls up their sleeves, leverages their networks, and solves the issues together.

As owners, PE firms provide both capital and expertise. Christian Trümpler added:

> We review financial results once a month. Our investment professionals focus on this; the non-executive directors usually join these reviews. We have everything in one place; it's an app, and everyone has access to it, so the financial figures and everything are transparent. The KPIs, the strategic initiatives, the progress, it's all in the system. And it is a thorough review from a financial and operational perspective.

A key strength of the PE model is the strong alignment of board members' incentives with the owner, propelled by substantial personal investments from directors. PE firms also pride themselves on their capability to drive rapid growth and strategic transformation.

On the downside, PE firms often focus on the short-term, may undervalue topics like sustainability or diversity, and may pursue overly aggressive strategies to deliver quick returns, at times at the cost of sustainable development of the company. Governance in PE-controlled firms has also been criticized as lacking in transparency. As Pauline Van der Meer Mohr, chair of the Dutch semiconductor equipment manufacturer ASM and director of Ahold Delhaize, NN Group, put it:

> In my view, there's an inherent tension between the long-term and the short-term interest of a PE company. For PE companies, their whole business model is that you have an exit plan before you go in. And those action plans, by definition, are never long-term. If you're thinking about a three or five-year exit plan, how can you seriously maintain that you have a superior model for long-term sustainable value creation?

A final point to note on the governance and board design of PE firms is that while they bring professional investment strategies to the board, they can often overlook, or simply ignore, broader stakeholder interests.

Widely held public firms

The third group comprises firms listed on stock exchanges with dispersed ownership. Because no single investor holds a controlling stake, these firms often lack a clear ownership strategy. A Nordic board chair observed:

> There are different ownership structures. The issue is that, in many cases, the way capital is distributed and managed in the Western world is not connected to the responsibility that you need to take as an owner.

There is a complete disconnect between the mutual fund manager and the hedge fund manager regarding what they invest in. Of course, they care about returns, but they have no ability, no toolbox, no mindset, no approach, not even ambition in most cases, to have a view on how the company is managed. They have given up that part of being an owner of a company. They are an asset manager and investor, but not an owner, because they need to keep the flexibility to trade in and out of securities. That is the approach that many take. They don't like to be seen as an active owner because they don't know how to do it.

Boards of widely held public firms must comply with strict regulations and maintain transparency, but often have high degrees of freedom due to weak oversight and control from dispersed shareholders and passive investors. Listing on a stock exchange means adherence to substantial reporting requirements and, in many jurisdictions, mandates around board diversity and stakeholder representation. While these regulations promote accountability, they can also impose a heavy compliance burden, leaving less room for board involvement in strategic planning.

Another pressure point for widely held public firms is the influence exerted by proxy advisors and analysts that can push boards toward standardized governance practices. These proxy advisors often exert influence using a template-based analysis of the business, sometimes without a deep understanding of the specifics of the company. This easily leads to a tick-box approach. As Riet Cadonau, experienced board chair and director and current director at the Zehnder Group AG, stated:

> As a listed company, we are also followed by people who either have little time for in-depth analysis or do not have the necessary experience. I am referring to proxy advisors, for example. If you are a mid-cap company, you are sometimes evaluated by juniors. And if you look at today's analysts, I think they have a challenging job because cross-subsidizing these roles is no longer possible. Today, an analyst sometimes must cover dozens of companies, which is hardly feasible given today's complexity. So, companies are sometimes followed by people who have a lot of influence in a listed environment, but hardly have the necessary resources to be able to evaluate you with the necessary depth.

Christoph Mohn, chair of the board of German Media giant Bertelsmann, shared a similar view:

> A significant challenge is that many publicly traded companies are overly influenced by proxy advisors, leading them to adopt a tick-box mentality. The thinking often becomes: "ISS wants us to fulfill criteria A, B, C, D, E, so we'll do it – whether it makes sense for us or not. If we don't comply, we risk facing difficulties, and we'll have to justify our decision not to."

The lack of an active owner who provides clear guidance and oversight may also lead to self-referential boards with a limited sense of direction. Without a clear owner strategy, boards may have too high a degree of freedom in choosing a strategy and their approach to governance. Greg Poux-Guillaume, board chair of Medmix, highlighted this risk:

> Large publicly-traded companies can become a vacuum of control. They often have a very fragmented shareholder structure where nobody speaks up. Your biggest shareholders end up being institutional shareholders, who vote with the proxy advisors because it is the simplest solution. In that case, the board has little accountability because you're not reporting to anybody. As a CEO or board chair, you can essentially be in control. It's divide and conquer. In effect, it becomes your company.

Widely held public firms also generally discourage directors from holding substantial personal stakes, in part due to modern definitions of independence. This can dilute the long-term alignment of directors with the company's performance.

Time horizons and strategic focus in different ownership structures

One of the central differences across the three ownership types is their varying time horizon and strategic focus. A board member of multiple European corporations highlighted:

> There is a fundamental challenge with the time horizon. Every owner has his or her own time horizon. And I think that it is very difficult sometimes to discuss projects that will be a long-term decision beyond a potential exit date for an owner.

Family-owned firms usually prioritize long-term goals and often include non-financial goals to guide their strategy, while PE-owned firms concentrate on short-to medium-term financial returns and a clear exit window due to their investment cycles. Publicly held companies contend with short-term market pressures from analysts and quarterly reporting, even as they attempt to maintain longer-range strategic perspectives.

Family- and founder-controlled firms

Family or founder-owned companies tend to take a generational view, enabling decisions that emphasize continuity, legacy, and values. Founders or family board members bring a long-term perspective, focusing on enduring value creation and intergenerational continuity. Family-controlled firms and other firms under the control of an individual shareholder (founder or anchor shareholder, for example) often find it easier to resist short-term market pressures and instead focus on enduring value creation. Christoph Mohn, chair of the board of German Media giant Bertelsmann, noted:

> As a family-owned business, we enjoy a distinct advantage: the ability to think long-term. We can make decisions without the pressure of constantly deferring to proxy advisors because we have the flexibility to plan across generations. This allows us to pursue the best solution for our situation, regardless of whether it's currently in vogue. Naturally, we must adhere to the legal and regulatory requirements of the market, but overall, we have more freedom to make strategic decisions.

Given the support by the controlling family or founder, boards in these firms are able to make decisions with a long-term outlook rather than chasing yearly or quarterly results. They also may find it easier to pursue strategies that may not yield immediate returns but may require long-term consistent investment compared to firms that face a diverse set of shareholders that they need to convince. Having a controlling family or founder can provide important stability and enable the company to engage in projects that may be difficult in a widely held or purely financial-investor-controlled company. Andreas Umbach, former chair of Swiss-based SIG Group AG, underscored this advantage:

> Having an anchor shareholder on the board is generally a huge advantage. Especially when times are not so good, or if you want to do something longer term or in a large M&A deal, and you know that you've already secured 10, 20, 30 percent of the votes. That's a huge advantage.

As the Roche example at the beginning of this chapter showed, family or founder-controlled companies may also prioritize goals other than financial, and the board members of these firms also enjoy more flexibility to drive investment in initiatives such as environmental conservation. In many family-owned firms, topics like sustainability and social responsibility have been central long before they appeared on the agenda of boards of public firms. Given that family firms often have a tighter connection to the communities in which they operate, community responsibility is a natural extension of their business activities. For instance, a board chair of a large European family business explained:

> The family has always been very concerned and aware of its responsibility vis-à-vis the towns where we operate and their citizens. We have invested a significant amount of money in young people, supporting sports, and in infrastructure such as kindergartens and educational

centers for underprivileged children. We practically built two different towns for the workers. We created vacation places for the children of the workers. There was always a strong sense of social responsibility towards the town and its people.

Yet, along with these benefits comes the potential for emotional entrenchment. A dominant family voice on the board may complicate strategic pivots if emotional or legacy considerations overshadow business realities. Family firms often find it difficult to abandon strategic directions that carry emotional weight for the family, or when business needs and family interests collide.

In addition, family firms often prioritize long-term and intergenerational interests, which can lead to conservative decision-making and risk aversion.[4] When necessary strategic changes conflict with family preferences, this cautious approach may create resistance. As a result, boards in family-controlled firms frequently face challenges when trying to implement strategic changes that the controlling family opposes. Similarly, an anchor shareholder can become a constraint or even threat to the board, as Andreas Umbach noted:

> Having an anchor shareholder on the board is great when your interests are aligned but it can become a bit difficult if the person representing the shareholder plays this off and creates a latent threat in the room. That can become counterproductive.

Private-equity-controlled firms

Where family-controlled firms think in generations, PE-controlled firms think in periods of three to five or, at most, seven years. The short holding period translates into a short time horizon in board decision-making and implies a strong emphasis on short to medium-term financial results, often at the expense of long-term sustainability. This focus can be a powerful driver for near-term performance, but may sacrifice long-term results and competitiveness.

An undeniable strength of the short-term focus is that it instills a strong sense of urgency on the board, prompting quick corrective actions. Underperformance is addressed swiftly due to the significant impact of any delay on investment returns, and firms drive results aggressively to meet exit timelines. For instance, Olof Faxander, Senior Partner at Nordic Capital Advisors, explained:

> When you have underperformance or any kind of challenges, action takes longer in a public company than in the PE world. I mean, one lost year for us is 20 per cent of our holding period. It's a lot of time lost there. I mean, one-fifth, it's difficult to catch up on that. And in a public environment, things can slip for quite some time before re-election, so it may take longer before anyone reacts.

He continued:

> We're valuing the company every quarter and looking at the perfor-
> mance. And it's quite a Darwinist environment in the PE world. The
> short time horizon is a much harder push in the PE environment. This
> means that focusing on results becomes clearer and we drive for results
> harder.

Some PE firms are adopting longer holding periods, recognizing the benefits of sus-
tained growth, often by rolling over investments into new funds to extend ownership. A PE-firm partner outlined this new logic:

> The industry and our limited partners that give us money are changing.
> "In three to five years, we're going to sell the company" used to be a reli-
> gion. Our investors, who give us money, are more open than they used to
> be to us owning a company longer. So we may say, "Listen, we know you
> want some returns, but this is a great company on a good trajectory. Let
> us sell half of it and keep the other half for another five years." So, we are
> increasingly looking at seven to eight years. Most of us are running multi-
> ple different funds, so we may sell the company from one fund to another.
> "In fund III, I have this investment; it's five years old, and it's a great
> company. It's been a good investment for the fund III investors. But we
> love the company, let me sell it to my fund V." So, I'm selling it basically
> to myself. Usually, there's a high correlation between the limited partners
> we have in fund III and the limited partners in fund V. So what we're
> fundamentally saying is, "This is a good company that has like a 20-year
> runway. None of us should get out at this point, let's find ways to keep it."

How widely this change will diffuse in the PE world and how it will affect governance in PE firms remains to be seen.

Widely held public firms

The time horizon and strategic focus for widely held public firms are often less clear,
given that their shareholder base may hold widely differing expectations. Some
shareholders, like family owners or anchor shareholders, may hold a long-term view
of the firm, while other investors, like hedge funds or activist investors, may have
extremely short-term time horizons, and analysts could push for a focus on quarterly
results. Johannes Huth, former partner at KKR, senior independent director of Coty
Inc., and director at Axel Springer, summarized this difficulty:

> In a listed company, it is also not quite clear which perspective the board
> should take. A long-term fund has one perspective as the owner, a hedge

fund that wants to turn shares has a different perspective as the owner, and individual shareholders have a third perspective. That makes it more difficult for a listed board. They have to evaluate these perspectives and then develop a strategy that satisfies all.

Similarly, proxy advisors that influence governance practices may emphasize short-term compliance over long-term strategy. Boards of widely held firms, therefore, often struggle with balancing short- and long-term goals, a skill that is particularly important in modern governance, as we highlighted in the first chapters of this book.

Board composition, diversity, and engagement across ownership structures

Board composition also varies significantly among different ownership structures. Whether it's the inclusion of family members, PE partners, or diverse directors in widely held firms, these factors can deeply influence board performance and governance quality.

Family- and founder-controlled firms

In family-controlled firms, founders and family members may play different roles, ranging from passive owners, investors, stewards, and governors, all the way to active operators.[5] Some of these roles are compatible with a seat on the board, while others are less so, and therefore, understanding the essence of these roles is essential to enhance governance by clarifying expectations and avoiding possible conflicts that impact board dynamics.

When family members join the board, they can help align family values and shareholder interests. They may also contribute to strategic resilience by bringing unique insights, ensuring continuity, and integrating the family's time horizon into strategic decisions. To fully realize these benefits, however, they need to balance family preferences with their fiduciary duties to the company. It is, therefore, important to appoint family members based on expertise rather than lineage. Selection based on expertise, combined with proper training, ensures family board members fulfill their roles effectively.[6]

In particular, regarding the board chair role, it is essential that appointments are made based on qualifications and the ability to meet professional requirements rather than family membership. Stefan Nöken, a member of the board at Vaillant, Vorwerk, and Peri Group, put it succinctly:

> In a family-controlled company, it is not automatically the best solution for a family member to be board chair simply because he or she bears the name. You have to ask yourself whether the professional, personal, and

leadership requirements are met. But it takes a certain degree of personal greatness to say: Yes, it's better for the company if I'm on the board but not the chairman, as there are people who can fulfill this role better.

Also, founders on the board can be a mixed blessing for the company. While founders typically hold deep experience of the business that can be valuable for the board and often drive forward-looking topics such as entrepreneurship and innovation on the board agenda, they are frequently also control-oriented and may dominate the board discussions and decision-making. This may make it more difficult for other directors to make value-adding contributions.

Private-equity-controlled firms

In PE-controlled firms, it is common practice for PE partners to sit on the board, bringing deep knowledge of the company from due diligence processes. While in many companies, the PE partner might serve as board chair, this should be considered not good practice since most PE partners lack the operational experience to be effective in this role. Instead, an independent board should be hired with recognized expertise in the business to select the board chair. In addition, PE firms typically recruit a number of independent directors based on specific expertise aligned with the company's strategic goals, as Christian Trümpler from Partners Group noted:

> The core element of this framework is actually how we, as owners, define, agree and support strategy together with the management teams of these investments. And this is where the board has a strategic role, and therefore the selection of these members is of strategic importance...We ask ourselves, who do we bring in to drive which value lever? And that can often be complementary know-how, things that you may not have covered in the management team but want to drive through the board.

Board tenures in PE-controlled firms tend to be shorter, as a PE-firm partner observed:

> PE companies are being sold on average every three to seven years, frequently after four or five. And every time, the boards are wiped out and reconstituted. Typically, the board doesn't travel along to the next owner. So you never have somebody who's on a board for ten years, or 15 years.

In addition, independent directors usually have substantial personal financial stakes, aligning their interests with company performance. Therefore, directors are expected to exhibit a high level of engagement and frequent interactions beyond formal board meetings. Erik Huggers, board member at Hexagon and several other privately-owned companies and former board member of ProSieben, noted: "Public boards can sometimes be about prestige; PE boards are about personal commitment.

Joining a PE-owned company board means investing significantly in terms of time and money, which tends to create a stronger alignment with company success."

While these arrangements encourage active board participation, when coupled with PE firms' tendency to repeatedly select the same individuals they know and trust, boards in the PE world often lack diversity. Efforts are therefore needed to broaden the pool of candidates and incorporate more diverse perspectives. A PE-firm partner highlighted that PE boards often have to work harder to achieve diversity:

> It's pretty common that you would find independent board members in a PE environment that might be on two or three boards for that particular PE firm. This makes it harder for PE firms to achieve diversity on the board. PE firms need to try harder. It might be like, "It's just easy to hire Joe to be on my board because he has already been on a bunch of boards for me. Where Mary down the street is a good candidate, but I don't know her and need to work harder to vet her." So it is not so much a question that you wouldn't have people who are qualified, but you may have to look harder or longer.

In addition to the higher effort required, increasing diversity may also force PE firms to rethink concepts such as "skin-in-the-game" as the PE-firm partner continued:

> In a diverse board, where you have diversity in economic background, gender, I think the challenge would be to define what "skin in the game" means. You could discuss the concept of a "meaningful investment," but for one person, that might be 20,000 dollars, and for someone else, that might be two million. What's meaningful to people depends on their circumstances. Obviously, that could get complicated to administer, but I think conceptually it could work.

Publicly held firms

In widely held corporations, the focus of conversations regarding board composition and selection of directors is often on the independence and diversity of directors. For regulators and proxy advisors, director independence is paramount, and significant shareholdings among directors are typically discouraged by these groups. As a result, directors may be less of an expert in the business of the company they oversee, and their incentives may be less aligned with company performance. As a result, board members tend to be less engaged and involved in day-to-day activities than in PE-held firms. In fact, where director engagement in day-to-day matters is often seen as a strength in PE-controlled firms, in publicly held corporations, there is a stronger distinction between the executive team and the board. Public boards could learn something from PE boards about increasing engagement and aligning director incentives with company performance.

On the upside, in widely held public firms, greater public scrutiny and regulatory requirements have driven diversity in gender, ethnicity, and experience, and the boards have begun to leverage this diversity into better decision-making. In this case, it is PE and family-controlled firms that could learn something about leveraging diversity for good governance from public corporations.

Decision-making processes and governance structures across ownership structures

Ownership types also affect how decisions are made and how boards are structured. Family-controlled firms may face unique challenges due to family dynamics influencing decisions. PE-owned firms often centralize decision-making among a small circle of key individuals. Public companies, meanwhile, adhere to more rigid governance protocols. Each of these models faces different hurdles in adapting to modern governance demands.

Family- and founder-controlled firms

In family-and founder-controlled firms and to some extent also in other firms with a dominant anchor investor, decision-making may be driven by family priorities or the priorities of the anchor investor rather than strictly by the board's sense of what is in the best interest of the company. In other words, boards are at risk of engaging in realpolitik and deciding what seems possible rather than what is perceived as best for the company. This approach can easily paralyze the board, especially when there are factions and conflicts in the controlling family. Kaj-Erik Relander, board member of Louis Dreyfuss Corporation, SES Satellites, and a number of other privately held corporations, explained:

> In family-controlled firms, e.g., in Asian culture, quite often the controlling family may treat the board as advisors rather than as decision-makers. As a board member, you need to decide for yourself if you can square that with your understanding of the fiduciary role.

To enable the board to respond to the dual challenges of modern governance and create the agility that is necessary to respond to discontinuous changes, family firms need to have clarity on the role of the family versus the board, the goals of both, and make a distinction between family governance and corporate governance. Good practice is to establish mechanisms like family trusts or councils to manage family-related issues clearly outside of the company governance, so that any board representation on the board projects a family-wide view. A critical function of these councils is to create a defined owner strategy[7] that explicitly outlines purpose, goals, and boundary conditions and can enable a structured strategy discourse. Kaj-Erik

Relander, board member of Louis Dreyfuss Corporation, SES Satellites, and a number of other privately held corporations, explained:

> You can tie the whole concept of board design around a theory of ownership strategies. Without an ownership strategy, it's difficult to design a board. For a family company, the long-term ownership strategy may be more focused on wealth preservation and slow but lower-risk building of wealth, and for the family legacy to survive over many generations. The owner, the chairperson, or a combination of the two needs to make sure that these basic elements are in place. And that can be broadly defined. It can include ESG – it is not limited to financial value – but could also include societal value. Families may emphasize that one of the important things is to engage the family members in the business. Or their most important thing is survival or prosperity development for the family.

Stefan Nöken, a member of the board at Vaillant, Vorwerk, and Peri Group, added:

> There is a big difference between widely-held public companies and family-run companies because the owner strategy provides a precise framework for the board of directors. If the owners are families who have clear views of the long-term family agenda, what is important to them, and what their expectations are, then that provides a valuable framework for the board. This is not usually the case with widely-held companies. There may be one or two major investors at the shareholders' meeting, but they are usually primarily involved and interested in the financial aspects of the company.

Founders on the board can often play an outsized role in the decision-making. While in some companies like Meta or Alphabet, founders hold a large share of the voting rights, even when founders no longer hold the majority of shares, it is often difficult for the board to make decisions against their will, given their strong relationships with stakeholders within and outside the company. Founders may, therefore, become an obstacle to change when the board needs to drive the organization into a direction that is not aligned with the founder's preferences.

Private-equity-controlled firms

By contrast, in PE-controlled companies, when compared with public firms (either widely held or family-controlled), the board has, at least nominally, more power in setting the agenda as a PE-firm partner noted:

> The balance of power between management and the board around things like setting the agenda for board meetings and what's going to

be discussed, are very different. The board of a PE-owned company has much more power and control over the management team. Because there is the owner on the board, who can say: "We own this company and these are the three things we want to talk about." Boards can be way more directive about board meeting content, whereas public company boards are much more consuming of what the management team gives them.

One common model of decision-making in PE-held firms is that decisions are made by the CEO, the board chair, and the PE partner overseeing the investment. This inner circle often meets much more frequently than the full board. It prepares and often de facto makes the decisions, relegating the full board to a formality without real decision-making authority. For instance, a Nordic PE partner described this structure:

> We thought how we can speed up the discussion and give the CEO counterparts to discuss. We developed an instrument that consists of the CEO, the chairman, and the owner's representative. It has no decision-making power. It's not the second board. It's rather a sounding board comprising these three individuals to help the CEO, to discuss and debate, to deal with tricky things, and basically to be an advisor to the CEO. But also gives the CEO the certainty of having the backing of the chairman, who leads the board, and the owner when going to the board. In some cases, they talk once a week. So it is like a shadow board, you could say, but there are no decision-making powers attached to it.

The advantage of this approach is that it can enable rapid action, allows firm alignment of decisions with the objectives of the PE company, and often involves less formal decision-making. However, this comes at the cost of a lack of transparency, reduced checks and balances, and a potential for sidelining independent directors who are outside of the inner circle, and, potentially, it ignores the interests of minority owners.

While these mechanisms, in theory, may not be designed to have any formal decision-making powers, in practice, in many organizations, they imply that decision-making shifts from the board into this inner circle, leaving the board as a formal mechanism that rubber-stamps the proposals of the inner circle. Greg Poux-Guillaume remarked: "The problem with many of the PE boards is that a lot of discussions are taking place outside of the board, and the board itself is a rubber-stamping exercise."

This risk is particularly high when individuals in the inner circle have a certain amount of ego, as is frequent in PE, and they do not perceive the need to involve others in decisions and ignore the board. In the worst cases, significant decisions are made solely by the PE partners. Unfortunately, some PE firms, or at least some individuals in them, still view ownership rights in a way that ignores the roles and rights of other stakeholders – a theory of the firm that dates back to the 1960s but is no longer appropriate today.

To align with modern governance expectations, PE boards must adopt transparent processes and robust checks and balances, including lessons from public boards. Here, PE firms should look to and learn from public firms that have long instituted more transparent decision-making processes and structures as a counterforce to overbearing individuals.

Widely held public firms

Where PE firms may overcentralize decision-making to an inner circle, widely held public firms often focus on strict adherence to regulatory requirements and formal governance protocols, given the public exposure of directors and the liability risks that arise from not following due process. On the positive side, this may lead to decision-making processes that are more structured and have a greater emphasis on compliance and transparency. On the negative side, such decision-making processes can become slow and overly formal, in particular in large boards that meet only infrequently and at times can suffer from a lack of engagement from the board members. Large boards can feel procedural and too little focused on strategy. Here, public boards could take cues from well-managed PE firms' more active engagement and strategic involvement

A second challenge in widely held public firms is that board decision-making might get disconnected from owners, given that widely dispersed owners have too little information and no credible mechanism to have their voice heard by a board that willfully ignores them. This is especially so where there is a risk of a dominant CEO and leadership team or a power-oriented board chair consolidating their control in the absence of active shareholders. For instance, a board chair of a large European corporation recalled a problematic experience:

> The worst board I attended was [NAME] because the chairman used to call every single member of the board before the board meeting. When you came to the board meeting, everybody knew how he had to vote. And those board members liked the job. It was not difficult, and it was well-paid, so they all accepted the decisions of the chairman. We never discussed anything on the board with different opinions. The time for questions was limited; he didn't want more than 15 minutes for any subject. It was a waste of time. A rubber-stamping exercise.

Such scenarios underscore why widely held public firms must devise mechanisms to prevent dominance by a single individual and to better incorporate genuine shareholder perspectives.

Some implications of ownership models

Our research underscores the profound impact of ownership structure on board governance, design, and effectiveness. Whether family-controlled, PE-owned, or publicly held, each configuration carries unique qualities that influence board composition, decision-making, and strategic priorities. Recognizing these differences is critical for crafting governance practices that align with a company's ownership context and strategic aims.

By addressing each ownership model's specific challenges – and capitalizing on its strengths – boards can fulfill their fiduciary duties more effectively and contribute to long-term organizational success.

Practical considerations for board chairs

In addition to the issues already discussed for board chairs, the differences arising from ownership models imply the need to engage in an open dialogue with all types of owners, whether they are family members, PE firms, or public shareholders. The goal is to understand expectations, align on strategy, and clarify time horizons. Ronnie Leten, board chair of Epiroc AB, former chair of Ericsson and Electrolux, and former member of the board of AB SKF, explained:

> As a board chair, I need to understand an investor's expectations. If I buy a share, what do I want? I want the share to pay a normal dividend and for it to grow constantly over a long period. Do I expect that it will go up 60 per cent in one year? No, because that's speculative and not sustainable. If it does go up 60 per cent, my question will be: "What about next year? Is this something that I want to keep? Will it drop down?" Then there are the activists. At Ericsson, we had one that you can call an activist. My approach has been to go and talk to them, and I want to understand what they want and what they mean. I said to them, "We have a mutual project to make the company stronger for all of us, but in the long run." They agreed so we could work through our differences in views. And I must say, most of the time when we sit together and talk about what they have seen and heard, I can only agree. But of course, if you have a shareholder who pushes you to have a result that is not sustainable but speculative, and I cannot work with them.

Practical consideration for the board as a whole

Governance structures and processes should be tailored to the ownership model, yet still meet high standards of accountability and transparency. Boards should look beyond their ownership type to adopt effective practices used elsewhere.

Practical considerations for individual board members

For individual board members, the differences across ownership models highlight the need to focus on upholding their fiduciary duties to the company and all its stakeholders. Balancing various interests appropriately is often a challenge in the high-powered, high-pressure situations that directors face on different boards. The tension between different stakeholder interests calls for balance, integrity, and a clear ethical stance.

By focusing on these themes, boards can navigate the complexities associated with different ownership structures, improve their governance practices, and better fulfill their roles in guiding their organizations toward success.

Notes

1. S. Meister and R. Palkhiwala, "The Rise of 'Governance Correctness': How Public Markets Have Lost Entrepreneurial Ground to Private Equity" (Baar: Partnersgroup, 2018).
2. Jeffrey M. Cohn, "What Boards of Public Companies Can Learn from Private Equity," *HBR.org*, *Harvard Business Review*, February 12, 2024, https://hbr.org/2024/02/what-boards-of-public-companies-can-learn-from-private-equity.
3. A classic study on the share of family firms among the largest companies in a country finds that in most countries the share of family-controlled companies among the 20 largest companies ranges between 20 percent and 40 percent. See Rafael La Porta, Florencio Lopez-de-Silanes, and Andrei Shleifer, "Corporate Ownership around the World," *Journal of Finance* 54, no. 2 (1999). More recent evidence confirms that family-controlled firms continue to be a major force among the large public and private enterprises in many economies. See https://familybusinessindex.com/ for a list of the largest family businesses globally.
4. Randall Morck and Bernard Yeung, "Family Control and the Rent–Seeking Society," *Entrepreneurship Theory and Practice* 28, no. 4 (2004).
5. Nick Di Loreto, "5 Kinds of Ownership Roles in a Family Business," *HBR.org*, *Harvard Business Review*, March 22, 2024, https://hbr.org/2024/03/5-kinds-of-ownership-roles-in-a-family-business.
6. Ivan Lansberg, "Why Your Family Business Needs Family Members on the Board," *HBR.org*, *Harvard Business Review*, September 22, 2022, https://hbr.org/2022/09/why-your-family-business-needs-family-members-on-the-board.
7. Nicolai J. Foss, Peter G. Klein, Lasse B. Lien, Thomas Zellweger, and Todd Zenger, "Ownership Competence," *Strategic Management Journal* 42, no. 2 (2021); William Schulze and Thomas Zellweger, "Property Rights, Owner-Management, and Value Creation," *Academy of Management Review* 46, no. 3 (2021); Thomas Zellweger, *Managing the Family Business* (Cheltenham: Edward Elgar, 2017).

Chapter 9

Board design in different strategic situations

How much does a company's situation influence the design and workings of its board? It is well established that the work of the leadership team and, therefore, the requirements for the type of CEO[1] and their leadership team[2] fundamentally vary in different organizational situations. We argue that the same holds true for the board: the configuration of the five dimensions of the board diamond depends upon the organization's context and circumstances.

Consider the example of Sulzer in 2022, which illustrates how a board's role can change dramatically during a crisis. Sulzer, the Swiss-based industrial engineering and manufacturing firm specializing in fluid engineering with sustainable pumping, agitation, mixing, separation, and application technologies, underwent a period of change between 2020 and 2022. After the COVID-19 pandemic hit, the company was hit by market declines in the oil and gas sector, which forced it to focus sharply on cost reduction. At the same time, it was also in the midst of a strategic refocusing, which culminated in 2021 with the spin-off of its Medmix division into a separate, publicly-listed company. In late 2021, there was a change in leadership, with Frederic Lalande replacing CEO Greg Poux-Guillaume. And early 2022 saw the appointment of a new board chair, Suzanne Thoma.

Sulzer had been under close scrutiny for several years due to the stake held in the company by the Russian Renova Group (led by Viktor Vekselberg). In 2018, it had repurchased about five million of its own shares from Renova to reduce Vekselberg's influence and to sidestep US sanctions. However, following the Russian invasion of Ukraine, any business linked to Russian investors was thrust back into the spotlight. Sulzer, with manufacturing, sales, and service operations in Russia – a major market for industrial and pumping equipment in oil, gas, and other heavy industries – had

DOI: 10.4324/9781003532200-13

to make complex decisions about suspending, restructuring, or selling its Russian operations. These decisions affected revenue streams and strategic planning at a time when the company was also facing increasing pressure from investors and stakeholders to comply with new sanctions, maintain high corporate governance standards, and protect Sulzer's global reputation. Meanwhile, broader market volatility in Europe raised concerns over supply chains, credit risk, and contractual obligations.

Against this backdrop, the board decided to step in and take control of the situation at the time (2022). Thoma explained:

> We then had a crisis situation where the board was very active because the situation went beyond the capacity of management. The board was then like a task force. The members had individual tasks, or at least co-sponsor topics with the executives, but they were in charge. We were a little bit like an executive committee for the special issues that we had taken control of.

Facing mounting pressure through 2022, Sulzer's board further consolidated its control by separating from Lalande as CEO and naming Thoma as executive chair. This move reflected the board's desire for unified leadership amid challenging circumstances. In her dual role, Thoma combined her responsibilities as chair of the board with active operational management authority. Changes were also made to the executive team to streamline decision-making and navigate ongoing sanctions and geopolitical uncertainties. Thoma's dual role allowed for quicker strategic pivots and direct board-level oversight of operational matters – a necessity in the light of legal and regulatory complexities arising from the sanctions.

This very hands-on approach of the board and its executive chair helped Sulzer restore confidence among its investors and business partners and navigate back to a period of calm.

Tailoring board design to the company's specific situation

While corporate governance codices and proxy advisor templates often suggest a one-size-fits-all approach, we argue that the design of a board must be tailored to each company's unique situation. For instance, Kaj-Erik Relander, board member of Louis Dreyfuss Corporation, SES Satellites, and a number of other privately held corporations, explained how the role of the board might depend very much on the specific situation and history of the company:

> What the board can do depends on the company situation. It depends on the role of the chair and the relationship between the chair and the CEO. You can't force a discussion on topics that don't align with the

circumstances. It is quite often actually the history of the company that determines what you can discuss. On one board I served on, the board acted traditionally as an advisor to the CEO, and the CEO made all decisions. Ultimately, the management paid no attention to the board. In another company, I have a very good executive team that says, "My job here is to maximize the opportunity in this particular space that I am in. My board will help me define what is the relevant space for me, and then I'll maximize that opportunity. My owners are fine with this because it puts the share price up, and I send them dividends." The working of these two boards is totally different.

Boards must be tailored to reflect the company's unique situation, strategic challenges, industry context, and stage of development, and the board leadership needs to be aligned with all of these. Customization ensures that the board possesses the necessary skills, expertise, and dynamics to guide the company effectively. This does not imply an anything-goes approach but rather a well-considered design strategy that takes unique circumstances into consideration and a leadership approach that adjusts to the situation at hand.

Situational board design begins with a thorough analysis of the company's current and future challenges and opportunities in its environment. In addition to the general challenges of corporate governance outlined at the beginning of this book, industry, geography, and company-specific challenges and opportunities also need to be identified. It is in light of these factors that the board should define the skills needed going forward and identify and recruit board members with expertise in the areas that are critical to address the challenges and capture opportunities. A situational approach to board design also implies that regular replacements should be made to at least part of the board, which should be staffed with individuals who, in addition to traditional board member skills, possess the specialized skills required to address specific strategic needs.

Given that it is often difficult to bring individuals with specific expertise fast enough onto the board to address emerging topics an alternative may be to bring them onto a relevant committee without making them full members of the board (at least initially). Whether this option is possible depends on the nature of the committee. Committees with delegated authority (audit, compensation, nominating/governance committees in a public company, for example) are typically required by corporate governance rules to consist exclusively of board members (see the SEC requirements in the US, for instance, or equivalent regulations elsewhere). In contrast, optional or temporary committees (such as strategy, technology, or innovation committees) often include non-board members if the committee's role is mostly advisory and does not exercise the board's legal authority. The exact rules in this respect vary by jurisdiction. Further limitations may arise from a company's bylaws that may explicitly allow or disallow non-board members on committees. A solution to this could be advisory boards, which often have less stringent rules.

There are several implications to consider in a situational approach to board design. First, it implies a willingness (for larger boards) to accommodate additional skills. Some board members we talked to suggested going so far as to temporarily overstaff the board to provide additional support during periods of significant growth or transformation.

Secondly, a situational approach to board design implies a horses-for-courses philosophy, where directors temporarily join a board to help the company overcome specific challenges, as is often the case with PE-controlled companies. Debbie Hewitt, chair of England's Football Association, noted:

> I think it is wrong to say every board should have a certain set of skills. Because every company is different, the directors' skills are likely to be different. Board composition must start situationally and with the context of the specific business. Across every sector, you have got startups; you have very well-established businesses; you have big businesses and small businesses; you have international businesses. I am a believer in horses for courses. The skill set of the directors should reflect the context of the business and its strategic priorities.

Thirdly, a situational approach to board design requires a strong focus on proactive planning and succession management. To remain relevant and effective, boards need to proactively plan board composition by deriving their skills matrix from future strategic challenges and the company's long-term strategic vision. Based on this skills matrix, the board should then identify potential board members early on as we discussed before. Stefan Nöken, a member of the board at Vaillant, Vorwerk, and Peri Group, explained:

> I think it's crucial that the company's situation is reflected in the board. It's not enough to cover the traditional domains – to have a lawyer, an engineer, and a salesperson. You have to go a lot deeper and ask: "What is the company dealing with today and tomorrow? What are the major strategic challenges? What are the changes in the economy, in competition, in customer behavior, in technology, and in business models? What are the changes in the labor market? What are the changes in value orientation that go hand in hand with the new generation?" You have to think about what kind of expertise you need to address these questions. There is no doubt that you need digital & AI expertise today, for example. I don't think there's any company that says it's none of my business. You need expertise in the area of sustainability. More than ever, you need expertise in cultural and employee development.

Also, in the situational approach to board design that we advocate, board design needs to achieve a balance between continuity and change. While boards need to renew, adjust to, or even anticipate changes in the environment and bring in new perspectives, they also need to keep a focus on stability and retain the institutional knowledge that creates resilience to withstand severe crises.

A situational approach to the board – and the bigger change it implies – needs to be supported by board dynamics. Adjusting to ever-changing situations requires an even stronger focus on collaboration within the board. As a result, they must focus even more on open communication, trust, and mutual respect among members.

The risks of misaligned board composition, structure, and involvement

A board that is not aligned with the company's strategic situation can impede transformation efforts. Members can resist change, delay initiatives, or completely undermine transformation efforts by remaining anchored to past approaches and successes. When the design of a board is not aligned with the firm's strategic situation, it could lack the necessary expertise and fail to provide appropriate guidance during critical periods, thereby exacerbating problems. Eric Huggers, board member at Hexagon and several other privately owned companies and former board member of ProSieben, provided an example:

> A mismatch between board expertise and company strategy is a serious issue. Take traditional broadcasters disrupted by Netflix, YouTube, or TikTok – digital transformation is essential. Yet many boards, dominated by finance-focused members prioritizing dividends, lack understanding of technology, culture, and talent needs. As a result, boards set narrow financial KPIs, harming long-term success.

A misaligned board tends to fixate on obsolete metrics, for example, by overemphasizing conventional financial indicators that can stifle innovation and hinder adaptation to strategic shifts in the business environment. This narrow focus may also prevent the board from detecting early warning signs of emerging crises. As a result, it operates reactively, responding to crisis situations by over-involving itself in day-to-day operations, undermining management authority, blurring governance lines, and creating confusion and inefficiency.

While it may be temporarily possible to run the company from the board level, as we saw in the case of Sulzer at the beginning of this chapter, this is not healthy or sustainable in the long run for any company, since it removes the necessary checks and balances of corporate governance. Without proactively adapting the board's roles, composition, structure, and processes, it is more difficult to maintain the clear boundaries that are essential for effective governance and organizational stability, and allow the board to support management without interfering in operational responsibilities.

Therefore, we advise that boards critically assess the alignment of the board design with evolving strategic needs at regular intervals and be prepared to adjust the board composition, structure, and dynamics to avoid misalignment.

Adapting the board to different stages of company growth and maturity

In this book, we focus on three strategic situations relevant to many companies: Growth, maturity, and crisis. In this subsection, we juxtapose the differences between growth and maturity, while in the next section, we focus on crisis situations. Our focus here is on later-stage growth companies, which are often owned by PE firms, rather than those in the early stages of growth, such as those backed by venture capital, which face different types of challenges.[3]

Companies at different stages of their lifecycle face fundamentally different strategic challenges, and these differences should be reflected in the roles of the board, its composition, structure, and dynamics.

Board roles

During the growth stage, the board's primary purpose and role are to help navigate rapid growth, overcome early challenges, manage transitions during different stages of growth, and pivot quickly when required. When a company is in a growth period, boards are often more hands-on, playing an active, sometimes operational role. They provide strategic guidance and support to management teams. Since the requirements for managing companies of different sizes fundamentally differ,[4] the leadership team and CEO may lack experience, which means the board must play an important role in filling in the gaps of expertise; not only guiding the leadership team but also identifying when replacements may need to be made. Boards of PE-controlled companies, which we discussed in Chapter 8, are often designed with this idea in mind.

As a company matures, the board's role shifts increasingly to strategic oversight, risk management, regulatory compliance, and ensuring robust internal controls. They take a more hands-off approach, focusing on strategic stewardship, long-term planning, and value creation. In mature companies, boards often delegate specific tasks to specialized committees to ensure efficiency and effectiveness in steering a more complex, but typically less dynamic, company.

Board composition

In growth-stage companies, boards are often dominated by founders and investors, such as PE partners, with independent advisors taking up the remaining seats. This composition ensures a strong focus on growth aligned with the company's strategic ambitions but it also risks reducing the independence of the board, as a board member of multiple European corporations noted: "One issue or challenge with growth-stage businesses is often that the board is typically congested with shareholder or investor representatives. So, you tend to underinvest in independent experts, and that is not healthy in the long run."

Board members in growth companies often come from two distinct backgrounds: either finance and business development (investors such as PE firms) or a CEO or executive background (independent members). This mix is designed to enable the board to take tight control of scaling strategies and operational agility. Additionally, due to the fast-evolving nature of the company, the board itself tends to be relatively small and highly flexible, enabling fast decision-making and a more hands-on approach. However, as the company grows, the board often needs to be adjusted to address its changing needs. One board chair explained: "When it comes to growth companies, over time, you need to change the board because you need different competencies. You need more breadth on your board."

Mature companies, in contrast, benefit from boards that are structured to incorporate a broader range of expertise. These boards are more likely to be dominated by independent directors who bring diverse backgrounds in areas such as finance, law, operations, and international markets, thus ensuring that complex issues are analyzed from multiple perspectives. A higher proportion of independent directors also helps to provide robust oversight, minimize conflicts of interest, and maintain rigorous checks and balances. The more diverse background in mature company boards supports long-term strategic decision-making and ensures that the board's guidance aligns with the company's broader objectives, more diverse shareholders and other stakeholders, and regulatory requirements.

Board structures

Regarding structure, boards in growth firms tend to be more informal and agile, reflecting a strong focus on growth and change. These boards often do not have the extensive committee frameworks found in more mature organizations, and they tend to meet more frequently in a less structured manner to respond quickly to emerging challenges and opportunities. The roles within the board and executive team can be more fluid, with board chairs temporarily taking on executive tasks. While this overlapping of roles can simplify decision-making and facilitate rapid action, it can also introduce potential conflicts of interest. The overall structure is designed to support rapid adaptation and quick pivots in strategy, which are essential in a fast-changing market environment.

In contrast, mature companies tend to rely on a more formalized board structure characterized by defined roles and responsibilities supporting enhanced oversight and ensuring balanced governance. Mature boards typically rely on a well-established committee framework, including specialized committees for audit, compensation, governance, and risk management. These committees operate within a framework of clearly defined processes, formal policies, and standardized reporting procedures, which serve to ensure accountability and transparency.

Board dynamics

Founders or investors often dominate the dynamics within a growth-stage board. However, they are otherwise collaborative and informal. Meetings are often designed to foster problem-solving, reflecting the company's need to adapt quickly to a rapidly evolving environment. The decision-making process, although led by one or several individuals, tends to be highly flexible and informal. While these dynamics allow the company to capture market opportunities, there is also the risk that dominant egos take control at the expense of inclusive processes and balanced decision-making.

The dynamics of a mature board, in contrast, are more deliberative, cautious, and formal, largely due to the increased complexity and regulatory oversight characteristic of mature firms. Discussions are typically more structured, with decisions emerging from extensive debate and comprehensive analysis. Boundaries between the leadership team and the board are maintained to ensure that while management handles day-to-day operations, the board focuses on oversight and strategic guidance. This separation often slows down decision-making but ensures a broader consideration of all angles of a problem. The board's discussions frequently have a strong emphasis on performance metrics, compliance issues, and risk management, which run the risk of focusing on the present and the past rather than the future.

These differences in style between boards of growth-stage and mature firms also suggest that a transition from growth to maturity, or new growth in a mature company, may demand a rethinking of the board. Directors need to be ready to adapt the board as companies evolve, to reflect the different competencies, structures, and dynamics that are required through the varying stages and circumstances.

The critical role of boards and board chairs during crisis situations

One situation that puts particular focus on the board is a crisis.[5] During a crisis, boards play an essential, heightened role, often taking more active leadership, as we saw in the Sulzer case at the beginning of this chapter. In a crisis, boards must take decisive action and also collaborate closely with management. The board chair, in particular, becomes a key force and stabilizing facilitator of communication between the board, management, and stakeholders.

Crisis situations may force the board to adapt all dimensions of its design. Faced with an extended crisis that requires an organizational transformation, the board may need to adjust its composition by, for example, bringing in temporary members as support. If a crisis situation triggers a larger transformation, it is often advisable to adjust the composition of the board to add the skills that transformation requires.

Crisis situations often also lead to structural changes in the board, for instance, when temporary structures such as new committees or working groups are formed to focus time and energy on the crisis.

Most importantly, in a crisis situation, the board needs to adjust, at least temporarily, how it operates. During a crisis, boards must go beyond traditional oversight to engage deeply with management, providing clear guidance and support to enable quick decision-making to address immediate threats and stabilize operations.[6] The board and management together need to adapt strategies in response to evolving circumstances while keeping long-term objectives in sight. Effective board work during a crisis requires strategic clarity on the company's purpose and values to be able to align any transformative efforts with them.

As an example, Stefan Nöken, a member of the board at Vaillant, Vorwerk, and Peri Group, explained:

> A frequently observed pattern is that whenever things get tight, be it because the financial performance is below expectations, the strategy is not working, or there are personnel issues, the board's immediate reflex is to move closer to the operational business. Right up to the point where they may take over responsibility. That's not by preference but due to the situation.

Whenever the board directly interferes in operational matters, as is often the case in a crisis situation, close alignment with management is critical so that the board's actions are not perceived by the executive team as a sign of mistrust, as one board chair explained to us:

> When you get involved in operational matters as a board, for the management, this easily signals mistrust. So, when things are not going well, it creates a fine line to walk. You have to get close enough to have a sufficient understanding of those operational areas that are not going well while maintaining trust with the management. It requires very careful communication.

To be effective during a crisis, the board needs to adjust its modus operandi. This often involves an increased reporting and meeting frequency to keep the board informed and able to respond promptly. Frequent updates facilitate timely interventions. More meetings allow for simplification of each meeting's agenda, focusing on the key operational and strategic issues that require immediate attention and enabling an emphasis on decision-making rather than reporting and extensive discussion.

One board member of a large European corporation explained:

> There are several things that are important during a crisis. Point number one is to keep the information gap as small as possible. Otherwise, we don't really stand a chance, and we can't fulfill our responsibility at all. In a crisis, the reporting cycles have to become shorter, whether that's weekly reporting

from management in writing or to the board of directors. And if the situation doesn't deteriorate, then you just continue. But you're constantly on the ball. This could be calls or more frequent meetings, but it's about increasing the reporting frequency. I think it is also important to reduce the complexity of the meetings. You have to focus on only three or four key topics, with more focus on operational questions. And try to deal with them conclusively. Not just discussion, but to make decisions and follow up on them. "Where is the progress report?" And that's where the board chair needs to be decisive. Following up and getting closer to operations.

Communication and stakeholder management also fall under the board's purview during crisis situations. The board must ensure that clear, consistent, and accurate information is communicated to all stakeholders, including employees, investors, customers, and regulatory bodies. This helps manage the immediate situation and maintain or rebuild trust, which is crucial for long-term recovery and stability.

During crises, the role of the board chair is of particular importance. Board chairs need to act as a decisive leader and main support for the CEO, a communication and information facilitator, and a stabilizing force. During crises, decision-making often requires one or a small group of individuals to take decisive leadership. This role naturally falls on the board chair. Although during a crisis the board chair needs to be the main supporter of the CEO, depending upon the situation, they may also need to be the individual who ensures that an underperforming CEO is held accountable.[7] This involves closely monitoring the CEO's response to the crisis, ensuring that both the CEO and the leadership team have the necessary resources to implement crisis management strategies, and continually assessing whether the CEO is able to deliver an effective response.

Crises require increased information flows between the board, the CEO, and the leadership team to be able to make swift decisions. Therefore, the chair's role is to be a facilitator of these flows, ensuring clear, transparent communication between the board, CEO, and stakeholders. The board chair must ensure that all relevant information is accurately disseminated and that discussions remain focused on the most critical issues at hand. This involves setting clear and highly prioritized agendas, fostering an environment where candid dialogue is encouraged, and quickly synthesizing insights to drive consensus and timely decision-making.

The final role of the board chair in a crisis, which is related to the task of communication, is to be a stabilizing and calming force. Given that crises often create uncertainty and anxiety throughout the organization, the board chair needs to act as a calming presence, addressing fears and questions throughout the organization. Therefore, they should take the lead in articulating the board's perspective on the crisis, outlining strategic actions, and providing reassurance that the organization is taking decisive measures to address the challenges. Through clear and consistent communication, they can maintain trust and confidence among investors, regulators, customers, and employees. This engagement of all stakeholders helps safeguard the company's reputation and ensures that stakeholder concerns are addressed.

Implications for board chairs, individual directors, and the board as a whole

The situational approach to the board underscores the importance of boards being adaptable, situationally tailored, and proactive in their composition, structure, and operations. During different stages of company growth and maturity, and in particular during crises, boards must adjust their roles, engagement levels, composition, and operational practices to guide the company effectively. Misaligned board composition and over-involvement in operations can hinder the company's ability to navigate challenges. Therefore, a strategic approach to board design, anticipating future needs, and aligning with the company's specific situation is essential for effective governance and organizational success.

For board chairs and the board as a whole, this implies the need to regularly assess their composition and structure in light of the strategic challenges and opportunities, and work toward aligning the board membership. The board, led by the chair, should regularly evaluate its members' skills and expertise relative to the company's strategic situation and proactively bring in new competencies when required. Also, board practices should be regularly evaluated and adjusted to re-align meeting structures, reporting frequencies, and engagement levels with the company's situation. To do so, the board must develop flexibility and adaptability in its operations.

Boards are also well advised to enhance crisis preparedness by developing protocols for increased engagement and communication during crises to ensure they are equipped to provide active leadership and decisive action when needed. To create resilience, crisis preparation needs to begin in times of relative stability, when the board should focus on identifying early signs of crisis. While specific shocks are unexpected, regular preparation and the development of crisis scenarios allow the board to build robust capabilities for crisis response, upon which responses to a specific shock can be built. Resilience in crisis response requires the board's ability to act decisively and make high-quality decisions under pressure. For this, the board needs a well-established culture of productive discussion and decision-making that balances the quality of decisions and their speed. Dealing effectively with crisis situations is a skill that boards can train and learn. Firefighters, crisis response teams, and disaster relief agencies build these skills through regular practice in times of stability so that when a crisis occurs, and stakes are high, decision-making processes and responses are well practiced and not left to chance.[8]

For individual directors, the situational approach to board design requires them to stay informed about industry trends and their company's evolving needs and pursue ongoing education to enhance relevant expertise. Since the situational approach implies shorter tenure of members, individuals must focus on continued development to retain their value in the market for corporate directors. In crises, the situational approach requires individual directors to be willing to step up their involvement during critical periods while respecting management's operational responsibilities. Directors may be required on short notice to increase their engagement with a corporation to address the challenges at hand.

Notes

1. Thomas Keil and Marianna Zangrillo, *The Next CEO: Board and CEO Perspectives for Successful CEO Succession* (London: Routledge, 2021).
2. Thomas Keil and Marianna Zangrillo, *The Next Leadership Team: How to Select, Build, and Optimize Your Top Team* (London: Routledge, 2023).
3. Nils K. Lang and Peter Wirtz, "Kicking Off the Corporate Governance Lifecycle: Seed Funding, Venture Capital and the Nascent Board," *British Journal of Management* 33, no. 1 (2022); Igor Filatotchev and Cristiano Bellavitis, "Venture Capital and Corporate Governance of Entrepreneurial Ventures," in *The Palgrave Encyclopedia of Private Equity* (Springer, 2025); Lutgart AA Van Den Berghe and Abigail Levrau, "The Role of the Venture Capitalist as Monitor of the Company: A Corporate Governance Perspective," *Corporate Governance: An International Review* 10, no. 3 (2002); Stefano Bonini, Senem Alkan, and Antonio Salvi, "The Effects of Venture Capitalists on the Governance of Firms," *Corporate Governance: An International Review* 20, no. 1 (2012).
4. Larry E. Greiner, "Evolution and Revolution as Organizations Grow," *Harvard Business Review* 50, no. 4 (1972); Ingrid Bonn and Andrew Pettigrew, "Towards a Dynamic Theory of Boards: An Organisational Life Cycle Approach," *Journal of Management & Organization* 15, no. 1 (2009); Igor Filatotchev, Steve Toms, and Mike Wright, "The Firm's Strategic Dynamics and Corporate Governance Life-Cycle," *International Journal of Managerial Finance* 2, no. 4 (2006); Elise Perrault and Patrick McHugh, "Toward a Life Cycle Theory of Board Evolution: Considering Firm Legitimacy," *Journal of Management & Organization* 21, no. 5 (2015); Neil Churchill and Virginia Lewis, "The Five Stages of Small Business Growth," *Harvard Business Review* 62 (1983).
5. Jordi Canals, *The Role of the Board of Directors in Corporate Transformation*, Case Study: SMN-0708-E (Barcelona: IESE Business School, April 5, 2022).
6. Rutger von Post and Robert C. Pozen, "Boards Can Guide Business through a Crisis," *sloanreview.mit.edu*, MIT Sloan Management Review, May 07, 2020, https://sloanreview.mit.edu/article/boards-can-guide-businesses-through-a-crisis/.
7. Achim Schmitt, Gilbert Probst, and Michael Tushman, "The Role of the Board Chair during a Crisis," *sloanreview.mit.edu*, MIT Sloan Management Review, 2020, https://sloanreview.mit.edu/article/the-role-of-the-board-chair-during-a-crisis/.
8. Thomas Keil and Marianna Zangrillo, "Building Organizational Resilience: When the Entire Organization Should Be Engaged and Power Unleashed," in *Building Resilient Organizations*, ed. Stuart Crainer (Newtown Square, PA: Thinkers50/Brightline, 2022).

Chapter 10

Board design and the institutional environment

In February 2023, SAP's board of directors nominated Punit Renjen, former CEO of Deloitte, to the board and designated him as successor to then-board chair Hasso Plattner, whose term was set to expire in May 2024. SAP is Germany's best-known technology company and the world's largest enterprise resource planning software vendor.

India-born Renjen had risen through the ranks at Deloitte, ultimately becoming the first Asian CEO of the company – a position he held for two consecutive terms. During his tenure as CEO, he is credited with developing and executing a global strategy that established Deloitte as one of the world's leading professional services organizations.

Renjen's nomination was part of a structured succession plan to ensure continuity in leadership at SAP following the departure of Plattner, one of the company's founders and the board's *éminence grise*. Following his nomination, Renjen was elected and appointed deputy chair in May 2023.

Renjen immediately set to work traveling around the world visiting SAP subsidiaries, signaling that he intended to take an active, hands-on role once he became chair. This interpretation of the role of chair is uncommon in German corporate governance, where the board is usually restricted to a supervisory role, leaving the executive team to run company operations. Observers stated that Renjen's approach quickly made him enemies on the board of directors, the executive board, and with SAP's top management.[1]

The different views and opinions and their resulting conflicts escalated rapidly, eventually prompting the board of directors to take a radical step. In February 2024, SAP announced that Renjen would resign from the board due to "differences in perspective on the role of SAP Supervisory Board chair."[2] Instead, the supervisory board nominated Pekka Ala-Pietilä, former president of Nokia Corporation and a former member of SAP's board of directors, to succeed Plattner for two years. In announcing the transition, SAP highlighted Ala-Pietilä's profound "understanding of the [...] complexities of European SE governance."[3]

While corporate governance is converging globally, board design continues to depend on the institutional environment and, therefore, important dimensions of board design differ across countries.[4] The design of the board always depends upon each country's laws, norms, and regulations, and, as the SAP example demonstrates, differences in views about the role of the board can lead to conflicts and undermine effective governance.

In relation to the topics discussed in this book, international differences in corporate governance add another layer of complexity. In this chapter, therefore, we discuss some of the key distinctions between corporate governance in Anglo-Saxon countries (such as the US, the UK, and Australia), the Nordics, and the nations of continental Europe (such as France, Germany, the Netherlands, and Switzerland), and how they affect the different dimensions of the board diamond. We will discuss important differences along all five dimensions of the board diamond, but will conclude with a brief discussion of how international proxy advisors have become an equalizing force, at least in large corporations (Table 10.1).

Board purpose and roles

In our conversations with directors, those with experience across multiple legislations repeatedly stated that board roles and responsibilities are perceived differently across countries, affecting all other dimensions of the board diamond. For instance, Xiaoqun Clever-Steg, director at multiple international corporations, highlighted some of these differences in board purpose and roles, using Germany, Switzerland, the UK, and Australia as comparisons:

> The Swiss board, the "Verwaltungsrat," has more say in strategy and the operational part. The German "Aufsichtsrat" is more about supervision and governance. And in the UK or Australian board, the company is really run by the CEO, the board tends to have more independent board members and oversees performance, governance, and risk, with a stronger focus on shareholder interests. So not every board has the same task since their role is defined differently.

The differences in the board's purpose and role don't stem just from the differences in countries' laws, norms, and regulations but also from the variety of perspectives that lead to distinct priorities. Despite the global shift toward incorporating all stake-holders into corporate governance, for example, the degree to which boards priori-tize shareholder value versus broader stakeholder interests continues to vary around the world. In the US, the UK, and Australia, corporate governance has traditionally emphasized maximizing shareholder returns as the key outcome of effective corpo-rate governance, focusing directors on financial oversight and risk management. This perspective typically leads boards to prioritize short-term financial metrics and stock performance at the expense of other stakeholders, such as employees, customers, and the community.

While growing investor pressure and regulatory developments have pushed companies toward a more stakeholder-inclusive approach incorporating sustain-ability considerations, the backlash in the US against many of the themes related to ESG and diversity, equity, and inclusion shows starkly that this novel perspec-tive may not be as deeply rooted in corporations and their boards as many observ-ers thought.

In contrast to the US, the UK, and Australia, governance frameworks in conti-nental Europe and the Nordic countries have long embedded stakeholder-oriented principles. Companies in these countries view themselves as integral parts of soci-ety, with responsibilities beyond profit maximization, and many boards incorpo-rate long-term value creation, sustainability, and social responsibility in addition to short-term financial performance. A Nordic board chair highlighted:

> In my view, it is also a matter of reducing the excessive emphasis on shareholder value that comes from the US and the Anglo-Saxon world. Some forms of value creation have always been much more present in the Nordics and the European continent than in the UK and the US. The same holds to a very large extent in Asia. In these regions, corpora-tions or private enterprises are seen as part of society with a mandate to benefit society. I would say we are moving away from the Anglo-Saxon focus on shareholder value as the only metric, which I think is a positive development.

German corporate law, for example, explicitly mandates employee representation on the board of directors, reflecting a broader commitment to balancing shareholder, employee, and societal interests. Similar stakeholder-driven approaches are evident in France, where governance traditions emphasize social responsibility alongside financial performance, and in Nordic economies, where consensus-building and employee participation play a central role in board deliberations.

Some of the continental European directors we interviewed noted that European boards have long considered the interests of wider stakeholders but have previously faced pressure from shareholders to narrow their focus to financial metrics. The grow-ing recognition by shareholders of the shift toward sustainability and the inclusion

Table 10.1 Comparison of key board dimensions across geographies

	United States	*United Kingdom*	*France*
Board role	– Primarily focused on shareholder value and strategic oversight – Emphasis on compliance and risk management, performance monitoring	– Must observe the UK Corporate Governance Code ("comply or explain") – Focus on long-term strategy, risk management, and stakeholder engagement	– Balances shareholder interests with broader stakeholder considerations – Influenced by civil law traditions and state-influenced economic model
Composition	– A significant majority of independent directors is common in listed companies – CEO duality remains frequent but under investor pressure	– Typically a non-executive chair distinct from the CEO– Emphasis on independence and diversity – Larger listed companies aim for a majority of non-executive, independent directors	– Single-tier (conseil d'administration) or two-tier (directoire + conseil de surveillance) – Independent directors are increasingly important, but not always in the same proportion as the US/UK
Structure and dynamics	– Single-tier board (executive + non-executive in one body) – Sarbanes-Oxley, Dodd-Frank, and stock exchange rules shape robust committee structures	– Also single-tier but with strong norms on chair–CEO separation – Chair often wields significant influence over agenda and board processes	– Single-tier boards can combine or separate chair and CEO roles (PDG or separated) – Larger firms must have employee reps if above certain thresholds

Germany	Other Continental Europe	Nordic Countries	Australia
– Stakeholder-oriented system, balancing the interests of shareholders, employees, creditors, and the public – Strong tradition of long-term stability and co-determination	– Often stakeholder-inclusive (similar to France and Germany), though specifics vary by country – Some mix of shareholder and stakeholder models, depending on local legal tradition	– Combines shareholder value with strong social responsibility, employee rights, and consensus-building – Emphasis on sustainability and inclusive governance	– Emphasis on shareholder returns and risk management – Growing attention to ESG and "social license to operate"
– Strict two-tier model: Management Board (Vorstand) for operations Supervisory Board (Aufsichtsrat) for oversight–Co-determination can fill up to half of the supervisory seats with employees	– Varies by country: some allow single-tier or two-tier boards – Independent directors are strongly encouraged in line with EU codes – Shareholder or state/family ownership can heavily influence board composition	– Mostly single-tier boards–Employee representation is widespread (e.g., Sweden and Norway) – Independence is emphasized, with controlling shareholders more common in family-owned enterprises	– Single-tier boards with a high proportion of independent directors, per ASX recommendations – Diversity (including gender diversity) is increasingly prioritized
– Two-tier is mandated, ensuring a clear separation between management and oversight – Co-determination fosters diverse perspectives but can slow decision-making	– Structures often rooted in local legal traditions – The Netherlands commonly uses a two-tier system; Italy/Spain more often single-tier – Growing trend toward independence and robust oversight	– Consensus-driven culture with less shareholder activism – Often high expectations for transparency and ESG – Notable for gender quotas on boards (e.g., Norway)	– Specialized committees (audit, remuneration, nomination, risk) akin to the US – Regulatory focus on director accountability heightened after misconduct inquiries

(*Continued*)

Table 10.1 (Continued)

	United States	United Kingdom	France
Chair and CEO roles	– CEO duality (CEO is also chair) still occurs, but there is growing pressure to split the roles	– Strong norm of separating chair and CEO – Chair leads the board, CEO manages operations	– Possible to combine roles as Président-Directeur Général (PDG) or separate into Président non-exécutif + Directeur Général
Employee representation	– No formal requirement for employee representation in most companies – Some voluntary initiatives, but uncommon	– No formal requirement for employee directors – Code encourages stakeholder engagement via other means	– Employee reps required in large companies (number depends on size) – Part of a stakeholder-inclusive approach
Evaluation and development	– Annual board and director evaluations are increasingly standard – Driven by investor scrutiny and best-practice guidelines	– Annual performance evaluations encouraged – External evaluations every three years for larger listed companies	– AFEP-MEDEF code recommends regular evaluations – Larger CAC 40 firms more likely to conduct rigorous reviews
Key governance highlights	– Robust regulatory influence from Sarbanes-Oxley, Dodd-Frank, and the SEC – Activist investors significantly shape board composition	– "Comply or explain" under the UK Corporate Governance Code – Institutional investors have a strong influence – Senior Independent Director acts as a balance	– Civil law basis; major influence from AFEP-MEDEF code – State influence can be significant for some firms – Emphasis on combining or separating PDG roles based on the firm's needs

Germany	Other Continental Europe	Nordic Countries	Australia
– Strict separation by law: The CEO belongs to the Management Board; the Supervisory Board is led by a distinct chair	– Practice varies: some jurisdictions allow combined roles, others prefer or encourage separation – Dependent on local codes and the presence of controlling shareholders or state influence	– Generally separated (chair vs. CEO), with the chair playing a strong oversight role – In some cases, major shareholders can have a direct say in who chairs the board	– Typically separated – ASX guidelines advise having an independent chair and a separate CEO
– Co-determination law can allocate up to 50 percent of supervisory board seats to employees in large firms – Integral to corporate governance	– Varies: the Netherlands has some co-determination features, while Spain/Italy have less so – Typically less extensive than Germany but more than in Anglo-American markets	– Widespread employee representation (e.g., in Sweden, Norway)	– No requirement for formal employee representation – Focus on stakeholder engagement without mandated board seats
– The German Corporate Governance Code encourages regular self-assessments – Not as standardized as in Anglo-American contexts	– Board reviews are increasingly common, often under "comply or explain" frameworks – Varies significantly by country	– Systematic evaluations guided by national governance codes – External or internal reviews are increasingly standard	– ASX Corporate Governance Council recommends regular evaluations – Often done internally, sometimes with external facilitation ("comply or explain" model)
– Mandatory two-tier system – Employee codetermination is a core principle – Balances long-term corporate interests with robust stakeholder protections	– Family or state ownership can be prominent in some regions (e.g., Italy, Spain) – Netherlands: strong stakeholder rules and partial co-determination – "Comply or explain" model grows across the EU	– Consensus culture with a focus on ESG, worker rights, and gender diversity – Norway led the mandatory gender quotas on boards	– Influenced by the ASX Corporate Governance Council's Principles and Recommendations – Emphasizes transparency, independence, risk oversight, and increasingly ESG

of other stakeholders has enabled boards to more openly address broader stakeholder interests. Pierre-André de Chalendar, former board chair of Saint-Gobain, explained:

> In Europe, we have been thinking about stakeholders for a long time. Many of our boards have been thinking that way, but a number of our shareholders have pressed us to state things differently, so a number of us have been trying to bend our speech a little bit when talking to the investors. What has changed, and that is a radical change, is that in the last few years, we have seen movement from the shareholder community to acknowledge all stakeholders. This is a radical shift from the shareholder base, and that makes us more at ease.

However, how this perspective will survive the current swing back toward the prioritization of shareholders, particularly in the US, remains to be seen.

The differences between countries in board purpose and roles have important implications for board design. Investors, stakeholders, and board members need to consider whether the board is the right mechanism to achieve specific goals. Empowering a board may, for instance, run counter to the governance culture of a country and may lead to conflicts and misunderstandings, as the SAP example at the beginning of this chapter highlights.

Board structure

One of the most fundamental differences in corporate governance across geographies is the board's structure, with the biggest difference being the use of single-tier versus two-tier boards. Pauline Van der Meer Mohr, chair of the Dutch semiconductor equipment manufacturer ASML and director of Ahold Delhaize, NN Group, explained:

> There is such a big difference between one-tier and the two-tier boards, in terms of the role of the board and its chair, the board composition, and the board's participation in decision-making. In a one-tier board, the board gets much more involved. In a two-tier board, the board of directors takes a backseat role and not the company leadership role.

Many countries with Anglo-Saxon governance traditions, such as the US, the UK, and Australia, operate under a single-tier board system, where executive and non-executive directors serve together. This structure facilitates direct interaction between management and independent directors, allowing for real-time oversight and strategic input. However, because the CEO – and possibly other inside directors – serve on the board, board independence is more difficult to achieve.

In contrast, several European countries – most notably Germany – mandate a two-tier board system. This creates a clear separation between the management board (Vorstand), responsible for day-to-day operations, and the board of directors (Aufsichtsrat), which provides oversight and represents broader stakeholder interests. This model, which is also present in varying forms in France, the Netherlands, and parts of the Nordic countries, is designed to ensure robust checks and balances, but it can also introduce complexities in decision-making and reduce the board's influence.

Structures such as committees and advisory boards also vary depending on a country's regulatory frameworks and governance traditions. In shareholder-centric models like the US, the UK, and Australia, board committees are highly formalized. Publicly traded companies typically maintain three core committees – the audit committee, the remuneration (compensation) committee, and the nominating committee – each composed predominantly of independent directors. In contrast, in countries with more stakeholder-oriented governance models, such as continental European and the Nordics, committee structures can be less rigid. France, along with other parts of continental Europe, follows a flexible approach. Here, audit and compensation committees are common, yet additional committees focusing on areas like corporate social responsibility or sustainability are increasingly being integrated, particularly among large listed firms. In Germany's two-tier system, employee representation can potentially influence committee dynamics, with worker representatives typically sitting on key committees. This reflects Germany's broader emphasis on balancing shareholder and stakeholder interests.

Advisory boards – providing non-binding strategic counsel – are also prevalent in entrepreneurial markets like the US and UK, where rapidly evolving sectors demand external expertise. They are also common in continental Europe, particularly in family-owned businesses and mid-sized firms, and serve as a bridge between corporate strategy, generational transitions, and external governance support. In the Nordic countries, where governance structures tend to be leaner and emphasize consensus-driven decision-making, advisory boards are less widespread, as directors and executives typically engage in direct, informal dialogue with stakeholders and external advisors.

Given the important role that board committees and other structures have in responding to the dual challenge of corporate governance, board chairs and board members need to consider how to leverage them within the constraints of the respective governance system. Depending on the flexibility the board has in creating and dissolving committees, the board structure they adopt to address efficiency requirements, in light of the lengthening list of a board's responsibilities, and to support strategy work may, therefore, differ from country to country.

Board composition

Requirements regarding the board composition also vary widely around the world, particularly in terms of board independence and employee representation. Markets with strong Anglo-Saxon governance traditions, such as the US, the UK, and Australia, prioritize independent directors and typically require a majority of non-executive board members to enhance oversight in their single-tier board. In these markets, shareholder activism, proxy advisors, and investor-driven pressure play an important role in shaping board composition. Over the past decade, these countries have seen a tremendous increase in the attention given to diversity in terms of gender, ethnicity, skills, and general demographic backgrounds. However, in the US, in particular, this trend has recently been reversed, with many companies rolling back their diversity initiatives.[5]

Director independence is increasingly becoming more important in continental Europe too, due to the pressures of proxy advisors that often bring US-based rules to the rest of the world. However, rules regarding independence are often less stringently followed compared to Anglo-Saxon companies. Instead, continental European companies typically have a strong tradition of family members on the board of directors in family-controlled companies, or state representatives in (at least partially) state-owned companies.

While board independence is less of a consideration in continental Europe, employee representation is deeply embedded in the governance systems of France, Germany, and the Nordics. In Germany, co-determination laws require large companies to allocate up to half of their board of directors seats to employee representatives, ensuring that labor interests are directly represented at the highest level of decision-making. Austria, Denmark, France, Norway, and Sweden also incorporate employee board representation as a standard governance feature, reflecting a broader cultural emphasis on social inclusion and corporate responsibility.

Strong employee representation can bring advantages to the discourse on the board, since employee representatives often bring a different perspective to the leadership team. In addition, decisions can be easier to implement if there has been buy-in from them during the board discussion. However, given that they often coordinate positions to collectively influence decisions, a strong block of employee representatives can also lead to factionalization and hamper the board's ability to function cohesively, or even at all. This was made evident by the long-running debates at German automotive firm Volkswagen, where employee representatives and representatives of the state were unconvinced by the strategy of the CEO and leadership team and blocked the transformative changes that were needed for the company to adapt to the evolving market in light of electrification and digitalization of the automotive industry.

As well as aligning board composition with a country's expectations of independence, diversity, and employee representation, the selection of board members must align with the purpose and roles of the board and the country's board decision-making culture. When board members bring different expectations of their role, as was the case in the SAP example, problems are inevitable, and even a board with a high degree of expertise may become ineffective. Erik Huggers, board member at

Hexagon and several other privately-owned companies and former board member of ProSieben, provided an illuminating example in this respect:

> Board composition must align with local board culture. I experienced a board split between German governance culture and Anglo-Saxon practices. This mismatch created confusion – particularly about who held ultimate responsibility, the CEO or the executive board. Despite the impressive individual skills of our board members, cultural misalignment weakened the board's effectiveness.

Finally, board composition may also be affected by the level of compensation. Principles of board compensation vary starkly across countries. While in some legislations (e.g., Belgium and the Netherlands), the compensation for a board member continues to be nominal compared to the qualifications that are required and the risks related to liability, in other countries like Switzerland, board positions are well paid and offer some financial incentives that are aligned with the responsibility of the position. For instance, Andreas Joehle, former CEO and now partner at the PE firm Ufenau Capital Partners, noted:

> We are currently looking for someone to join a board in the Benelux region. While the regulatory limit is set at 12.000 euros a year for compensation and expenses, it will cost me more to pay for the D&O insurance than for the brain power they're supposed to bring to the table. So, I'm on the lookout for someone who's driven by a sense of altruism and who's excited to dive into the challenge, not just the compensation.

Research[6] shows that such differences in compensation can create problems in either finding the right caliber of board members or, when people feel underpaid, lead to a lack of motivation to take risks, as several directors shared with us in confidence. For example, one said:

> I don't know why I'm doing this. I'm really not paid very much. This is a lot of work, and there are really other things I could be doing. The next time I get asked, maybe I'll just give it a miss.

Board dynamics

Board dynamics also vary across countries, adding complexity to board design and leadership. These variations are often shaped by factors such as board purpose and role, structure, and composition (as discussed above), as well as differences in norms, culture, and legal frameworks. For instance, in countries that follow a common law tradition (the US, the UK, and Australia), a greater emphasis on litigation risk often leads to boards behaving more cautiously, with directors focusing on compliance and risk avoidance due to potential civil or criminal liability. In contrast, boards in countries with a civil law tradition (such as France, Germany, and Switzerland) may be less subject to aggressive shareholder litigation and, therefore, more concerned with reputational risks rather than legal liability. A board member with experience across different legal systems explained:

> People on boards behave differently depending on the legal system. In the US, the fines are very big, both criminal and civil. We aren't used to that in Europe, especially in the civil law countries. In common law legislation, people are a little more careful about some of the financial risks that come with that. So, even before getting into the criminal risks, people tend to be more careful on boards.

Boardroom dynamics are also significantly affected by the distribution of power. In CEO-dominated systems like the US and, to a certain extent, France, the CEO often wields significant influence, sometimes doubling up as board chair, which leads to a top-down approach where executives set the agenda and independent directors provide oversight rather than control. In contrast, the UK and Australia exhibit a more balanced power structure, with influential independent non-executive directors and a clear separation between the CEO and board chair to ensure accountability. Power is often even more decentralized in Germany, the Netherlands, and Nordic countries, where employee representation on boards and a consensus-driven governance approach integrate multiple stakeholder perspectives.

Boardroom dynamics also vary based on the common discussion styles of different countries. These can range from confrontational and performance-driven to collaborative and consensus-oriented. In the US and UK, board discussions are data-driven and investor-focused, often involving frequent challenges to executives, especially in response to financial performance concerns or pressure from activist shareholders. In contrast, France and Southern Europe tend toward more hierarchical yet strategic discussions, shaped by elite networks and government influence. Germany and Nordic countries, which emphasize stakeholder inclusion, favor deliberate, analytical discussions, where long-term stability and employee interests weigh heavily in boardroom debates. Nordic boards, in particular, exhibit a flat hierarchy and transparency-driven culture, where ethical considerations can carry as much weight as financial metrics.

Lastly, boardroom dynamics across countries differ starkly in terms of decision-making style. US and UK boards tend to move quickly to align with shareholder interests, prioritizing market-driven, performance-based strategies, often responding to activist investors and quarterly financial results. In Australia, boards often aim to balance rapid decision-making with long-term sustainability concerns. In contrast, Germany, the Netherlands, and the Nordics take a slow, consensus-driven approach, where decisions must align with employee participation laws, stakeholder interests, and long-term corporate health. France and other continental European nations fall in between, with state influence and labor unions playing an important key role in decision-making.

Board chairs and board members need to take these important differences into consideration to be able to achieve the board's purpose and roles and utilize the members of the board effectively. In particular, when the board is expanded to include members from another governance system, training and coaching may be required to avoid misunderstandings and conflicts.

Board leadership: chair and CEO roles

Another area of divergence in board design across countries is the strength of the role of the board chair and the distribution of power between it and the CEO. In the US, CEO duality – where one individual holds both the CEO and chair positions – has traditionally been the norm, even though investor pressure and corporate governance reforms have led to increased scrutiny of this practice and an increasing number of independent chairs. When the roles are separated, power often rests with the CEO, though the power of the independent chair can vary substantially.

The relative influence of the CEO in the US may have important implications for the board's role in the governance system. For instance, a board chair noted:

> The CEO has a lot of power to shape what the board will do. If the board is treated as a necessary evil, something you have to live with for governance and regulatory reasons, then it's going to be a passive board. If the CEO views the board as a dozen people around the table with unique experiences and perspectives, then it can help them think through difficult questions and be a sounding board and an asset.

Problems emerge when a board tries to take a role that is not aligned with the power distribution that board members, executives, or stakeholders are expecting. For instance, Christian Trümpler of the Partners Group, shared with us:

> An active governance approach is not always embraced by the CEOs. First, there are regional differences regarding the understanding and role of the CEO. In certain parts of the world, it is not common for the supervisory board to take an active role in shaping strategy and partnering with executive teams on executing it. Second, and irrespective of geography, the ability of a CEO to embrace and leverage a strong supervisory board is often a factor that sets strong CEOs apart from weak ones.

In contrast, in the UK and Australia, there is a strong preference for separating these roles, ensuring that the board retains an independent check on executive management. For example, the UK Corporate Governance Code sets clear expectations that the chair should be an independent director upon appointment, distinct from the

CEO, to promote effective oversight. Board chairs in the UK are actively involved in governance, strategy, and stakeholder engagement and interact with management regularly, often weekly, providing leadership and direction.

Separating the two roles is also the norm in continental Europe and the Nordics. In Germany, for example, where the board system is two-tiered, the Corporate Governance Code defines a clear separation between the roles of CEO (Vorstandsvorsitzender) and board chair. Where the ultimate decision power rests, however, is not always clear, since a board chair may represent a family owner or major shareholder and, therefore, wield considerable power.

Some continental European countries allow for both a combination and a separation of the two roles. France, for instance, offers a hybrid approach, where companies can choose between a unified leadership model (Président-Directeur Général – PDG) and a structure that separates the two roles. In the unified model, power is centralized with the PDG, whereas in the separate model it is shared between the board chair (Président) and the CEO (Directeur Général).

In Switzerland, the role is often separated, though it is also possible that an executive chair plays both board chair and CEO roles, especially in holding structures. When the roles are separated, however, the board chair (Verwaltungsratspräsident) wields considerably more power than in most other continental European countries because the board holds full responsibility for strategy and organization. Paul Bulcke, chair of Nestlé, described this as follows:

> In Switzerland, the board chair has a more important role to play in governance than in most countries because the board's role is not only oversight, it's setting the strategy and caring for the overall "health" of the company. As a board chair, you are responsible with the board for the "what," the "how," and the "why" of the company.

As our earlier example from SAP shows, candidates for board chair positions are well advised to reflect on these substantial differences in the expectations and power of the role, to avoid misaligning their expectations and plans for the board, or misunderstanding how the board is structured according to the governance system of the country. Nevertheless, it is important to note that the power and the possibilities of the board chair position often do not arise from the formal rules of governance but rather from the informal support of major shareholders or a majority of the board members. What is written in the law regarding the limits of the role is not necessarily the practice lived in organizations.

Board evaluation and development

While the practice of board evaluations is gaining traction globally, its rigor and frequency vary across jurisdictions. Regular board assessments are a well-established practice in the US and UK and are often conducted annually, with larger firms engaging external consultants for independent evaluations every few years. The UK's "comply or explain" framework encourages transparency, requiring companies to disclose how they assess board effectiveness.

In continental Europe, board evaluation practices are evolving but are often less standardized. In France, governance codes recommend regular self-assessments, though external reviews remain less frequent than in Anglo-American markets. In Germany, board evaluations are encouraged under the German Corporate Governance Code, but the process tends to be less formalized than in the US or UK. In the Nordics, systematic board reviews are increasingly common, aligning with broader governance expectations around transparency and accountability. In the rest of continental Europe, systematic board evaluations are also becoming increasingly common, especially in larger firms, but the form and rigor of these evaluations still differ substantially. In fact, improving the quality of board evaluations continues to be one of the main levers for improving the board, as we argued in Chapter 7.

The equalizing effect of international proxy advisors and compliance pressures

In today's international corporate governance environment, proxy advisory firms, such as ISS or Glass Lewis, wield significant influence over practices in corporate governance, independent of the country's corporate governance rules. Proxy advisors have a powerful influence on board design in companies reliant on an international investor base, where institutional investors often look to them for recommendations. As a result, proxy advisors play an oversized role in shaping board compositions, executive compensation, and governance policies across global markets.

The influence of proxy advisors is often a double-edged sword. On the one hand, they play an essential role in diffusing good governance practices across international markets. On the other hand, one of the most common criticisms is their one-size-fits-all approach, which applies standardized guidelines without adequately considering the unique circumstances of individual companies. Given the vast number of votes that proxy advisory firms must cast, they often lack the resources to conduct in-depth, independent assessments of each company's governance structure. Riet Cadonau, experienced board chair and director and current director at the Zehnder Group AG, noted:

> In a public company, you are also being covered by people who either have little time for in-depth analysis or little experience. I'm referring to proxy advisors and analysts. If you're a mid-cap company, you're sometimes being judged by people who are checking the box out of necessity. And if you look at today's analysts, they have a challenging job: Today, an analyst sometimes must cover dozens of companies, which is hardly feasible given

today's complexity. The result is that it happens that you are covered by people who have a lot of influence but few resources and sometimes little experience to evaluate companies with the depth needed.

Lack of resources and experience is not limited to the proxy advisors; it can also be a constraint for the investors making their decisions based on the proxy advisors' suggestions. Jeff Campbell, former vice chairman and CFO of American Express, former CFO of McKesson and American Airlines, and current director at AON plc, Marathon Petroleum Corp., and Hexcel Corp, explained:

> When you look at a BlackRock or Vanguard, you have twenty people who focus on governance and are trying to figure out how to vote on the proxies. And when you have five thousand proxies to vote, the only way to manage five thousand proxies with twenty people is to say: "I am going to come up with a template and some simple rules and check-marks." And that is really dangerous because organizations are all so different. It is dangerous to assume there is one simple answer to most issues. In my view, you want a group of investors and a group of board members who are entrusted to be thoughtful about what is appropriate at any point in time for any organization based on the range of regula-tory, strategy, business, social, and governmental requirements.

In some cases, this can lead to counterproductive outcomes – rejecting directors with substantial shareholdings, for example, because they are not considered properly independent, despite their deep vested interest in the company's success. Similarly, rigid tenure limits intended to keep boards fresh can inadvertently strip companies of experienced directors who bring long-term strategic insight and stability. A board member of a large European corporation expressed this starkly:

> The funny thing about proxy advisors is that they don't appreciate it if someone has skin in the game because they don't consider them inde-pendent. That's a very strange rule. Second, they do not recommend you vote for someone who has been in office for over ten years. As a result, the two people with the most skin in the game, who bring the most experience, are always recommended as "no" at the Annual General Meeting. They then automatically have the fewest votes, and I have the most votes, even though I know the least about the business by far. In principle, I believe these proxy advisor guidelines are good, even if they are not always correct in individual cases. However, regarding these two points, that someone who invests themselves is supposed to be a bad board member and that experience counts for nothing, I think they are fundamentally wrong in the current assessment. I see so many board members who actually have no idea and no commitment.

Proxy advisory firms also often base their recommendations predominantly on US governance practices.[7] However, as this chapter highlights, the governance systems outside of the US, or at least the Anglo-Saxon context, are often different along important dimensions. What works in the US, with its intense focus on shareholder value and the legal system's focus on litigation, may not work equally well in Europe, with its different board purpose and role, and different legal traditions.

This pressure to conform to proxy advisor standards may also impact board design in unintended ways. Companies might prioritize policies that align with advisory firm recommendations rather than those that best serve their business needs. For instance, transparency and accountability requirements provide essential guardrails, ensuring ethical corporate behavior. However, when taken too far, the proxy advisors' rules can shift the focus away from strategic decision-making and toward a compliance-driven, "tick-box" mentality. Governance is most effective when it balances regulation with flexibility, enabling companies to operate efficiently while maintaining proper oversight.

Our interviews with board directors reinforce these concerns. Many directors expressed unease about the disproportionate influence of proxy advisors, warning that their rigid and often mechanistic application of governance standards could erode board effectiveness rather than enhance it. They emphasized the need for a more nuanced approach – one that recognizes the diversity of governance needs across companies and industries. Striking the right balance between regulation, proxy advisor influence, and strategic governance is essential to ensuring corporate boards remain accountable and effective in a rapidly evolving business landscape.

Notes

1. Peter M. Färbinger, "Two Years Lost for Sap," *E3 Magazine*, February 22, 2024, https://e3mag.com/en/two-lost-years-for-sap/.
2. Martin Beyer, "Sap Has a New Succession Plan," *CIO*, Feb 12, 2024, https://www.cio.com/article/1306972/sap-has-a-new-succession-plan.html.
3. Peter M. Färbinger, "Sap and Punit Renjen Have Mutually Agreed to Part Ways," *E3 Magazine*, February 13, 2024, https://e3mag.com/en/sap-and-punit-renjen-have-decided-to-part-ways-by-mutual-agreement/.
4. For a discussion on the differences in corporate governance across countries see, for instance, Martin K. Welge and Marc Eulerich, *Corporate-Governance-Management*, 2nd ed. (Wiesbaden: Springer Gabler, 2014); David Larcker and Brian Tayan, *Corporate Governance Matters: A Closer Look at Organizational Choices and Their Consequences*, 3rd ed. (London: Pearson/FT Press, 2020); Richard Leblanc, *The Handbook of Board Governance: A Comprehensive Guide for Public, Private, and Not-for-Profit Board Members* (Hoboken, NJ: John Wiley & Sons, 2020); Thomas Clarke, *International Corporate Governance: A Comparative Approach* (Routledge, 2007); Kevin Keasey, Steve Thompson, and Michael Wright, *Corporate Governance: Accountability, Enterprise and International Comparisons* (Chichester: John Wiley & Sons, 2005); Toru Yoshikawa and Abdul A. Rasheed, "Convergence of Corporate Governance: Critical Review and Future Directions," *Corporate Governance: An International Review*

17, no. 3 (2009); Ruth V. Aguilera and G. Jackson, "Comparative and International Corporate Governance," *Academy of Management Annals* 4 (2010); Ruth V. Aguilera, Valentina Marano, and Ilir Haxhi, "International Corporate Governance: A Review and Opportunities for Future Research," *Journal of International Business Studies* 50 (2019); Craig Doidge, G. Andrew Karolyi, and René M. Stulz, "Why Do Countries Matter So Much for Corporate Governance?," *Journal of Financial Economics* 86, no. 1 (2007). Felix Lessambo, *The International Corporate Governance System: Audit Roles and Board Oversight* (Springer, 2016).

5. Richa Naidu and Simon Jessop, "Before Trump's Return, Some Top U.S. Firms Had Already Gone Cold on Diversity Pledges," *Reuters*, January 27, 2025, https://www.reuters.com/world/us/before-trumps-return-some-top-us-firms-had-already-gone-cold-diversity-pledges-2025-01-27/; The Conference Board, *Corporate Boards Are More Diverse Than Ever, but Growth in Racial Diversity among New Directors Is Slowing*(New York: The Conference Board, December 03, 2024).

6. Yuval Deutsch, Thomas Keil, and Tomi Laamanen, "A Dual Agency View of Board Compensation: The Joint Effects of Outside Director and CEO Stock Options on Firm Risk," *Strategic Management Journal* 32, no. 2 (2011).

7. Even where proxy advisors may try to incorporate international academic research as a basis for their recommendations, there are practical limitations such as that the most widely studied context for corporate governance research is the US with substantially less research on other countries given more limited data availability.

Part IV

Envisioning the future of governance

Chapter 11

Making boards efficient, agile, and resilient to disruption

In a fast-changing business environment, boards must evolve to sustain their contribution to the competitive advantage of the companies they govern. In this final chapter, we highlight key areas of development that emerged from our research, where many boards have untapped potential. While the best boards we studied already excel in many of these areas, most still have several opportunities for growth.

The imperative for efficiency, agility, and resilience

The dual challenge of modern governance, the central theme of this book, highlights the need for boards to evolve from static, loosely managed groups of peers into efficient, agile, and resilient teams. They must be prepared to anticipate and respond swiftly to crises, technological disruptions, and evolving strategic challenges while effectively managing today's expanding set of responsibilities. Quite simply, the increased complexity and uncertainty in today's business environment demand a new approach to how boards operate. Xiaoqun Clever-Steg, director at multiple international corporations, summarized the new challenges that boards face:

> Boards will need to develop a different approach going forward. Until recently, we operated in a relatively stable, rule-based environment

where optimizing performance was the primary focus. You had fairly predictable outcomes and could focus on managing them effectively, for example, with financial KPIs and other traditional metrics. Now, we have entered a new era marked by heightened geopolitical dynamics, uncertainty, and rapid technological advancement, at an unprecedented scale. As a result, the focus must shift from managing outcomes to managing leading indicators that drive those outcomes. And those leading indicators are often linked to national interests, behavior or culture, which are much more challenging to influence.

She continued to explain:

In this new environment, resilience, adaptability and the ability to navigate unplannable shocks have become critical capabilities. Boards must ensure that organizations can not only withstand disruptions but also anticipate and pivot quickly in response to unforeseen challenges. If that is the organization you aim to build, what does the board need to bring to the table? Far more than just a deep understanding of the balance sheet, and being able to challenge the profit and loss or capital allocation. Boards need to foster unconventional thinking, bring in outside-in perspectives, and incorporate diverse skill sets and experiences. Boards need to understand the complexities of a multigenerational workforce, embrace new technology and new business models, and understand human psychology and behavioral shifts. if your board continues to operate in an old-fashioned manner, you will not be able to deal with all these demands.

The agile board

Strategic agility is becoming increasingly imperative. Board composition, structure, processes, and practices need to be designed for agility and adaptability. Boards need to adopt agile methodologies[1] to be able to respond rapidly to emerging crises, risks, and opportunities. Embracing such agile methodologies may help boards speed up decision-making and engage in the strategic pivots that a highly uncertain business environment demands.

An agile board also needs to be supported through structural mechanisms that allocate certain tasks to specialized committees, advisory boards, and work groups that focus on specific challenges or opportunities and empower these to drive work on behalf of the board, as we argued in Chapter 5. Flexible structures enable the board to concentrate expertise where it's most needed and respond rapidly to new issues as they arise, while protecting its valuable time for discussions on strategy.

Resilience at the top

A second consideration in the development of boards should be driving organizational resilience. The ongoing multi-crisis landscape, which looks to shape the business environment for the foreseeable future, demands a new level of resilience. Boards play an increasingly central role in driving organization-wide resilience but are often ill-equipped to do so.[2] They should, therefore, incorporate resilience considerations into governance: conducting stress tests, planning for worst-case scenarios, and investing in robust supply chains that can withstand disruptive shocks. Only through a proactive approach to disaster planning can boards significantly improve organizational resilience, prevent critical disruptions, and ultimately support sustainable value creation.[3]

The board's role as an anchor of stability and efficiency

While boards need to adopt agility and resilience to be able to respond quickly to crises, they also must continue to be an anchor of stability. They need to keep the organization and its leadership team grounded in a long-term perspective that bridges the problems and challenges of today with a clear view towards the opportunities of tomorrow.

As we have argued throughout this book, the traditional static model of boards as a loosely managed group of peers is becoming increasingly inadequate. The new challenges of today call for a more dynamic model. Boards need to become high-performance teams that can reconfigure themselves and the organization to align with the company's shifting demands and leverage structure, process, and practices to efficiently deal with the requirements of today and prepare the organization for the opportunities and challenges of tomorrow.

Evolving board purpose and roles

Becoming a catalyst for corporate experimentation

A core theme of this book has been the evolving purpose and roles of the board. With the business landscape changing so fast, boards have to be future-oriented to stay relevant. This means they may need to play a central role in driving experimentation and exploration of potential new opportunities.

To take on this duty, they need to embrace the inherent uncertainty and discontinuous change in today's markets. Uncertainty and change provide not only challenges to the status quo but also create opportunities for the organization to become a driver of change. To capture these opportunities and counter the challenges, companies and their boards need to invest time and resources to experiment and develop competitive advantages proactively.

In our view, the board's role in this is threefold. First, together with the leadership team, boards need to engage with the underlying forces of change. Foresight and strategic vision are inherently rooted in a deep understanding of key trends in the business environment. Boards must foster a robust dialogue with the leadership team to identify and interpret these trends, establish a process for developing effective solutions, and define a clear path for integrating these solutions into the company's core strategy and operations. Kathleen Bailey Lord, chair at ed-tech company Janison and member of the board at Datacom, AMP, and St Vincent's Health Australia, described how this differs from past behaviors of boards:

> In a time when we were in effect dealing with known problems, the wisdom that boards brought often were ready solutions. Boards were tapping into the wisdom of members who had been doing the same job before, and you could be wise and dispense their experience and wisdom. Today, we do not have the answers. So, the role of the board is shifting to be more of a catalyst, to test potential solutions and help the management assess the risks of different solutions or scenarios. It's much more dynamic and hypothesis-testing-based, looking at probabilities. Of course, you're still drawing on their experience in order to help formulate the questions and think about what might be possible. But it is a very different dynamic.

To fulfill their role as the central force guiding exploration, boards must enable the entire organization to assess and pursue new strategies. They should foster openness to new approaches across all levels of the company, encouraging experimentation and the testing of strategic hypotheses – even if some tests result in failure. Only through learning and experimentation can the board and leadership team effectively evaluate risks and the likelihood of success for different courses of action.

Balancing breadth of roles with focus: identifying overarching board mandates

To respond to the dual challenge of modern governance, boards have redefined their purpose and expanded their roles. However, there is a natural limit to this expansion, and no board can focus its full attention on all its responsibilities all of the time. Instead, we argue that boards need to define temporary mandates that guide the focus of their work, as do the CEO and leadership team. Mandates should be derived from the strategic opportunities and challenges the company faces and its strategic vision. A mandate then helps the board to proactively prioritize its tasks rather than passively responding to external events. It goes without saying that in today's world, mandates need to be flexible and evolve in response to the company's new challenges and shifting priorities, to ensure the board remains relevant and effective.

Implications for board work

The evolving roles of the board also have implications for the nature of the work of board members. Expanded roles and mandates require board members to invest more time (if temporarily) in their roles, to position themselves not just as overseers of management but as proactive advisors, strategic partners of the leadership team, and potentially leaders themselves on certain critical issues. This increased involvement of board members has several implications. First, their roles are becoming more demanding, reducing the number of roles each individual can realistically fulfil. Secondly, they also need to engage in continuous self-education to remain up to date on emerging risks, technologies, and industry trends, to ensure that they can provide valuable insights into strategic decision-making.

More work for the same compensation?

Given the increasing demands on board members, we believe that boards around the world, and the regulators setting compensation rules, will need to rethink their approach to remuneration. While financial incentives should not be the primary driver for members, it is not realistic to assume that highly qualified experts will take on increasingly demanding tasks that involve potential personal liability without adequate compensation.

Toward a dynamic approach to board composition

To remain effective and respond to crises and strategic discontinuities, boards must transition from a static composition to a dynamic one, proactively adapting their membership to align with the company's evolving strategic needs and emerging challenges. Rod Adkins, board member at United Parcel Service (UPS), PayPal, Grainger, and Avnet, summarized this idea:

> Going forward, boards must think about a dynamic versus a static model. In the past, board members may have been on the board for as much as twenty or thirty years. However, given the competitive nature and complexity associated with today's businesses, boards will have to rethink that. Rethink how they source directors and then also maintain directors. The model is going to be much more dynamic moving forward. High-performance boards will always have to focus on the types of skills, backgrounds, and experiences of the directors needed at any time. It must be consistent with the pace of change in the marketplace.

To adopt a more dynamic approach, boards must engage in proactive succession nning and management, facilitate more frequent turnover of members with varied tenure limits, and bring in directors with specialized expertise for specific phases of the company's development while maintaining a core group of long-serving members.

Balancing continuity and change

As their role evolves, boards benefit from both continuity and change in their membership. To effectively support and oversee the CEO and leadership team in today's complex landscape, boards require deep institutional knowledge and long-standing expertise. Veteran board members who understand the company and industry inside out provide essential institutional memory, contributing to stability. However, they also risk a loss of independence and objectivity and some aspects of their experience becoming obsolete, as the business landscape changes. Implementing tenure limits of 10–12 years helps mitigate the risk of stagnation and ensures a steady influx of fresh perspectives.

New board members bring valuable insights and play a crucial role in helping the board, CEO, and leadership team focus on the future and embrace innovation. However, they often lack in-depth knowledge of the organization and industry and require time to be able to fully contribute. Creating agile and adaptable boards requires balancing the benefits of stability with the need for change. Historically, boards have tended to overemphasize stability. We therefore advocate for increasing the pace of change in board composition to ensure continued effectiveness.

Addressing emerging skill gaps

Many boards still need to actively address expertise gaps in areas such as AI and digitalization, new technologies, sustainability, and geopolitical change. Continuous learning and development are essential if board members are to remain relevant and capable of making strategic decisions on subjects where they may lack experience. Boards should therefore provide access to training, workshops, and educational resources that focus on emerging trends. They should also engage consultants, academics, or industry specialists to educate their members on specific topics. As we discussed in detail in Chapter 7, board chairs play a central role in this by fostering an environment and culture where directors can freely admit to knowledge gaps and seek to fill them.

However, there are limits to the continuous learning and development of existing board members. So instead of a board where all members are long tenured, it is worth considering a model where some directors are selected according to the strategic priorities and specific skills needed at a given time, and serve for a relatively brief period. For example, during a period of rebranding, a director with branding expertise might be brought in first, followed by someone with retail experience to support market expansion, as Christian Trümpler from Partners Group explained:

> In one of our investments, we knew that we had to reposition the brand within the first two years because although it was successful in Europe,

it was not known in the US. So, rebranding was important. We needed an American with brand experience on the board to support this project because we had to reposition it globally. But from the outset, we also knew that the best person to help us with rebranding would not be the same person who would continuously drive our go-to-market efforts in the US. We communicated this to the board members right from the start: we need one person on this board to help us rebrand, then in two years' time, we will need somebody else to get us into Walmart and Target. That was the plan from the beginning, and it's now being executed one-to-one without any bad blood because it was made clear to everyone from the start.

Another point on this balance between stability and change is that a dynamic board model does not mean regular replacement of all its members. Instead, boards should maintain a stable core while incorporating new members with targeted expertise on a more rotational basis. Additionally, board composition can be made more dynamic by proactively engaging external experts through committees, ad hoc working groups, and advisory boards. This approach not only brings in specialized knowledge but also provides an opportunity to evaluate potential future board candidates and allows potential new members to familiarize themselves with the organization, ultimately streamlining the onboarding process if they join the board at a later date.

Succession planning and effective onboarding

A dynamic approach to board composition is only possible when the board engages in systematic succession management and proactively develops how the board is composed. Succession management naturally starts with the long-term vision and strategy of the organization, which provides the basis for regularly assessing the board's skills, identifying gaps, and planning for future needs. Succession management enables the board to anticipate transitions and retirements and prepare for rotations of directors in advance, rather than reacting to them.

Another key consideration with a dynamic approach to board composition is the need for reducing the time allocated to onboarding, to ensure board members add value, as Johannes Huth, former partner at KKR, senior independent director of Coty Inc, and director at Axel Springer, explained:

It's certainly a good thing to regularly bring fresh blood into a board, but you have to be mindful of the time it takes before a board member is effective. If you join the board of a complex company, it takes some years before you fully understand it and have spent some time getting to know the management. And if you have to say goodbye again after five years, then you don't really have that much time to work effectively.

As we discussed in Chapter 7, this requires both a significant time commitment from incoming directors as well as systematic and effective onboarding processes from the company, to enable new directors to contribute sooner and prevent short tenures from compromising the board's effectiveness.

Cognitive diversity as the lever enabling shifting the board's purpose and roles

As boards shift their purpose and roles increasingly toward strategic advice and the creation of strategic responses to a dramatically changing world, a broader range of perspectives is needed, and diversity within boards is crucial to creating a high-quality dialogue on future strategies and supporting strategic innovation.[4] To leverage this diversity, boards need to develop a culture of valuing and respecting different viewpoints and be willing to work through the often-difficult process of reconciling them, as we emphasized in Chapters 5 and 6.

From demographic to cognitive diversity

In the current political environment, diversity has become a highly political topic that is often supported or rejected based on ideological perspectives. While the heated political discourse on diversity all too often focuses on demographic factors like gender, ethnicity, or sexual orientation, it is not these demographic characteristics themselves that matter for the quality of board work, but rather the underlying differences in perspective that they may generate. In other words, rather than focusing first and foremost on demographic diversity, boards should emphasize cognitive diversity that focuses on different experiences and ways of thinking.[5] Debbie Hewitt, chair of England's Football Association, noted: "Boards need people who think in different ways and who bring different experiences to their discussions. True cognitive diversity is essential to an effective board."

To achieve cognitive diversity, you need differences in upbringing, education, life, and work experience, as well as variations in demographics. Boards that are diverse along all these dimensions can usually engage in richer and more robust discussions and decision-making processes.

However, simply bringing varied viewpoints to the table is not enough in itself. Board members must embrace all the differences in perspectives, thought processes, and problem-solving approaches as opportunities to make better decisions, rather than perceive them as hurdles. A culture that values differences in thinking is not only central to effectively leveraging a diverse board, it is also a core skill that underlies the board's ability to embrace uncertainty and change. A board that cannot engage fundamentally different viewpoints will not be able to constructively respond to changes that challenge the status quo of the organization. To enable management to explore and assess new strategies, the board needs to accept the uncertainty and novelty inherent in strategic discontinuities and the resulting likelihood of failures. Rather than rejecting what is different and untested, boards need to embrace the novelty and foster experimentation with new approaches, and the failures that such experiments invariably create.

Beyond the status quo: experimentation with new structures and practices

To enhance efficiency, agility, and resilience, boards should also actively experiment with new structures such as shadow boards and fluid committee structures, models of interaction within the board and in its collaboration with management, novel tools and practices, and, more generally, explore different governance models.

Like any organizational structure, boards need to invest time and energy in continually optimizing their own workings. They should periodically evaluate their structures, processes, and culture and adapt to industry trends, governance best practices, and emerging changes. This requires open-mindedness and the willingness to experiment with new approaches and technologies. For many boards, this will also require a change in culture away from the board as a source of stability and towards a culture of constant change, continuous improvement, and innovation, something that does not come easily to many boards and may run counter to the incentives of some of their members. Greg Poux-Guillaume, a chairman at Swiss-based Medmix, explained:

> One of the problems with board evolution is that it is often reactive. In an ideal world, you would like to see a board reflecting proactively about its structure, its composition, and its practices. So when you have a new CEO or you start a transformation, you would like the board to ask: "How should we transform? What new skills do we need?" It rarely happens because what is your incentive to make yourself obsolete?

Experimenting with adaptive structures

The dynamic approach to boards that we advocate also implies continuous experimentation with novel structural solutions to the tasks of the board. The structure of committees, working groups, and advisory boards needs to be regularly adjusted to align with the company's strategic needs. This could involve the creation and dissolution of committees, working groups, and advisory boards, or at least the redefinition of their mandate and changes to their composition. Many boards continue to be too slow-paced in adjusting their structure and responding to changes, and they need effective mechanisms to facilitate timely renewal.

Beyond these regular adjustments of their existing structural tools, boards should experiment with innovative structural solutions. For instance, some boards have started to use shadow boards consisting of younger employees or emerging leaders to provide competing views on strategic issues on the board's agenda. These shadow boards work on the same agenda and problems, providing an unencumbered view, fresh insights, and often alternative approaches. Debbie Hewitt, chair of England's Football Association, introduced this idea to us:

> We created a shadow board in one of the businesses that I chaired. It was a board to which we appointed young people we considered to have the potential to be executives in the future. We appointed an individual to each board position. So I had an equivalent who was the chair, plus there was someone appointed as the chief executive, someone as the finance director, and a similar number of non-executive directors as the main board. This shadow board received most of our board papers. They had their board meeting with the same agenda as our main board. We would then meet with them to debrief. It was time-consuming, but it provided excellent insights about how they tackled a topic and what they saw as important. It provided both mentoring for the shadow board candidates and reverse mentoring for our board. They certainly challenged some of our assumptions.

A second area of experimentation is often around the formation of temporary structures, such as temporary working groups. These break up the traditional distinction between the board and the leadership team to develop solutions to strategic issues in a truly collaborative manner. Kathleen Bailey Lord, chair at ed-tech company Janison and member of the board at Datacom, AMP, and St Vincent's, provided an example:

> On one of my boards, we now experiment with new ways of working together with the management through working groups. It is an experiment, and we don't know yet if it will work. Boards have to be prepared to experiment and take some risks in trying new things, even if some may fail. Of course, there is the inherent risk that you will change the role of a director and management at that moment. You do need directors who are very mindful of the red lines so that whilst you're having a conversation as equals, you still stay in your own domain and respect the principles of governance. So you're not trying to tell management what to do.

More generally, we advocate for boards to experiment with more flexible approaches to committees, ad hoc groups, and advisory boards. Whenever governance rules allow, boards should regularly rethink committee mandates, structures, and compositions as business needs evolve and complement the longer-lasting (and often more tightly regulated) mandatory committees with temporary structures that provide the agility to address specific issues.

Meeting models

A second domain of experimentation involves meeting models. The pandemic accelerated the adoption of virtual meetings, prompting boards to redefine processes to maintain effectiveness in a remote environment. As we discussed in Chapter 5, however, there are good reasons why boards should be skeptical about moving to a fully virtual meeting mode. Boards should instead experiment with advancements in technology that may enhance engagement and interactivity in remote meetings and enable effective mixed or hybrid modes of working. Phoebe Wood, Invesco, Ltd., PPL Corporation, and Leggett and Platt Corporation, explained:

> What's the right balance between physical and virtual meetings going forward? Boards are answering this question in their own way. A clear trend is that many more committee meetings are being held online, often with a commitment to meet at least once a year in person. The percentage of board meetings that are held in person will depend on the CEO, the chair, the industry, and the ease of getting together, and there is no "right" answer. However, the value of the board gathering in person includes the informal conversations that occur over dinner, in the hallway, or in the bathrooms. Those aren't occurring naturally in a virtual setting, so you need to create time for them.

AI tools

Emerging AI technologies have the potential to transform many aspects of board work, including strategic analysis, risk assessment, trend scouting, generation of board materials, and decision-making support, to name a few. Boards must not only guide the company in its adaptation of AI and other digital technologies and their implications for the company's business model, but directors should themselves stay abreast of the technological advancements to leverage these tools for more effective and efficient board work. Directors need to understand the opportunities but also the limits of AI capabilities and limitations to leverage them effectively. One of the key advantages that AI tools provide for board members is that they allow them to engage in analysis tasks that traditionally would have required business development or consulting resources that typically have not been under control or even available for board members.

Innovative governance models

While regulatory rules in every country set limits that need to be respected, boards should nevertheless reconsider their traditional board structures and processes and actively learn from other countries or other company types, as we suggested in Chapters 8 and 10. Even if regulatory limits prevent direct implementation, fundamentally questioning current governance models may provide insights on how to evolve the existing structures. For instance, some directors we interviewed proposed completely separating strategic oversight from compliance and monitoring functions. Kaj-Erik Relander, board member of Louis Dreyfuss Corporation, SES Satellites, and a number of other privately held corporations, explained:

> You might want to separate the compliance topics from discussions on business and strategy. Often, what happens is you spend too much time on compliance and, after three and a half hours on audit and compliance, you don't have much energy left to be disruptive around technology and strategy.

In a similar vein, Thomas Thune Andersen, chair at Lloyd's Register Group and VKR Holding and member of the board at BW Group and IMI plc, explained:

> Conceptually, as we move forward, maybe there will be a governance board for reporting and compliance, and then a strategic board for the future. So you have a board that looks backward and a board that looks forward. But then you would need to work out who signs the accounts and makes the important decisions. It is an interesting model but has lots of unanswered questions.

While in publicly listed companies, such radical departures from established governance may be difficult or even impossible from a regulatory perspective, it is often the lived reality in PE-held firms. A segmentation of the main tasks of the board can enhance focus and effectiveness in each area. However, it also poses challenges around decision integration and clarity of authority. As such, boards might experiment with variations of this idea and integrate aspects of it into their governance model.

Redefining interaction with management

Finally, boards should experiment with different models of interaction with management. In many boards, interaction with management continues to be formal and limited to the classical board presentation and discussion format. The most innovative boards, however, have started to experiment with novel ways to engage with management while respecting governance boundaries. For example, when directors need to act as advisors and actors in strategy creation, formal modes of interaction do not make sufficient use of their expertise and skills, and they may need to consider temporarily breaching the traditional divide between board members and executives. However, board chairs and board members also need to recognize the risks of overstepping governance boundaries and taking on operational tasks, and ensure that directors always remain mindful of their governance role.

Concluding remarks

We began this book with the observation that the role of the board of directors in corporations has never been more critical than it is today. At the same time, the tasks that boards must accomplish have become increasingly complex and challenging. Although boards have become more effective and efficient over the past decade, this process of professionalization has been chasing a moving target. As a result, there are still many areas where boards can improve. We hope that this book has provided frameworks, ideas, and suggestions on how to further develop this essential component of the strategic apex of any organization and that board chairs and directors will find inspiration in them for their daily board work.

Notes

1. William B. Joiner and Stephen A. Josephs, *Leadership Agility: Five Levels of Mastery for Anticipating and Initiating Change* (San Francisco, CA: Jossey Bass, 2006).
2. National Association of Corporate Directors (NACD), *The Future of the American Board Report: A Framework for Governing into the Future*, NACD (Arlington, USA, October 13, 2022).
3. Seymour Burchman and Blair Jones, "How Boards Can Plan for the Disasters That No One Wants to Think About," *HBR.org*, Harvard Business Review, September 04, 2020, https://hbr.org/2020/09/how-boards-can-plan-for-the-disasters-that-no-one-wants-to-think-about.
4. Heng An, Carl R. Chen, Qun Wu, and Ting Zhang, "Corporate Innovation: Do Diverse Boards Help?" Journal of Financial and Quantitative Analysis 56, no. 1 (2021); Amy J. Hillman, "Board Diversity: Beginning to Unpeel the Onion," Corporate Governance: An International Review 23, no. 2 (2015); Renée B. Adams, Jakob De Haan, Siri Terjesen, and Hans Van Ees, "Board Diversity: Moving the Field Forward," Corporate Governance: An International Review 23, no. 2 (2015).
5. Scott E. Page, *The Difference: How the Power of Diversity Creates Better Groups, Firms, Schools, and Society* (Princeton, NJ: Princeton University Press, 2008).

Bibliography

Abraham, Chon, Sasha Cohen O'Connell, Iria Giuffrida, and Ronald R. Sims. "Adding Cybersecurity Expertise to Your Board." *MIT Sloan Management Review* 65, no. 2 (2024): 1–6.

Adams, Renée B., Jakob De Haan, Siri Terjesen, and Hans Van Ees. "Board Diversity: Moving the Field Forward." *Corporate Governance: An International Review* 23, no. 2 (2015): 77–82.

Adams, Renée B., and Daniel Ferreira. "Women in the Boardroom and Their Impact on Governance and Performance." *Journal of Financial Economics* 94, no. 2 (2009): 291–309.

Agrawal, Ajay, Joshua Gans, and Avi Goldfarb. "How AI Will Change Strategy: A Thought Experiment." *HBR.org. Harvard Business Review,* October 3, 2017, https://hbr.org/2017/10/how-ai-will-change-strategy-a-thought-experiment.

Aguilera, Ruth V., J. Alberto Aragón-Correa, Valentina Marano, and Peter A. Tashman. "The Corporate Governance of Environmental Sustainability: A Review and Proposal for More Integrated Research." *Journal of Management* 47, no. 6 (July 2021): 1468–1497.

Aguilera, Ruth V., and Alvaro Cuervo-Cazurra. "Codes of Good Governance." *Corporate Governance: An International Review* 17, no. 3 (May 2009): 376–387.

Aguilera, Ruth V., Kurt Desender, Michael K. Bednar, and Jun Ho Lee. "Connecting the Dots: Bringing External Corporate Governance into the Corporate Governance Puzzle." *Academy of Management Annals* 9, no. 1 (2015): 483–573.

Aguilera, Ruth V., and Gregory Jackson. "Comparative and International Corporate Governance." *Academy of Management Annals* 4 (2010): 485–556.

Aguilera, Ruth V., Valentina Marano, and Ilir Haxhi. "International Corporate Governance: A Review and Opportunities for Future Research." *Journal of International Business Studies* 50 (2019): 457–498.

Allayannis, George (Yiorgos), Boban Markovic, and Gerry Yemen. *The End of Credit Suisse,* Case Study: UVA-F-2064. Charlottesville, VA: Darden Business Publishing, December 20, 2023.

Altman, Steven A., and Caroline R. Bastian. "The State of Globalization in 2023: Data Disproves the Notion That the World Has Become More Regionalized in Recent Years." *HBR.org. Harvard Business Review,* July 11, 2023, https://hbr.org/2023/07/the-state-of-globalization-in-2023.

An, Heng, Carl R. Chen, Qun Wu, and Ting Zhang. "Corporate Innovation: Do Diverse Boards Help?." *Journal of Financial and Quantitative Analysis* 56, no. 1 (2021): 155–182.

Anderson, George, James M. Citrin, Cassandra Frangos, and Zachary Morfín. "5 Moments That Make or Break a CEO-Board Chair Relationship." *HBR.org. Harvard Business Review*, August 23, 2024, https://hbr.org/2024/08/5-moments-that-make-or-break-a-ceo-board-chair-relationship.

Anderson, George M., and David Chun. "How Much Board Turnover Is Best?." Editorial Material. *Harvard Business Review* 92, no. 4 (2014): 26.

Anthony, Scott D., Clark G. Gilbert, and Mark W. Johnson. *Dual Transformation: How to Reposition Today's Business While Creating the Future*. Boston, MA: Harvard Business Review Press, 2017.

Banerjee, Anup, Mattias Nordqvist, and Karin Hellerstedt. "The Role of the Board Chair - A Literature Review and Suggestions for Future Research." *Corporate Governance: An International Review* 28, no. 6 (2020): 372–405.

Barton, Dominic, and Mark Wiseman. "Where Boards Fall Short." *Harvard Business Review* 93, no. 1 (2015): 19.

Ben-Amar, Walid, Claude Francoeur, Taïeb Hafsi, and Réal Labelle. "What Makes Better Boards? A Closer Look at Diversity and Ownership." *British Journal of Management* 24, no. 1 (2013): 85–101.

Bennigson, Larry, and Frank S. Leonard. "Bringing Opportunity Oversight onto the Boards Agenda." *MIT Sloan Management Review* 54, no. 3 (2013): 57–61.

Beyer, Martin. "SAP Has a New Succession Plan." *CIO*, February 12, 2024, https://www.cio.com/article/1306972/sap-has-a-new-succession-plan.html.

Bezemer, P. J., A. Pugliese, G. Nicholson, and A. Zattoni. "Toward a Synthesis of the Board-Strategy Relationship: A Literature Review and Future Research Agenda." *Corporate Governance: An International Review* 31, no. 1 (January 2023): 178–197.

Bjørnåli, Ekaterina S., and Magnus Gulbrandsen. "Exploring Board Formation and Evolution of Board Composition in Academic Spin-Offs." *The Journal of Technology Transfer* 35 (2010): 92–112.

Boivie, Steven, Michael K. Bednar, Ruth V. Aguilera, and Joel L. Andrus. "Are Boards Designed to Fail? The Implausibility of Effective Board Monitoring." *Academy of Management Annals* 10, no. 1 (2016): 319–407.

Boivie, Steven, Michael C. Withers, Scott D. Graffin, and Kevin G. Corley. "Corporate Directors' Implicit Theories of the Roles and Duties of Boards." *Strategic Management Journal* 42, no. 9 (2021): 1662–1695.

Bonini, Stefano, Senem Alkan, and Antonio Salvi. "The Effects of Venture Capitalists on the Governance of Firms." *Corporate Governance: An International Review* 20, no. 1 (2012): 21–45.

Bonn, Ingrid, and Andrew Pettigrew. "Towards a Dynamic Theory of Boards: An Organisational Life Cycle Approach." *Journal of Management & Organization* 15, no. 1 (2009): 2–16.

Boyd, Brian K., and Angelo M. Solarino. "Ownership of Corporations: A Review, Synthesis, and Research Agenda." *Journal of Management* 42, no. 5 (2016): 1282–1314.

Brissett, Leslie, Mannie Sher, and Tazi Lorraine Smith. *Dynamics at Boardroom Level: A Tavistock Primer for Leaders, Coaches and Consultants*. London: Routledge, 2020.

Brown, Gerry, and Randall S. Peterson. *Disaster in the Boardroom: Six Dysfunctions Everyone Should Understand*. Cham: Springer/Palgrave McMillan, 2022.

Burchman, Seymour, and Blair Jones. "How Boards Can Plan for the Disasters That No One Wants to Think About." *HBR.org. Harvard Business Review*, September 04, 2020, https://hbr.org/2020/09/how-boards-can-plan-for-the-disasters-that-no-one-wants-to-think-about.

Byron, Kris, and Corinne Post. "Women on Boards of Directors and Corporate Social Performance: A Meta-Analysis." *Corporate Governance: An International Review* 24, no. 4 (2016): 428–442.

Canals, Jordi. *Can the Board of Directors Be an Effective Team?* Case Study: SMN-0709-E. Barcelona: IESE Business School, March 4, 2024.

Canals, Jordi. *The Role of the Board of Directors in Corporate Transformation*, Case Study: SMN-0708-E. Barcelona: IESE Business School, April 5, 2022.

Carey, Dennis, Ram Charan, Joseph Griesedieck, and Michael Useem. "8 Questions to Ask before Selecting a New Board Leader." *HBR.org. Harvard Business Review*, January 17, 2023. https://hbr.org/2023/01/8-questions-to-ask-before-selecting-a-new-board-leader.

Carpenter, Mason A., Wm. Gerard Sanders, and Hal B. Gregersen. "Bundling Human Capital with Organizational Context: The Impact of International Assignment Experience on Multinational Firm Performance and CEO Pay." *Academy of Management Journal* 44, no. 3 (2001): 493–511.

Chamorro-Premuzic, Tomas, and Darko Lovric. "How to Decide If AI Should Be Part of Your Growth Strategy." *HBR.org, Harvard Business Review*, March 20, 2024, https://hbr.org/2024/03/how-to-decide-if-ai-should-be-part-of-your-growth-strategy.

Charan, Ram, Dennis Carey, and Michael Useem. *Boards That Lead: When to Take Charge, When to Partner, and When to Stay out of the Way.* Boston, MA: Harvard Business Review Press, 2014.

Cheng, J. Yo-Jud, and Boris Groysberg. "Gender Diversity at the Board Level Can Mean Innovation Success." *MIT Sloan Management Review* 61, no. 2 (2020): 1–8.

Churchill, Neil, and Virginia Lewis. "The Five Stages of Small Business Growth." *Harvard Business Review* 62 (1983): 30–39.

Ciampa, Dan, and Adam Bryant. "Power, Influence, and CEO Succession." *Harvard Business Review* 103, no. 7–8 (2024): 44–52.

Clark, Cynthia E., and Jill A. Brown. "Meet the New Board: Same as the Old Board." *MIT Sloan Management Review* 64, no. 1 (2022): 56–59.

Clarke, Thomas. *International Corporate Governance: A Comparative Approach.* London: Routledge, 2007.

Cliffe, Sarah, and Barbara Hackman Franklin. "The Board View: Directors Must Balance All Interests a Conversation with Corporate Governance Expert Barbara Hackman Franklin by Sarah Cliffe." Editorial Material. *Harvard Business Review* 95, no. 3 (2017): 64–66.

Cohn, Jeffrey M. "What Boards of Public Companies Can Learn from Private Equity." *HBR.org. Harvard Business Review*, February 12, 2024, https://hbr.org/2024/02/what-boards-of-public-companies-can-learn-from-private-equity.

Coles, Jerilyn W., and William S. Hesterly. "Independence of the Chairman and Board Composition: Firm Choices and Shareholder Value." *Journal of Management* 26, no. 2 (2000): 195–214.

The Conference Board. *Corporate Boards Are More Diverse Than Ever, but Growth in Racial Diversity among New Directors Is Slowing.* New York: The Conference Board, December 03, 2024.

Cook, Scott, Andrei Hagiu, and Julian Wright. "Turn Generative Ai from an Existential Threat into a Competitive Advantage." *Harvard Business Review* 102, no. 1 (2024): 118–125.

Cossin, Didier. *High Performance Boards: Improving and Energizing Your Governance.* Chichester: John Wiley & Sons, 2024.

Cossin, Didier, and Estelle Metayer. "How Strategic Is Your Board?." *MIT Sloan Management Review* 56, no. 1 (2014): 37–43.

Creary, Stephanie J., Janet Foutty, and Kwasi Mitchell. "How Diversity Can Boost Board Effectiveness." *MIT Sloan Management Review* 64, no. 3 (2023): 1–4.

Crowley, Daniel F. C., and Robert G. Eccles. "Rescuing Esg from the Culture Wars." *HBR.org. Harvard Business Review*, February 09, 2023, https://hbr.org/2023/02/rescuing-esg-from-the-culture-wars.

Dalton, Dan R., Catherine M. Daily, Alan E. Ellstrand, and Jonathan L. Johnson. "Meta-Analytic Reviews of Board Composition, Leadership Structure, and Financial Performance." *Strategic Management Journal* 19, no. 3 (1998): 269–290.

Dalton, Dan R., and Catherine M. Dalton. "Integration of Micro and Macro Studies in Governance Research: CEO Duality, Board Composition, and Financial Performance." *Journal of Management* 37, no. 2 (2011): 404–411.

Deb, Palesh, Vipin Sreekumar, Prothit Sen, Augustine Duru, and David L. Brannon. "New Venture Governance: An Integrative, Multidisciplinary Review." *Academy of Management Annals* 18, no. 2 (2024): 831–861.

Deutsch, Yuval, Thomas Keil, and Tomi Laamanen. "A Dual Agency View of Board Compensation: The Joint Effects of Outside Director and CEO Stock Options on Firm Risk." *Strategic Management Journal* 32, no. 2 (2011): 212–227.

Deutsch, Yuval, and T. W. Ross. "You Are Known by the Directors You Keep: Reputable Directors as a Signaling Mechanism for Young Firms." *Management Science* 49, no. 8 (2003): 1003–1017.

Doidge, Craig, G. Andrew Karolyi, and René M. Stulz. "Why Do Countries Matter So Much for Corporate Governance?" *Journal of Financial Economics* 86, no. 1 (2007): 1–39.

Eccles, Robert G., and Tim Youmans. "Why Boards Must Look Beyond Shareholders." *sloanreview.mit.edu. MIT Sloan Management Review*, 2015, https://sloanreview.mit.edu/article/why-boards-must-look-beyond-shareholders/.

Edelman, David, and Vivek Sharma. "It's Time for Boards to Take AI Seriously." *HBR.org. Harvard Business Review*, November 2, 2023, https://hbr.org/2023/11/its-time-for-boards-to-take-ai-seriously.

Edmondson, Amy C. *Teaming: How Organizations Learn, Innovate, and Compete in the Knowledge Economy*. San Francisco, CA: John Wiley & Sons, 2012.

Eirola, A., P. J. Bezemer, and S. Reinhold." Boardroom Dissent: An Integrative Review and Future Research Agenda." *Corporate Governance: An International Review* 33, no. 3 (2024): 389–406.

Elvira, Marta, and Marta Villamor. *Diversity in Boards of Directors: A Synthesis and Review*, Case Study: DPON-0159-E. Barcelona: IESE Publishing, January 31, 2020.

Faleye, Olubunmi. "The Downside to Full Board Independence." *MIT Sloan Management Review* 58, no. 2 (2017): 87.

Faleye, Olubunmi, Rani Hoitash, and Udi Hoitash. "The Trouble with Too Much Board Oversight." *MIT Sloan Management Review* 54, no. 3 (2013): 53–56.

Färbinger, Peter M. "Sap and Punit Renjen Have Mutually Agreed to Part Ways." *E3 Magazine*, February 13, 2024, https://e3mag.com/en/sap-and-punit-renjen-have-decided-to-part-ways-by-mutual-agreement/.

Färbinger, Peter M. "Two Years Lost for Sap." *E3 Magazine,* February 22, 2024, https://e3mag.com/en/two-lost-years-for-sap/.

Feakin, Tobias. "Navigating the New Geopolitics of Tech." HBR.org. *Harvard Business Review,* November 11, 2024, https://hbr.org/2024/11/navigating-the-new-geopolitics-of-tech.

Federo, Ryan, Yuliya Ponomareva, Ruth V. Aguilera, Angel Saz-Carranza, and Carlos Losada. "Bringing Owners Back on Board: A Review of the Role of Ownership Type in

Board Governance." *Corporate Governance: An International Review* 28, no. 6 (2020): 348–371.

Ferreira, Daniel. "Board Diversity." In *Corporate Governance: A Synthesis of Theory, Research, and Practice*, edited by H. Kent Baker and Ronald Anderson, 225–242. Hoboken, NJ: Wiley, 2010.

Filatotchev, Igor, and Cristiano Bellavitis. "Venture Capital and Corporate Governance of Entrepreneurial Ventures." In *The Palgrave Encyclopedia of Private Equity*, edited by Douglas J. Cumming and Benjamin Hammer, 1203–1207. Cham: Palgrave MacMillan, 2025.

Filatotchev, Igor, Steve Toms, and Mike Wright. "The Firm's Strategic Dynamics and Corporate Governance Life-Cycle." *International Journal of Managerial Finance* 2, no. 4 (2006): 256–279.

Finkelstein, S., D. C. Hambrick, and A. A. Cannella. *Strategic Leadership: Theory and Research on Executives, Top Management Teams, and Boards.* New York: Oxford University Press, 2009.

Foss, Nicolai J., Peter G. Klein, Lasse B. Lien, Thomas Zellweger, and Todd Zenger. "Ownership Competence." *Strategic Management Journal* 42, no. 2 (2021): 302–328.

Fubini, David, Suraj Srinivasan, and Patrick Sanguineti. *Board Director Dilemmas: The Tradeoffs of Board Selection*, Case Study: 9-425-023. Boston, MA: Harvard Business Publishing, September 5, 2024.

Garfield, David. "Supply Chains Belong at the Top of a CEO's Agenda: Five Ways Leaders Can Navigate the Growing Risks of Instability and Disruption without Getting Bogged Down in Tactical Issues." *HBR.org. Harvard Business Review*, September 30, 2024, https://hbr.org/2024/09/supply-chains-belong-at-the-top-of-a-ceos-agenda.

Ghemawat, Pankaj. "Globalization in the Age of Trump: Protectionism Will Change How Companies Do Business—But Not in the Ways You Think." *Harvard Business Review* 95, no. 4 (2017): 112–123.

Gómez-Mejía, Luis R., Katalin Takács Haynes, Manuel Núñez-Nickel, Kathryn JL Jacobson, and José Moyano-Fuentes. "Socioemotional Wealth and Business Risks in Family-Controlled Firms: Evidence from Spanish Olive Oil Mills." *Administrative Science Quarterly* 52, no. 1 (2007): 106–137.

Govindarajan, Vijay, Anup Srivastava, Hussein Warsame, and Luminita Enache. "Tech Giants, Taxes, and a Looming Global Trade War." *HBR.org. Harvard Business Review*, August 24, 2020, https://hbr.org/2020/08/tech-giants-taxes-and-a-looming-global-trade-war.

Gregory, Holly J., and Sidley Austin LLP. "Establishing Norms for Director Behavior to Enhance Board Culture and Effectiveness." *corpgov.law.harvard.edu. Harvard Law School Forum on Corporate Governance*, November 8, 2022, https://corpgov.law.harvard.edu/2022/11/08/establishing-norms-for-director-behavior-to-enhance-board-culture-and-effectiveness/.

Greiner, Larry E. "Evolution and Revolution as Organizations Grow." *Harvard Business Review* 50, no. 4 (1972): 29–37.

Groysberg, Boris, and Deborah Bell. "Dysfunction in the Boardroom." *Harvard Business Review* 91, no. 6 (2013): 89–97.

Hagelgans, Andrea, and Lex Suvanto. "How Boards Can Guide Company Strategy on Social Issues." *HBR.org. Harvard Business Review*, December 15, 2022, https://hbr.org/2022/12/how-boards-can-guide-company-strategy-on-social-issues.

Henisz, Witold J. "The Value of Corporate Purpose." *HBR.org. Harvard Business Review*, November 20, 2023, https://hbr.org/2023/11/the-value-of-corporate-purpose.

Hernandez, Morela. "Game-Changing Strategies for Corporate Boards." *sloanreview.mit.edu. MIT Sloan Management Review*, October 17, 2018, 2018, https://sloanreview.mit.edu/article/game-changing-strategies-for-corporate-boards/.

Hilb, Martin. *Integrierte Corporate Governance.* 6th ed. Berlin: Springer, 2016.

Hilb, Martin. *New Corporate Governance: Successful Board Management Tools.* 5th ed. Heidelberg: Springer, 2016.

Hillman, Amy J. "Board Diversity: Beginning to Unpeel the Onion." *Corporate Governance: An International Review* 23, no. 2 (2015): 104–107.

Hooijberg, Robert, and Nancy Lane. "How Boards Botch CEO Succession." News Item. *MIT Sloan Management Review* 57, no. 4 (2016): 14–16.

Hosanagar, Kartik, and Ramayya Krishnan. "Who Profits the Most from Generative AI?" *MIT Sloan Management Review* 65, no. 3 (2024): 24–29.

Hrebiniak, Lawrence G. *Making Strategy Work: Leading Effective Execution and Change.* Upper Saddle River, NJ: Wharton School Publishing, 2005.

Huse, Morten. *Boards, Governance and Value Creation: The Human Side of Corporate Governance.* Cambridge: Cambridge University Press, 2007.

Janahi, Mohamed, Yuval Millo, and Georgios Voulgaris. "Age Diversity and the Monitoring Role of Corporate Boards: Evidence from Banks." *Human Relations* 76, no. 10 (2023): 1599–1633.

Johnson, Scott G., Karen Schnatterly, and Aaron D. Hill. "Board Composition beyond Independence: Social Capital, Human Capital, and Demographics." *Journal of Management* 39, no. 1 (2013): 232–262.

Joiner, William B., and Stephen A. Josephs. *Leadership Agility: Five Levels of Mastery for Anticipating and Initiating Change.* San Francisco, CA: Jossey Bass, 2006.

Katsiampa, Paraskevi, Paul B. McGuinness, and Hanxiong Zhang. "The Role of Board Age Diversity in the Performance of Publicly Listed Fintech Entities." *The European Journal of Finance* 30, no. 11 (2024): 1295–1326.

Keasey, Kevin, Steve Thompson, and Michael Wright. *Corporate Governance: Accountability, Enterprise and International Comparisons.* Chichester: John Wiley & Sons, 2005.

Keil, Thomas, and Marianna Zangrillo. "Building Organizational Resilience: When the Entire Organization Should Be Engaged and Power Unleashed." In *Building Resilient Organizations,* edited by Stuart Crainer, 87–93. Newtown Square, PA: Thinkers50/Brightline, 2022.

Keil, Thomas, and Marianna Zangrillo. "Don't Set Your Next CEO up to Fail." *MIT Sloan Management Review* 61, no. 2 (2020): 87–88.

Keil, Thomas, and Marianna Zangrillo. *The Next CEO: Board and CEO Perspectives for Successful CEO Succession.* London: Routledge, 2021.

Keil, Thomas, and Marianna Zangrillo. *The Next Leadership Team: How to Select, Build, and Optimize Your Top Team.* London: Routledge, 2023.

Keil, Thomas, and Marianna Zangrillo. "Why It's Not Enough for Your CEO to Be a Superstar." *Fast Company,* 2023, https://www.fastcompany.com/90909667/why-its-not-enough-for-your-ceo-to-be-a-superstar.

Khanna, Tarun, Mary C. Beckerle, and Nabil Y. Sakkab. "Boards Need a New Approach to Technology." *Harvard Business Review* 103, no. 9–10 (2024): 128–137.

Kiron, David, and Michael Schrage. "Strategy for and with AI." *MIT Sloan Management Review* 60, no. 4 (Summer 2019): 30–35.

Kiron, David, Michael Schrage, François Candelon, Shervin Khodabandeh, and Michael Chu. "Governance for Smarter KPIs: Effective Governance Enables Kpis to Evolve, Remain Aligned with Strategic Goals, and Gain Workers' and Managers' Trust." *sloanreview.mit.edu. MIT Sloan Management Review,* November 06, 2023, https://sloanreview.mit.edu/article/governance-for-smarter-kpis/.

Kolev, Kalin D., David B. Wangrow, Vincent L. Barker III, and Donald J. Schepker. "Board Committees in Corporate Governance: A Cross-Disciplinary Review and Agenda for the Future." *Journal of Management Studies* 56, no. 6 (2019): 1138–1193.

Krause, Ryan. "Being the CEO's Boss: An Examination of Board Chair Orientations." *Strategic Management Journal* 38, no. 3 (2017): 697–713.

Krause, Ryan, Matthew Semadeni, and Albert A. Cannella. "CEO Duality: A Review and Research Agenda." *Journal of Management* 40, no. 1 (2014): 256–286.

Krause, Ryan, Matthew Semadeni, and Michael C. Withers. "That Special Someone: When the Board Views Its Chair as a Resource." *Strategic Management Journal* 37, no. 9 (2016): 1990–2002.

Krause, Ryan, Michael C. Withers, and Mary J. Waller. "Leading the Board in a Crisis: Strategy and Performance Implications of Board Chair Directive Leadership." *Journal of Management* 50, no. 2 (2024): 654–684.

Krause, Ryan, Michael C. Withers, and Mary J. Waller. "Reducing Bias through Board Decision-Making: An Information-Processing Model of Board Decision Synergy." *Academy of Management Review* (2024), forthcoming. https://doi.org/10.5465/amr.2022.0271.

La Porta, Rafael, Florencio Lopez-de-Silanes, and Andrei Shleifer. "Corporate Ownership around the World." *Journal of Finance* 54, no. 2 (1999): 471–517.

Landaw, Jared L. *Maximizing the Benefits of Board Diversity: Lessons Learned from Activist Investing*, DN-V11N2. New York: The Conference Board, June 2020.

Lang, Nils K., and Peter Wirtz. "Kicking Off the Corporate Governance Lifecycle: Seed Funding, Venture Capital and the Nascent Board." *British Journal of Management* 33, no. 1 (2022): 181–210.

Lansberg, Ivan. "Why Your Family Business Needs Family Members on the Board." *HBR.org. Harvard Business Review*, September 22, 2022, https://hbr.org/2022/09/why-your-family-business-needs-family-members-on-the-board.

Larcker, David, and Brian Tayan. *Corporate Governance Matters: A Closer Look at Organizational Choices and Their Consequences*. 3rd ed. London: Pearson/FT Press, 2020.

Lawler, Edward E., and Christopher G. Worley. "Why Boards Need to Change." *MIT Sloan Management Review* 54, no. 1 (2012): 10–12.

Leblanc, Richard. *The Handbook of Board Governance: A Comprehensive Guide for Public, Private, and Not-for-Profit Board Members*. Hoboken, NJ: John Wiley & Sons, 2020.

Lessambo, Felix. *The International Corporate Governance System: Audit Roles and Board Oversight*. London: Palgrave Macmillan, 2016.

Levin, Blair, and Larry Downes. "Every Company Needs a Political Strategy Today." *MIT Sloan Management Review* 64, no. 2 (2023): 7–9.

Levy, Cindy, Shubham Singhal, and Matt Watters. *A Proactive Approach to Navigating Geopolitics Is Essential to Thrive*. www.mckinsey.com. McKinsey & Company, November 12, 2024, https://www.mckinsey.com/capabilities/geopolitics/our-insights/a-proactive-approach-to-navigating-geopolitics-is-essential-to-thrive#/.

Loreto, Nick Di. "5 Kinds of Ownership Roles in a Family Business." *HBR.org. Harvard Business Review*, March 22, 2024, https://hbr.org/2024/03/5-kinds-of-ownership-roles-in-a-family-business.

Lorsch, Jay William. *The Future of Boards: Meeting the Governance Challenges of the Twenty-First Century*. Boston, MA: Harvard Business Review Press, 2012.

Lorsch, Jay William, and Robert C. Clark. "Leading from the Boardroom." *Harvard Business Review* 86, no. 4 (2008): 104–111.

Markovitz, Gayle, Kate Whiting, and Spencer Feingold. "5 Takeaways from Davos 2025." *World Economic Forum*, January 24, 2025, https://www.weforum.org/stories/2025/01/5-key-takeaways-davos-2025/.

McDonald, M. L., J. D. Westphal, and M. E. Graebner. "What Do They Know? The Effects of Outside Director Acquisition Experience on Firm Acquisition Performance." *Strategic Management Journal* 29, no. 11 (2008): 1155–1177.

Meister, S., and R. Palkhiwala. "The Rise of 'Governance Correctness': How Public Markets Have Lost Entrepreneurial Ground to Private Equity." Baar: Partnersgroup, 2018. https://www.partnersgroup.com/~/media/Files/P/Partnersgroup/Universal/perspectives-document/2018-partners-group-white-paper-the-rise-of-governance-correctness.pdf.

Mendiratta, Esha. "Faultlines: Understanding How Board Composition May Influence Team Dynamics and Subgroup Formation in Corporate Boards." In *Research Handbook on Diversity and Corporate Governance*, edited by Sabina Tasheva and Morten Huse, 162–178. Cheltenham: Edward Elgar Publishing, 2023.

Menz, Markus, Robert Langan, and Ryan Krause. "Does Your Board Need an Executive Chair?" *HBR.org. Harvard Business Review*, November 25, 2022, https://hbr.org/2022/11/does-your-board-need-an-executive-chair.

Michael, Withers C., and Fitza, Markus A. "Do Board Chairs Matter? The Influence of Board Chairs on Firm Performance." *Strategic Management Journal* 38, no. 6 (2017): 1343–1355.

Miller, C. Chet, Sana Chiu, Curtis L. Wesley II, Dusya Vera, and Derek R. Avery. "Cognitive Diversity at the Strategic Apex: Assessing Evidence on the Value of Different Perspectives and Ideas among Senior Leaders." *Academy of Management Annals* 16, no. 2 (2022): 806–852.

Minichilli, Alessandro, Jonas Gabrielsson, and Morten Huse. "Board Evaluations: Making a Fit between the Purpose and the System." *Corporate Governance: An International Review* 15, no. 4 (2007): 609–622.

Miric, Milan. "Strategy, Not Technology, Is the Key to Winning with GenAI." *HBR.org. Harvard Business Review*, December 6, 2023, https://hbr.org/2023/12/strategy-not-technology-is-the-key-to-winning-with-genai.

Morck, Randall, and Bernard Yeung. "Family Control and the Rent–Seeking Society." *Entrepreneurship Theory and Practice* 28, no. 4 (2004): 391–409.

Moyo, Dambisa. "Are Businesses Ready for Deglobalization?". *Harvard Business Review*, December 6, 2019, https://hbr.org/2019/12/are-businesses-ready-for-deglobalization.

Moyo, Dambisa. *How Boards Work: And How They Can Work Better in a Chaotic World*. London: Bridge Street Press, 2021.

Nahmias, Omri. "Deglobalization." *MIT Sloan Management Review* 65, no. 3 (2024): 5.

Naidu, Richa, and Simon Jessop. "Before Trump's Return, Some Top U.S. Firms Had Already Gone Cold on Diversity Pledges." *Reuters*, January 27, 2025, https://www.reuters.com/world/us/before-trumps-return-some-top-us-firms-had-already-gone-cold-diversity-pledges-2025-01-27/.

Nambisan, Satish, and Yadong Luo. "Think Globally, Innovate Locally." *MIT Sloan Management Review* 63, no. 3 (2022): 79–84.

National Association of Corporate Directors (NACD). *The Future of the American Board Report: A Framework for Governing into the Future*. Arlington, TX: NACD, October 13, 2022.

Naughton, James. *Fiduciary Duties and Corporate Disclosure*, Case Study: UVA-C-2484. Charlottesville, VA: Darden Business Publishing, Jul 30, 2024.

Neville, François, Kris Byron, Corinne Post, and Andrew Ward. "Board Independence and Corporate Misconduct: A Cross-National Meta-Analysis." *Journal of Management* 45, no. 6 (2019): 2538–2569.

O'Keeffe, Dunigan, Karen Harris, and Austin Kimson. "How to Succeed in an Era of Volatility. (Cover Story)." *Harvard Business Review* 102, no. 2 (2024): 53–57.

O'Reilly III, Charles A., and Michael L. Tushman. "The Ambidextrous Organisation." *Harvard Business Review* 82, no. 4 (April 2004): 74–82.

O'Reilly III, Charles A., and Michael L. Tushman. *Lead and Disrupt: How to Solve the Innovator's Dilemma.* 2nd ed. Palo Alto, CA: Stanford Business Books, 2021.

Ormazabal, Gaizka. "Risk Oversight: What Every Director Should Know." *IESE Insight* 28, no. 28 (2016): 23–28.

Page, Scott E. *The Difference: How the Power of Diversity Creates Better Groups, Firms, Schools, and Society.* Princeton, NJ: Princeton University Press, 2008.

Paine, Lynn S. "The Business Roundtable's Stakeholder Pledge, Five Years Later." *HBR.org. Harvard Business Review*, August 19, 2024, https://hbr.org/2024/08/the-business-roundtables-stakeholder-pledge-five-years-later.

Paine, Lynn S., and Will Hurwitz. *Brief Note on Staggered Boards*, Case Study: 9-323-040. Boston, MA: Harvard Business Publishing, December 2022 (Revised May 2024).

Paine, Lynn S., and Suraj Srinivasan. "A Guide to the Big Ideas and Debates in Corporate Governance." *HBR.org. Harvard Business Review*, October 14, 2019, https://hbr.org/2019/10/a-guide-to-the-big-ideas-and-debates-in-corporate-governance.

Parsons, Richard D., and Marc A. Feigen. "The Boardroom's Quiet Revolution." *Harvard Business Review* 92, no. 3 (2014): 98–104.

Paruchuri, Srikanth, Erik A. Hoempler, Amanda P. Cowen, Albert A. Cannella, and Peter Inho Nahm. "Governance Failure and Governance under Failure: Reviewing the Role of Directors in Organizational Misconduct." *Journal of Management* 50, no. 6 (2024): 2237–2265.

Pavićević, Stevo, Jerayr Haleblian, and Thomas Keil. "When Do Boards of Directors Contribute to Shareholder Value in Firms Targeted for Acquisition? A Group Information-Processing Perspective." *Organization Science* 34, no. 5 (2023): 1759–1776.

Pavićević, Stevo, and Thomas Keil. "Research: How Boards Can Increase CEO Accountability." *HBR.org. Harvard Business Review*, February 4, 2025, https://hbr.org/2025/02/research-how-boards-can-increase-ceo-accountability.

Pavićević, Stevo, and Thomas Keil. "The Role of Procedural Rationality in Debiasing Acquisition Decisions of Overconfident CEOs." *Strategic Management Journal* 42, no. 9 (2021): 1696–1715.

Pavićević, Stevo, Thomas Keil, and Gerry McNamara. "Debiasing the Literature on Executive Decision-Making Biases." *Academy of Management Annals* (2025), forthcoming. https://doi.org/10.5465/annals.2022.0152.

Pavićević, Stevo, Thomas Keil, and Zahra Shaker. *A Board Capital Perspective on Corporate Entrepreneurship in Technology-Intensive Firms*, Working Paper. Frankfurt: Frankfurt School of Finance and Management, 2025.

Perrault, Elise, and Patrick McHugh. "Toward a Life Cycle Theory of Board Evolution: Considering Firm Legitimacy." *Journal of Management & Organization* 21, no. 5 (2015): 627–649.

Peterson, Randall S., and Pedro Fontes Falcão, "6 Kinds of Board Members — And How to Influence," *HBR.org. Harvard Business Review*, December 20, 2023, https://hbr.org/2023/12/6-kinds-of-board-members-and-how-to-influence-them.

Peterson, Randall S., and Pedro Fontes Falcão. "Build a Better Board." *sloanreview.mit.edu. MIT Sloan Management Review* September 26, 2024, https://sloanreview.mit.edu/article/build-a-better-board/.

Peterson, Randall S., and Heidi K. Gardner. "Is Your Board Inclusive—Or Just Diverse?" *HBR.org. Harvard Business Review*, September 28, 2022, https://hbr.org/2022/09/is-your-board-inclusive-or-just-diverse.

Pick, Katharina. "Can You Hear Me Now?" *Harvard Business Review* 86, no. 8 (2008): 23–24.

Post, Corinne, and Kris Byron. "Women on Boards and Firm Financial Performance: A Meta-Analysis." *Academy of Management Journal* 58, no. 5 (2015): 1546–1571.

Post, Rutger von, and Robert C. Pozen. "Boards Can Guide Business through a Crisis." *sloanreview.mit.edu. MIT Sloan Management Review*, May 07, 2020, https://sloanreview.mit.edu/article/boards-can-guide-businesses-through-a-crisis/.

Pozen, Robert C. "The Case for Professional Boards." *Harvard Business Review* 88, no. 12 (2010): 50–58.

Pugliese, Amedeo, Peter Jan Bezemer, Alessandro Zattoni, Morten Huse, Frans A. J. Van den Bosch, and Henk W. Volberda. "Boards of Directors' Contribution to Strategy: A Literature Review and Research Agenda." *Corporate Governance: An International Review* 17, no. 3 (2009): 292–306.

Rothrock, Ray A., James Kaplan, and Friso Van Der Oord. "The Board's Role in Managing Cybersecurity Risks." *MIT Sloan Management Review* 59, no. 2 (2018): 12–15.

Sama, Linda M., Abraham Stefanidis, and R. Mitch Casselman. "Rethinking Corporate Governance in the Digital Economy: The Role of Stewardship." *Business Horizons* 65, no. 5 (2022): 535–546.

Schmitt, Achim, Gilbert Probst, and Michael Tushman. "The Role of the Board Chair during a Crisis." *sloanreview.mit.edu. MIT Sloan Management Review*, 2020, https://sloanreview.mit.edu/article/the-role-of-the-board-chair-during-a-crisis/.

Schulze, William, and Thomas Zellweger. "Property Rights, Owner-Management, and Value Creation." *Academy of Management Review* 46, no. 3 (2021): 489–511.

Sharma, Vivek, and David C. Edelman, "It's Time for Boards to Take AI Seriously." *HBR.org. Harvard Business Review*, November 02, 2023, https://hbr.org/2023/11/its-time-for-boards-to-take-ai-seriously.

Sherman, H. David, Dennis Carey, and Robert Brust. "The Audit Committee's New Agenda." *Harvard Business Review* 87, no. 6 (2009): 92–99.

Sonnenfeld, Jeffrey, Melanie Kusin, and Elise Walton. "What CEOs Really Think of Their Boards." *Harvard Business Review* 91, no. 4 (2013): 98–106.

Stadler, Christian, Julia Hautz, Kurt Matzler, and Stephan F. von_den_Eichen. *Open Strategy: Mastering Disruption from Outside the C-Suite*. Boston: MIT Press, 2021.

Stengel, Jakob. "Board Succession, Evaluation, and Recruitment: A Global Perspective." In *The Handbook of Board Governance*, edited by Richard Leblanc, 301–318. Hoboken, NJ: Wiley 2020.

Stiles, Philip. *Board Dynamics*. Cambridge: Cambridge University Press, 2021.

Stuart, Toby E. "Could Gen AI End Incumbent Firms' Competitive Advantage?" *HBR.org. Harvard Business Review*, November 21, 2024, https://hbr.org/2024/11/could-gen-ai-end-incumbent-firms-competitive-advantage.

Stybel, Laurence J., and Maryanne Peabody. "How Should Board Directors Evaluate Themselves?" *MIT Sloan Management Review* 47, no. 1 (2005): 67–72.

Subramanian, Guhan. "Corporate Governance 2.0." *Harvard Business Review* 93, no. 3 (Mar 2015): 96–105.

Terjesen, Siri, Ruth Sealy, and Val Singh. "Women Directors on Corporate Boards: A Review and Research Agenda." *Corporate governance: An International Review* 17, no. 3 (2009): 320–337.

Thomas, Chris, David Kidd, and Claudio Fernandez-Araoz. "Are You Underutilizing Your Board?" *MIT Sloan Management Review* 48, no. 2 (2007): 71–76.

Thomas, Robert J., Michael Schrage, Joshua B. Bellin, and George Marcotte. "How Boards Can Be Better—A Manifesto." *MIT Sloan Management Review* 50, no. 2 (2009): 69–74.

Tingle, Bryce, "The Case for More Company Insiders on Boards." *HBR.org. Harvard Business Review*, September 30, 2024, https://hbr.org/2024/09/the-case-for-more-company-insiders-on-boards?

Tuggle, Christopher S., Karen Schnatterly, and Richard A. Johnson. "Attention Patterns in the Boardroom: How Board Composition and Processes Affect Discussion of Entrepreneurial Issues." *Academy of Management Journal* 53, no. 3 (2010): 550–571.

Tuggle, Christopher S., David G. Sirmon, Christopher R. Reutzel, and Leonard Bierman. "Commanding Board of Director Attention: Investigating How Organizational Performance and CEO Duality Affect Board Members' Attention to Monitoring." *Strategic Management Journal* 31, no. 9 (2010): 946–968.

Useem, Michael. "How Well-Run Boards Make Decisions." *Harvard Business Review* 84, no. 11 (2006): 130–138.

Useem, Michael, Dennis Carey, and Ram Charan, "How Boards Can Innovate." *HBR.org. Harvard Business Review*, May 21, 2014, https://hbr.org/2014/05/how-boards-can-innovate.

Van Den Berghe, Lutgart A. A., and Abigail Levrau. "The Role of the Venture Capitalist as Monitor of the Company: A Corporate Governance Perspective." *Corporate Governance: An International Review* 10, no. 3 (2002): 124–135.

Van Ees, Hans, Jonas Gabrielsson, and Morten Huse. "Towards a Behavioral Theory of Boards and Corporate Governance." *Corporate Governance: An International Review* 17, no. 3 (2009): 307–319.

Weill, Peter, Thomas Apel, Stephanie L. Woerner, and Jennifer S. Banner. "It Pays to Have a Digitally Savvy Board." *MIT Sloan Management Review* 60, no. 3 (2019): 41–45.

Welge, Martin K., and Marc Eulerich. *Corporate-Governance-Management.* 2nd ed. Wiesbaden: Springer Gabler, 2014.

Westphal, James D., and Edward J. Zajac. "A Behavioral Theory of Corporate Governance: Explicating the Mechanisms of Socially Situated and Socially Constituted Agency." *Academy of Management Annals* 7, no. 1 (2013): 607–661.

Whelan, Tensie, "Research: Boards Still Have an Esg Expertise Gap—But They're Improving." *HBR.org. Harvard Business Review*, April 18, 2024, https://hbr.org/2024/04/research-boards-still-have-an-esg-expertise-gap-but-theyre-improving.

Wiersema, Margarethe, and Marie Louise Mors. "How Women Improve Decision-Making on Boards." *HBR.org. Harvard Business Review*, November 17, 2023, https://hbr.org/2023/11/research-how-women-improve-decision-making-on-boards.

Winston, Andrew. "Why Business Leaders Must Resist the Anti-ESG Movement." *HBR.org. Harvard Business Review*, April 05, 2023, https://hbr.org/2023/04/why-business-leaders-must-resist-the-anti-esg-movement.

Witt, Michael A. "Prepare for the U.S. And China to Decouple." *HBR.org. Harvard Business Review,* June 26, 2020, https://hbr.org/2020/06/prepare-for-the-u-s-and-china-to-decouple.

Yoshikawa, Toru, and Abdul A. Rasheed. "Convergence of Corporate Governance: Critical Review and Future Directions." *Corporate Governance: An International Review* 17, no. 3 (2009): 388–404.

Zangrillo, Marianna, Thomas Keil, and Benedetto Vigna. "Build the Right C-Suite Team for Your Strategy." *MIT Sloan Management Review* 66, no. 1 (2024): 36–40.

Zellweger, Thomas *Managing the Family Business.* Cheltenham: Edward Elgar, 2017.

Index

Note: **Bold** page numbers refer to tables and *italic* page numbers refer to figures.

For Product Safety Concerns and Information please contact our EU
representative GPSR@taylorandfrancis.com
Taylor & Francis Verlag GmbH, Kaufingerstraße 24, 80331 München, Germany